# The W

# at the Crossroads

Sustainable development demands a complete reappraisal of global economic and political priorities. To achieve a sustainable, liveable world, we must begin to take an holistic view of the interlocking problems the world faces. Rather than seek one-dimensional and simplistic answers, we must acknowledge that five centuries of North–South domination have created national and international structures which are fundamentally unsustainable and inequitable, with poverty and indignity for the majority contrasting with over-consumption and resource waste by the minority. Mankind is clearly on the wrong fork of the crossroads – the fork leading to disaster.

*The World at the Crossroads* looks at the steps which must be taken in order to get onto the right fork. Food and energy constraints on paths towards sustainability are thoroughly treated, but the contributors also deliver a telling critique of the statecentric economic and political institutions which are based on a fundamentally unsustainable growth paradigm and block the path towards a liveable world for future generations. Together they present a pragmatic, but normative, programme, which cuts through the rhetoric and poses a timely challenge to current thinking.

The contributors: Frank Amalric • Tariq Banuri • Wouter Biesiot • Priya Deshingkar • Hans-Peter Dürr • Anne Ehrlich • Grazia Borrini Feyerabend • Andrew Haines • Robert Hinde • Omar Masera • D L O Mendis • Henk Mulder • Samuel Okoye • Philip Smith • Jaap de Wilde

*The World at the Crossroads* derives from a study group constituted at the 41st Pugwash Conference on Science and World Affairs held in Beijing in 1991.

# The World at the Crossroads

## Towards a Sustainable, Equitable and Liveable World

A Report to the Pugwash Council

Edited by Philip B Smith, Samuel E Okoye, Jaap de Wilde and Priya Deshingkar

**Earthscan Publications Ltd, London**

First published in 1994 by
Earthscan Publications Limited
120 Pentonville Road, London N1 9JN

A catalogue record for this book is available from the British Library

ISBN: 1 85383 201 4

Typeset by Saxon Graphics Ltd, Derby
Printed by Biddles Limited, Guildford and King's Lynn
Cover design by Lucy Jenkins

Earthscan Publications Limited is an editorially independent
subsidiary of Kogan Page Limited and publishes in association with
the International Institute for Environment and Development and the
World Wide Fund for Nature.

# Contents

## Contents

# About the Authors

**Franck Amalric** (1966) is of French nationality. He was educated at the Ecole Polytechnique (Paris) and Harvard University. He has an MA in economics from Harvard and is working there for his PhD. He worked in Pakistan for a year and a half on the interlinkages between population growth and environmental degradation.

**Tariq J Banuri** (1949) is of Pakistani nationality. He was educated at Peshawar University (BE, 1970), Punjab University (MA, 1972), Williams College (MA, 1978), and Harvard University (PhD, 1986). He was a Ford Foundation Fellow from 1978–81, and received the Allyn Young Teaching Prize at Harvard University in 1983. He held various positions in the government of Pakistan from 1972 to 1977, had a number of teaching positions in the US (1980–92), was a research fellow of UNU-WIDER in Helsinki (1989–90), and has fulfilled adviser/consultant functions in Finland and Pakistan. In 1992 he became the director of the Sustainable Development Policy Institute (SDPI) in Islamabad.

**Wouter Biesiot** (1951) is of Dutch nationality. He has a PhD in physics and since 1980 has been a staff member of the Centre for Energy and Environmental Studies of the University of Groningen, The Netherlands. As senior lecturer at the Centre, he is in charge of the energy and materials research unit. His major areas of research interests are dynamic energy analysis and materials substitution problems.

**Priya Deshingkar** (1960, Delhi) is of Indian nationality. She has post-graduate qualifications in agriculture, economics and development studies. She has undertaken research on the links between poverty and natural resources since 1983 in India at the Centre for Science and Environment and subsequently in the UK at the Institute of Development Studies where she received her PhD in 1992. Her doctoral research was on entitlements of the poor to fuel and fodder resources in an Indian village. She is currently a Fellow at the Stockholm Environment Institute and is working on the impact of climate change on the forests of the Himalaya and local communities.

**Hans-Peter Dürr** (Germany, 1929) is a nuclear physicist. He received his education at the Technical University, Stuttgart (Diploma of Physics, 1953), University of California, Berkeley (PhD 1956) and Ludwig Maximilian University, Munich (Habilitation, 1969). He has done theoretical research work with Werner Heisenberg on unified quantum field theories of elementary particles and gravitation (1958–76), and was elected scientific member of the Max Planck Society (1963) and member of the board of directors of the Max-Planck-Institut für Physik und Astrophysik (1970). He has also engaged in activities in the fields of international cooperation and development, energy, peace and security, ecology, and economy, and has been associated with many international organisations. He received the Award of Merit 1956, Oakland, Right Livelihood Award 1987, Stockholm (alternative Nobel prize), Natura Obligat Medal 1991, Munich, and the Elise and Walter A Haas International Award, University of California.

**Anne H Ehrlich** (USA, 1933) is a senior research associate in biology and policy coordinator of the Centre for Conservation Biology at Stanford University, California. She has written extensively on issues of public concern such as population control, environmental protection, and the environmental consequences of nuclear war. She has coauthored *Ecoscience; Population, Resources, Environment* (Freeman & Co, 1977); *The Golden Door* (Ballantine Books, 1979); *Extinction* (Random House, 1981); *Earth* (Franklin Watts, 1987); *The Population Explosion* (Simon & Schuster, 1990); *Healing the Planet* (Addison-Wesley, 1991); and coedited *Hidden Dangers* (Sierra Club Books, 1990). She served as a consultant to the White House Council on Environmental Quality's Global 2000 Report (1980). She has taught a course in environmental policy for the Human Biology Program at Stanford since 1981. She received the Humanist Distinguished Service Award (jointly with Paul Ehrlich) and the Raymond B Bragg Award for Distinguished Service (1985) from the American Humanists Association. In 1988, she was elected an Honorary Fellow in the California Academy of Sciences. In 1989, she was selected for the United Nations' Global 500 Roll of Honour for Environmental Achievement. Bethany College awarded her an Honorary Doctorate Degree in 1990.

**Grazia Borrini Feyerabend** (1952) is of Italian nationality. She has a PhD in physics and an MSc in public health. She has held research and teaching positions at Stanford University, at the University of California at Berkeley and the Istituto Superiore di Sanità (Rome), as well as consultancy positions with the International Institute for Environment and Development (London), the UN Food and Agricultural Organization (Rome), and the Direzione Generale della Cooperazione allo Sviluppo (Rome). Her present position is coordinator of Social Policy Service at the headquarters of the International Union for the Conservation of Nature and Natural Resources in Gland, Switzerland.

**Andrew Haines** (UK, 1947) graduated in medicine from Kings College, University of London. He has worked in a number of countries including Nepal, Jamaica and the US. More recently he has developed a collaborative programme on community health care with colleagues in Brazil. Following a period as an epidemiologist with the UK Medical Research Council and as a general practitioner in an inner-city health centre, he was appointed professor and head of the department of Primary Health Care at University College London School. He has written many papers on a range of topics including prevention of cardiovascular disease and alcohol problems, care of the elderly and environmental issues.

**Robert A Hinde** (UK, 1923) BA Cambridge, DPhil Oxford, ScD Cambridge, Fellow of the Royal Society. Previously Royal Society research professor and honorary director of the Medical Research Unit on the Development and Integration of Behaviour. Currently master, St John's College, Cambridge. Research interests include animal and human social behaviour, and its development. Recent publications: *Individuals, Relation-*

*ships and Culture* (Cambridge University Press, 1987); *Cooperation and Prosocial Behaviour* (ed with J Groebel) (Cambridge University Press, 1991); *The Institution of War* (Macmillan, 1991).

**Omar Masera** (Mendoza, Argentina, 1961) has a BS in physics, and an MSc and a PhD in Energy and Resources from the University of California at Berkeley. He has held positions in Mexico in the fields of energy studies and of science, technology and development. In the US he has held positions at Berkeley, and has held several consultant appointments, most recently with the United Nations Economic Commission for Latin America (ECLAC). At present he is a professor at the Centro de Ecología, Universidad Nacional Autónoma de México (UNAM).

**D L O Mendis** (Sri Lanka, 1931) has a BS in engineering and an MSc in agriculture. For more than four decades he has been studying the ancient irrigation systems in Sri Lanka. He retired prematurely from the post of adviser (techniques) when the Ministry of Planning and Economic Affairs was abolished in 1979.

**Henk A J Mulder** (1964) is of Dutch nationality. He holds an MSc in chemistry and has been affiliated since 1989 with the Centre for Energy and Environmental Studies of the University of Groningen, The Netherlands. He is, as a research associate in the energy and materials research unit within that centre, working for his doctorate. His major areas of research interest concern life-cycle analysis and materials substitution problems.

**Samuel Ejikeme Okoye** (Nigeria, 1939) received his BSc (physics) from the University of London and his PhD (radio astronomy) from Cambridge University. He worked at the University of Ibadan, Nigeria, as a lecturer in Physics, and since 1966 at the Department of Physics and Astronomy, University of Nigeria, Nsukka. He received a chair in Radio Astronomy at Nsukka in 1976. He has published various articles in the field of high energy astrophysics and cosmology, an edited volume, *Basic Science Development in Nigeria: Problems and Prospects* and a monograph, *Viable and Affordable Policy Objectives for a Nigerian Space Programme in the 1980s.*
    He is currently science attaché to the High Commission of Nigeria in London and was until recently a Senior Visiting Fellow at the Institute of Astronomy, University of Cambridge (UK). He is a fellow of the Royal Astronomical Society, London, a member of the International Astronomical Union, and until 1992 a member of the Pugwash Council. He was consultant to the Nigerian delegation to the World Administrative Radio Conference (Geneva, 1978) and member of the Nigerian delegation to the United Nations Conference on the peaceful uses of space (Vienna, 1982).

**Philip Bartlett Smith** (USA, 1923) has dual (Dutch–American) citizenship. He has a PhD in experimental nuclear physics from the University of Illinois (1950). He has held teaching and research positions at the University of Illinois, the University of São Paulo, the University of Utrecht and until his retirement in 1988, at the University of Groningen, The Netherlands. He is the author of a number of research articles and the coeditor of a book on nuclear reactions. He was the founding chairperson of the Centre for Environmental Studies at the University of Groningen in 1973, and is at present associated with its successor, the Centre for Energy and Environmental Studies of this University. From 1963 up to the present he has been on the board of Pugwash Nederland. He was a member of the Pugwash Council from 1987 to 1992.

*About the Authors*

**Jaap de Wilde** (The Netherlands, 1957) studied history at the University of Utrecht, specializing in Peace Research and International Relations. He was a staff member of the Polemological Institute (1985–92) of the University of Groningen where he received his PhD on the dissertation, *Saved from Oblivion: Interdependence Theory in the First Half of the Twentieth Century* (Aldershot: Dartmouth, 1991). He has been interim editor of the monthly, the *Internationale Spectator*, and has worked in the section policy and management of international organizations of the University of Groningen, The Netherlands. He is a member of the editorial board of the international relations quarterly, *Transaktie*, board member of the European Peace Research Association (EuPRA) and of the Foundation for International Studies on Peace and Security, and has been board member of Pugwash Nederland. He is at present a Senior Research fellow at the Centre for Peace and Conflict Research in Copenhagen.

# Introduction

## Samuel E Okoye and Philip B Smith

### GOALS AND DEFINITIONS

This book is called *The World at the Crossroads* because the authors wish to present the choice which confronts humanity: will humankind take the fork leading to disaster or the fork leading to survival? Humankind is already a long way down the wrong fork of the crossroads. Most of this introduction is devoted to a description of this fork, and of the forces leading down it. In fact, disaster is not a threat in the offing, but is already being experienced by a great number of those now alive. It is indefensible for humankind to allow itself to head down the wrong fork, yet survival for all, as such, is only meaningful if it carries with it the connotation of an existence that provides opportunities for all of the inhabitants of the earth to live in dignity in an environment which allows for self-fulfilment and creativity. Such a world must not only be equitable and liveable, but must also be sustainable over an indefinite period in the future. The main goal of this study is to delineate, to the best of our capacity, not merely the requirements for getting on to the right fork (towards survival), but also the requirements for a survival that leads to a sustainable, equitable and liveable world. In this introduction, therefore, we set the scene, and the following chapters present the viewpoints of the contributors on the possibilities for, and the obstacles against, changing course and getting on to this fork. The concluding chapter gives a summary of the conclusions, together with concrete recommendations which may contribute to a pragmatic yet normative political programme.

The contributors to this volume are convinced that if a sustainable world is to be achieved it must be an equitable and a liveable one. There must be enough to go around, and how much that is, or can be, is the topic of several chapters. But an equitable world means more than just a world with a reasonably fair distribution of the material means of livelihood. It also implies the right to live in dignity and not suffer humiliation. To be liveable the world cannot be a place where eking out a bare existence is the lot of large portions of humankind. A liveable world also means a world in which all enjoy security of life and limb, a world in which fear of violence is largely absent. The socio-political and economic facets of equity and liveability are the subject of the largest part of this book.

Sustainability must be built, in the first place, on an equitable and liveable society because, in the final analysis, no world order can be sustainable unless it is politically stable, and a politically stable world order cannot be achieved in any meaningful fashion without equity and liveability. Sustainability itself relates essentially to the time horizon of an equitable and liveable society. Ideally, every activity of human beings should be of such a sort and on such a scale that if continued indefinitely the viability of the ecosystem will not be diminished. In myriad ways the present activities of human beings do not satisfy this criterion. There will have to be a transition period during which human activities are still unsustainable. This makes the restriction on the duration of unsustainable activities a central theme. We need to know when conversion must be realized in order to avoid causing so much irreversible damage to the ecosystem that sustainability can never be achieved. Additionally, we need to know the costs (the damage) of the conversion itself, as it still takes place within, and depends upon, unsustainable structures. This duration problem applies, in particular, to energy, water and food supplies, and to long-lasting pernicious pollution. In turn, it sets time limits on how long the restructuring of those socio-political and economic institutions which at present block the conversion can be postponed.

## VALUE PREMISES

The idea that those writing on societal issues are, or should be, obliged to state their own value premises at the outset was introduced by Gunnar Myrdal (1944). Though we cannot speak for the other contributors, we have found that there is general agreement on the main lines.

### Holism

Wholeness is a key word behind this work. It may be a commonplace that everything is connected with everything else, but any attempt at forming a total picture requires that we use this as a working principle. Dividing up the problem, or the world, into non-overlapping compartments in the classic reductionist approach of the physical sciences generally leads to sterile answers, although it can be useful in defining the 'space' or 'spaces' in which analyses of the problem will have to search for solutions.

The methodology followed is to treat problems together with their interrelations, especially the interrelations between bio-physical and societal problems. Pollution (including ozone layer depletion), energy shortage and global warming, lack of fresh water, loss of soil fertility and extinction of species, to mention a few in the first category, cannot sensibly be treated without simultaneously discussing problems in the second, such as the politico-economic structures which in the Third World reduce whole peoples to abject misery and in the First World create an economic juggernaut doomed to disastrous collapse whenever the production of an endless variety of (frequently quite unnecessary) commodities stops growing. Nor can these structures be discussed separately from the cultural and behavioural reasons why they exist and endure.

Consistent with a holistic point of departure is the idea that situations and occurrences should not be approached statically as a collection of facts, but rather as processes which are intricately intertwined. One can make more sense of the power structures in the world today if they are not viewed as the static outcome of North–South domination, but rather as a process that began five hundred years ago, and still continues today, differing only in appearance over the centuries. It is also fruitful to relate, as Polanyi (1944) does, the creation of so-called free markets to the destruction of community bonds in Third World societies, which has played an important role in the maintenance of Northern hegemony.

One example may serve to illustrate the futility of one-dimensional approaches or policies. The waves of 'economic refugees', causing such serious xenophobic reactions in some rich countries in Europe that the very basis of their democratic structure may be threatened, are just a foreboding of nightmares to come unless Northern societies are capable of realizing that treating problems in isolation by, in this example, clamping down on illegal immigrants is fruitless in the long run. The reasons why there are economic refugees must be addressed, ie the global inequity resulting in a world which is inherently unstable. The growing pressure of immigration is a symptom of this instability. To solve the problem of immigration the inequity itself must be removed by restructuring trade and financial institutions. Concretely this will mean a considerable sobering of the material life-style of the affluent, concomitant with a lessening of the dominance of the industrialized nations. No other course will stop the rising tide. Civilizations in the past have succumbed to waves of migration. It can happen again if the basic conditions causing immigration are not eliminated.

## *Expanded humanism*

Our point of departure is humanistic. Conventional humanism is, however, strictly anthropocentric. An expansion of humanism is needed which views human life as an integral part of all life. Whereas only a few years ago discussions of development and sustainability were almost entirely anthropocentrically oriented, as evidenced by such expressions as 'ecosystem services' (referring to services to human beings), the accent may now be shifting towards viewing life on earth from a holistic perspective. In this emerging paradigm, human life is seen not as outside the ecosystem, living on and at the expense of it, but rather as an integral part of it. We embrace this new paradigm wholeheartedly. Such a shift in ethical values may well even be a necessary condition if sustainability is to be achieved, since the present destruction of other life forms by human activity, if continued unabated, will otherwise eventually lead to the destruction of human life itself. The recognition of humankind's dependence on the infinite interconnectedness of all forms of life is in accord with biological science. This is directly relevant, of course, to the present disastrous extinction of species. In more general terms it could lead to a new development paradigm in which environmental health and development are no longer in conflict.

## *Gender and dignity*

Another tenet of the paradigm which has guided most of the authors of this book is that there must be a shift of accent away from hardness, aggressiveness and competitiveness, towards gentleness, compassion and sharing; in a word, away from the supremacy of masculine values and towards feminine values. Having, in principle, enough to go around will not provide for an equitable and liveable world if people do not learn to care for, and share with, others to a much larger extent than is accepted as the norm today. One consequence of such a shift in values would be a higher valuation of women in society, thus creating political and cultural conditions in which 'both halves' of humankind enjoy optimal chances to develop their talents on the basis of individual, independent choices. But in the present world order it is not only women who, almost all over the globe, cannot live their lives in dignity. It is not too strong a statement to say that the great majority of humankind suffers indignity. For some it is due to race or skin colour, for others the stigma and degradation of poverty itself, for still others religious faith, and frequently all three are combined to force countless numbers of human beings to live lives of indignity. There is a close connection between human dignity and what we have called feminine values. They go hand in hand, and are good bedfellows with expanded humanism.

## THE WRONG FORK: A DIVIDED WORLD

### *The economic dimension*

The description that modern economic theory gives of society is formulated by abstracting from human life only that which is expressible in monetary terms. Economics denies significance to affective values without which human life would have no meaning. Conceived, in principle, as a study of the production and consumption of goods (more exactly scarce goods, in the sense that there is a limited supply), it has in the course of its development become in practice a formalization of greed. Since the 'laws of economics' portray the accumulation of wealth as being in the interest of the whole, the stigma on greedy behaviour is removed. In the formulation of HRH Prince Claus of The Netherlands,[1] economics is '... basically concerned with the question of how those who are already rich, especially through their control of capital and land, can increase their wealth still further'. If it were just an intellectual exercise there could be no objection to it, but economic theory

---

1. 'One World or Several, or One World or Many', opening address at the twentieth World Conference of the Society for International Development, Amsterdam (1991: 8, mimeo).

justifies structures and behaviour incompatible with those needed for sustainability and equity. It also justifies the idea that endless growth is a normal, even a necessary, characteristic of society. Besides being ridiculous from an elementary mathematical point of view, the idea of endless material growth is the antithesis of sustainability. Finally, by denying value to the myriad forms of life of the ecosphere, which in the last analysis make human life possible, it promotes a mentality that is antithetical to life itself.

A view of life in which everything is valued in monetary terms has very negative consequences for the attainability of the goals espoused in this book. In the words of Keynes (1936) '... the ideas of economists and political philosophers, both when they are right and when they are wrong, are more powerful than is commonly understood. Indeed the world is ruled by little else. Practical men, who believe themselves to be quite exempt from any intellectual influences, are usually the slaves of some defunct economist.' In this view the concepts of *homo economicus* and the market, as well as the measurement of success (ie the gross domestic product (GDP) of a nation and the bank balance of an individual), are not just abstract ideas. They govern the lives of people and thus to a large extent the future of humankind. Can they be changed? One cannot rewrite economic theory without 'rewriting' society. The societies in the North were not created in the image of modern economic theory, but have, in the course of one or two centuries, been transformed into that image; an image in which increasing one's material possessions is the dominant goal in life for a vast majority of the population. Once societies are organized on the basis of continually increasing production (and therefore waste) based on the exhaustion of non-renewable (and renewable) resources one cannot just put on the brakes without inducing total collapse. Any proposal for economic reform which does not confront this fact is devoid of meaning. New extensions to national accounting in which values other than monetary transactions are introduced may turn out to have worthwhile consequences if taken seriously by powerful institutions. But the transformations that according to our lights are necessary to bring about a sustainable, liveable and equitable world go much deeper. Economic theory has alienated community values from economic activities (Polanyi, 1944; Daly and Cobb, 1990) and introducing environmental values into economic accounting will not in itself restore community values to economic activities.

## The technological fix

Perhaps the greatest irony of the dilemma confronting humankind is that on the one hand the unsustainability of the present situation would not have come about without technology and on the other escaping from it will require much more (and much better) technology. But frequently the solutions to problems which are human and societal are being sought in technology. All too often the faith in the 'technofix' puts blinkers on people's eyes which shield them from the real dilemmas. This faith provides policy makers with an excuse not to confront the societal problems which will have to be confronted if the world is to move along a path towards sustainability, equity and liveability. Very few problems confronting humanity are basically technological in nature. That is, if human overuse of nature is causing waste or pollution, the problem is human, and the solution should not be sought in improving the technology so that the overuse can continue with less harmful effects, but rather in reform measures, and in educating people to recognize and discontinue the overuse. Seeking a technological fix is really an escape mechanism to avoid difficult value-loaded differences of opinion. The world, rich and poor alike, needs good technology, but past experience also shows that technology will not discover a universal panacea or 'silver bullet'. It may introduce as many problems as it solves, as has turned out to be the case with chlorofluorocarbons (CFCs) which were once hailed as the ultimate beneficial technofix with no harmful side effects. Our reaction is not at all to reject technology; new good technology can provide a badly needed breathing space to solve human problems. But such new technology should not be used, as it usually is, to postpone or avoid entirely the political decisions needed to solve the problems.

## *The poverty/affluence phenomenon*

The difference between the 'poor' world, lying roughly between the tropic of Cancer and the tropic of Capricorn, and the 'rich' world, lying north and south, is deeper than it has ever been. At present, much of the former 'Second World' is on its way to join the South. Though the Central European and the Baltic countries may to some extent become linked to the West, the rest of the former Soviet Bloc seems to be in a process of 'Latin Americanization' (Werner et al, 1993). The lip service paid to cooperative solutions of the linked problems of the environment and poverty during the United Nations Conference on the Environment and Development (UNCED) stands in sharp contrast to the reality of a divided world, where on one side vast numbers live in a blind alley of hopeless poverty and on the other millions seem to be condemned to empty consumerism. Any analysis must take into account the fact that the obstacles to achieving a sustainable, equitable and liveable world are quite different on the two sides of the divide, while the processes creating the obstacles couple them inextricably.

What is most alarming is that although poverty is usually a relative concept, one discerns the emergence in many parts of the globe of a level of absolute poverty unprecedented both in its depth and extent. Absolute poverty means a level of existence that imposes real physical suffering on people through hunger and disease, denying them the opportunity to realize their potential as human beings and leading to premature death. Absolute poverty is on the increase, both in total numbers and in the proportion of the population afflicted. Today, the majority of the world's 1500 million absolute poor reside in the Third World, two-thirds in Asia alone (UNDP, 1991).

It is tempting, when considering the phenomenon of poverty or affluence among nations today, to assume that it is almost a natural phenomenon; that is, as if it were the unintended outcome of unfortunate mistakes, or as an inevitable but temporary stage in the path towards economic development of every nation. This idea comes from a distortion of history. Poverty on today's world scale is a product of a number of factors, one of which is what Polanyi (1944) called 'The Great Trans-formation' of world society from a variety of social economies to a market econ-omy. In the industrializing nations of Europe, in particular in England, the 'enclosures movement' destroyed the informal community in which the village economies were embedded. This made it possible to create national and later inter-national commodity markets and also a labour market, by expropriating the rights to the commons and driving villagers to the factories. The same type of alienating process occurred later in the colonies, but more rapidly, so that the loss of self-suf-ficiency of the village economies could not be compensated for, leading to terrible famines, particularly in India. The hunger of the multitudes of disenfranchised peoples next door to the extravagant luxury of the rich is not a natural phenome-non; it is made by human beings (Josué de Castro, 1951). Hunger and misery have, of course, always been a part of humankind's history, through wars or natural dis-asters such as drought, floods or pestilence, and also through the exploitation of human beings by human beings. What is new in the present world order is that hunger and misery are not only built into the economic structure, specifically the world-wide market structure, but they are also a vital component without which the structure could not function effectively.

## Domination

All three continents of what is now the Third World were once the homes of sophisticated civilizations. Many of their cities were centres of fabulous wealth more advanced than their first European visitors were used to at home. Time, however, has seen the reversal of this old order to one in which at present the large majority of people in those three continents are poor, while a small minority of humanity, mostly in Europe, North America and Japan, are rich. The stage for this world order was set by the emergence in Europe of industrial capitalism and the market economy, ushering in the period of colonialism.

The disasters staring the Third World in the face at the end of the twentieth century are of a complicated nature and of diverse character. The 'Third World' does not, of course, exist as an entity and the problems of each poor country have their own characteristics. Yet it is useful as a conceptual entity because there is a thread that runs through the history and structure of all poor countries, ie the human domination of human beings. Colonization of great parts of the world by the Western powers, and imitated by Japan, led at the end of the nineteenth cen-tury to a relatively stable power structure in the world. The poor were to remain poor, the rich, rich. In fact, the motivation behind the empire building of the Euro-pean industrializing countries was initially more commercial than political. The empires arose, more often than not, as a by-product of the individual pursuit of wealth by a class of entrepreneurs free to act independently of the state, but with the support, when needed, of the state. The early successes of colonization were made possible by military and organizational superiority on land and on sea. Once, however, the economic life of the colony had been forcibly harnessed to the needs of the colonial power, military and political control became an unnecessary burden and expense since the system was able to perpetuate itself, at least until the second half of the twentieth century.

The function of the newly colonized territories was to supply raw materials and to purchase the manufactured goods of the 'mother' country. In this way, the colonial powers laid the foundation of the present division of the world into the rich industrial nations on the one hand and the poor, so-called underdeveloped or developing countries on the other. In the process of colonization, indigenous industry was wiped out and self-sufficiency of the colonies was not tolerated.

The result was a world economic order which, while being extremely diverse, is on the whole characterized by a prosperous industrial centre and a poverty-stricken periphery relegated to primary production. Although the fundamental metropolis–satellite relationship between industrialized and developing countries has persisted, the basis of metropolitan domination has changed over the centuries. During the mercantilist period, the basis was military force and consequently the satellites were denied the freedom to trade. During the nineteenth century, liberalism permitted or even enforced the satellites' freedom to trade, but did not permit them to industrialize. Decolonization in the third quarter of the twentieth century did not come about through any change in policy, but because of a growing awareness on the part of the poor of their political rights, leading to rebellion which made the old system untenable without expensive and bloody military confrontations, difficult to justify on the home front. At first it appeared as if decolonization was destined really to change the world, but one after the other the colonial powers discovered that replacing military might and/or political control by less visible economic controls was 'cleaner' as well as less expensive. The domination was not changed, only its appearance. Financial and trade institutions have replaced the gunboats and neo-colonialism, ie economic colonialism, has led to the extension of the domination even to hitherto uncolonized regions. Sometimes things threaten to go awry and military action, sometimes covert, and frequently relying on the collaboration of the élite of the country in question, is necessary to restore control. As examples of 'surgical' operations one can think of the removal of Mohammed Hedayat Mossadeq in Iran (1953), the military defeat of the Arbenz government in Guatemala (1954), the murder of Patrice Lumumba in the Congo (1961) and the particularly bloody coup against Salvador Allende in Chile (1973).

## The global market economy
Under the hegemony of European capitalism a global market economy was created and the nexus of capital now encompasses the entire globe. The net result was an almost irreversible process in which poverty became self-perpetuating and inequality self-reinforcing. Once a country became poor, it tended to stay that way. However, it should be noted that two to three hundred years ago, judged by modern standards, all countries were poor. The process of colonization made possible a tremendous increase in the wealth of the colonial powers, while almost guaranteeing that the colonies could never rise out of their poverty. There are ways out, as developments in South-East Asia indicate, but the structure of the global economy

is hostile instead of adaptive towards newcomers. The colonial powers employed their capital to take the rights and resources from the colonies (aided and abetted by the élites of the poor countries themselves). It is therefore inevitable that the poor stay poor and, because they are poor, they are less able to organize with others in a similar predicament to improve their lot. No matter what the poor do, the dice of development are loaded against them. Indeed, as Harrison (1979) put it, 'to the developing countries, the great world market place must often seem like a casino where all the wheels, dice and decks are rigged, loaded and marked so that the Banks of the West always win.'

But, to be fair, one must not forget that the poor bear a share of the responsibility for their predicament. After all, the challenges and opportunities of decolonization still beckon. Instead of rising to the occasion, most post-colonial leaders of the developing countries were thoroughly acculturated to Western mores so that external colonialism has been replaced by internal colonialism. This has been accompanied by a poverty of vision in which the only model of development seriously considered was a replication in the developing countries of the Western industrial way of life together with its flaws: preoccupation with material goods, excessive consumption and the emphasis on the privileged individual. This kind of development enriches, and is naturally supported by, the local élite that directly serves the interests of the ex-colonial powers, simultaneously with its own (Brown, 1974). There is nothing new or unexpected in this 'unholy alliance'. Whether we are speaking of colonialism in the mercantilist period, or neo-colonialism today, it is important to realize that a stable system of domination/subordination can only exist if there is a ruling class in the subordinated country that, as it were, turns over the riches of their own countries to the dominating powers in return for wealth and (derived) power at home.

## Global and local inequality
A further consequence of this preoccupation with Western models of development is that inequalities are just as glaring inside Third World countries as in the world at large. The clearest dichotomy in this game of inequality is that between the winners and the losers in the development game, ie between those who benefit from economic growth and those who do not. The winners are those with access to the modern, Westernized sector, state or private. These are the town and city dwellers such as government employees, and the owners, managers and employees of modern style enterprises, national and multinational, as well as owners of urban property and estates. The losers are mainly the ordinary rural dwellers and the urban unemployed. Indeed the relationship between the urban and rural countryside within the Third World is not unlike that between the rich and poor countries, in that the rural areas tend to have 'poor terms of trade'; their produce fetches excessively low prices compared to the cost of the urban products. Further, the city's advantage derives from what Michael Lipton (1979) termed the urban bias of development, meaning that most of the developmental capital is lavished on the urban centres to the neglect of the rural areas.

The rural poor lack the muscle of organization and coordination with which to exact higher prices for their products, and as a consequence government employees and organized workers are able to maximize their incomes at the expense of the rural masses. As Julius Nyerere of Tanzania has observed, much of the money spent in the towns comes from foreign loans that have to be repaid with foreign exchange that is usually obtained by exporting the farmers' produce (Harrison, 1979). The farmers bear the costs, while the city dwellers reap the benefits, as it were.

## Repercussions of poverty on development

When all is said and done, inequitable development, intranational and international, has left behind a great mass of the poor. But this is not without its repercussions. For this very inequality now imposes limits on the pace of future equitable and sustainable development. Thus the modern (Westernized) sector of a poor country tends to be slowed in its further development precisely by the poverty of the other neglected sectors. In the same way, the industrialized countries will ultimately be braked in their growth (whatever the consequences of this may be) by the poverty of the developing countries who are being bled by the seemingly impersonal forces of the world market. Not only is the Western model of development patently unsustainable, locally and globally, but the present poverty–affluence phenomenon which derives from it must be seen as an inherently unstable arrangement. Indeed the reality of the prevailing geopolitics and the global economy is that a zero-sum game is now being played between the industrialized and developing countries: what one side wins, the other side must lose. This is why it seems so difficult to even contemplate a stable and sustainable world order that is also liveable and equitable. The rules of the game must be changed since, according to the Cocoyoc declaration (Harrison, 1979), '[a] growth process that benefits only the wealthiest minority and maintains or even increases the disparity between and within countries is not development. It is exploitation.' Economic growth of a more balanced and equitable kind is as essential as social justice, if absolute poverty is to be eliminated and equity achieved.

The existing international values are not of a high ethical standard. Partly because the international system is perceived to be basically anarchic, immoral values of might, greed and profit travel almost unhindered under the cover of 'national interest' or ideological rhetoric. In order for the Third World to escape from the indignity of its poverty in a rapid tempo, a new ethical code in international relations is needed. Such a code should allow for some redistribution of wealth while recognizing the value of compassion and equity, and of cooperation and participation. Such a change in the ethics which govern international relations will only come about when people, policy makers in particular, begin to realize that it is ultimately in the national interest of all states to have an equitable world. The ultimate aim of all would become a sustainable development strategy that ensures that the needs of the present generation are met without compromising the ability of future generations to meet their own needs.

# THE ISSUE OF POPULATION GROWTH

We hold it to be self-evident that on whichever side one is of what, for simplicity, we have called the rich–poor divide, it is undeniable that prospects for the future would be more favourable if there were fewer people on earth. Since reducing this number, certainly in the short term, is not a humanly acceptable alternative, the best that one can hope for is a stable world population not much larger than the present one.

For several million years the effect of humanity and its forebears on the environment was, in global terms, negligible, and although massive migrations have changed the course of history, and the development of agriculture has permanently changed the face of the earth, 'population' as a problem has only come into public perception in the second half of the twentieth century. In this period a tremendous increase in the number of human inhabitants of the globe has taken place, most of it in the Third World. This has led to the accusation, voiced in particular in the affluent countries where population growth has slowed to almost zero, or has even become negative, that it is this burgeoning population which is the greatest threat to the achievement of sustainability on a global level. Seen from the perspective of the South, the idea that people have to put limits on the number of children that they may have not only sounds patronizing but seems to represent a threat to their freedom, if not an outright interference in the most intimate aspect of their family life. These different perspectives could explain why discussions of population growth quite often arouse emotional reactions.

Frequently, the obviously correct but irrelevant statement is made – in view of the realities confronting the billions who live in poverty – that it is physically impossible for the poorest four-fifths of the world's population to ever achieve the 'standard of living' of the middle classes in the Organization for Economic Cooperation and Development (OECD) countries. This is a red herring serving to distract attention from the fact that even if there were no Third World at all, the integrated damage to the environment, together with the exhaustion of raw materials and fossil fuels, caused by the affluent nations alone would probably be sufficient to cause the collapse of the life support systems of the world within a century.

The problem of population growth is closely connected with poverty, but also with religion and cultural values. Poverty itself, as we have seen earlier, cannot be divorced from the operation of the trade and financial institutions which have evolved over centuries; particularly the institutions involved in North–South domination.

## EDUCATION OF WOMEN, PRIMARY HEALTH CARE AND BIRTH CONTROL MEASURES

The fact remains that in many places on earth the number of people is reaching a limit beyond which there will simply not be enough to go around. In other places displacement of populations (towards cities or other countries) is leading to too few people to care for the land. Both have potentially irreversible environmental consequences. On a global scale these consequences are not as serious as the destruction of the environment by the consumerism of the affluent, but they are certainly deadly serious for the populations involved.

Education of women, primary health care and birth control measures are frequently key words in 'population control' programmes. Treating them as isolated 'instruments' jibes with the dominant tendency towards simplification of complex problems. It renders them tractable to policy decisions. It would be absurd, of course, to be against them. In great parts of the world the education of women lags far behind that of men. It is obvious that this gap should be eliminated, since that would play a positive role in giving women more voice in the determination of their own and their children's destinies. The promotion of better primary health care, and the education and empowerment of women wherever they are deficient, as is the case in most of the poor parts of the world, should be recognized as an inherently human good. The same is true of the availability of methods of birth control which give women, particularly poor women, more control over their own wombs and lives, and well-being of their children. Yet there is more to be said on the subject.

The promotion of policies such as these can help create a society in which people can lead their lives in optimal fulfilment of their individual and social potentials. There is ample evidence that these policies are correlated with lower birth rates (causality is difficult to prove). They turn sour, however, if the human value of these 'key words' is subjugated to their usefulness as policy measures to control population growth. This is not just nit-picking. Much more is implied when these policies are implemented, as Dei ex machina, in ways isolated from the multitude of other factors effecting human well-being. Trying to achieve a specific numerical goal (birth rate reduction) while leaving intact the institutional causes of misery and insecurity must in the end be self-defeating. Women should be given the opportunity to become educated, children's health care should be improved and methods of birth control should be made available as part of the redefinition of social priorities called for in this book, in order to enhance the value of human life and liberate people from bondage, not to achieve the one-dimensional goal of reducing population growth.

Summing up, the number of people living on earth is only one facet of the many problems which confront humanity. It cannot be considered separately from the interlocking relationships between the economic, political and cultural/social systems under which people live. Indeed, population growth is a symptom of a maladjusted world society. It is illusory, therefore, to prescribe simplistic solutions or one-dimensional treatment of women's education, primary health care and birth control measures as means for achieving, in a sustainable fashion, an equitable world society in which life is liveable.

## OVERVIEW

The ordering of the chapters in this volume was a difficult task. It should be clear by now to the reader that we reject narrow disciplinary boundaries. But the readability is undoubtedly improved if there is at least a semblance of logical ordering. To achieve this minimum we have chosen to begin with the more physical and biophysical facets, going on to the political and social aspects in the later chapters. The many cross-references are witness to the interconnections, however, and the division is not really sharp. This is as it should be; the whole is more than the sum of its parts. In a final chapter the principal results and recommendations are collected.

In Chapter 1, by Anne Ehrlich, it is stated that it is impossible to answer the question of how many people could inhabit the earth without defining what one means by inhabit, ie what demands the inhabitants place on the biosphere. One may speak of ultimate bio-physical limits, determined by the inflow of energy (actually syntropy) from the sun, by the availability of fresh water and fertile soil, by the availability of materials, and by the living and eating habits of people all over the earth. Almost half of the primary production of photosynthesis is now appropriated directly and indirectly by human beings, so that the limits are certainly not far away, especially if one takes into account that humans cannot live alone on the earth. But the significance of such limits will depend on the way in which human societies are organized. In order to function in a way which will lead to a sustainable world society the economic regime under which production and distribution operate will have to be fundamentally changed. In Chapter 2, by Hans-Peter Dürr, it is argued that this will demand considerable moderation in the use of natural resources in order to avoid irreversible destruction of the biodiversity essential for the earth's life-support system. The concept is introduced of a personal 'eco-budget', ie the amount of energy that each individual can use without causing such irreversible damage. Means of promoting adherence to this budget, without coercion, are discussed. The specific constraints on possible future development laid down by the limited reserves of fossil fuels and (probably) the greenhouse effect are treated in Chapter 3, by Wouter Biesiot and Henk Mulder. There it is shown, approaching the subject from another angle, that the moderation in lifestyle of the affluent necessary to maintain biodiversity is also necessary to conserve sufficient fossil fuel reserves to be able to build up renewable energy systems. In addition it is shown that there is very limited time available to commence an all-out conversion programme on a world scale, and that besides moderation a very large improvement in the efficiency of energy use will also be necessary.

There are countries, whole regions, where various limits seem clearly in sight. This is particularly the case for fresh water, for which there is no substitute. But changing usage patterns, such as employing less wasteful irrigation practices and reintroducing less energy-intensive, sustainable agriculture, could change this picture (see also Chapter 1). Changes must, however, be carried out in the right way. In Chapter 5, D L O Mendis gives an example of an efficient irrigation system which existed in ancient times in Sri Lanka, but which has been replaced by modern hydraulic engineering projects to the great detriment of the country. In Chapter 4, by Omar Masera and Priya Deshingkar, it is shown how an apparent limit on firewood availability, calculated on the basis of over-simplified aggregate assumptions and ignoring societal factors, led to the implementation of unwise, purely technologically based projects with severe negative consequences for both people and the environment. Innovative schemes are also discussed by which people have reorganized their communities to protect their environment and livelihoods.

With proper reorganization the earth can sustainably support a large population on an equitable and liveable footing. That is no justification for complying with the admonition of Genesis 1:28 to 'Be fruitful, and multiply'. It is ridiculous to advocate a world in which there are as many people as possible, or to waste time and words in fruitless discussions on how many that might be. Reductionist discussions of population, pollution, food production or any single factor are fruitless. What is needed is a discussion on how those who do inhabit this earth can live together in such a way that the world community is sustainable, equitable and liveable. The subject of the following chapters is this way of living together. In Chapter 6, by Franck Amalric and Tariq Banuri, colonization is shown to be the root cause of unsustainability. The commons of the earth are essentially all colonized. The present trend, underlined by UNCED, is the 'colonization of the future'. Since future generations cannot be empowered, the only means of preventing this colonization is self-restraint. Achieving this is an economic problem, the solution of which is constrained by socio-economic structures, basically predicated not on the satisfaction of needs but on creating an ever-increasing desire for more.

In Chapter 7, by Grazia Borrini Feyerabend, it is shown that taking control of lands, forest and wildlife out of the hands of local people, as has occurred on a wide scale in the second half of the twentieth century, has overnight made poachers of whole populations who had previously lived for centuries in equilibrium with their animal and plant environment. The pressing need is for (re-)empowerment of local populations as a condition for a sustainable world in which there is room for both people and wildlife. The experience in Zimbabwe is encouraging, where this process of re-empowerment is beginning to take place.

In Chapter 8, by Andrew Haines, human health is presented as one of the essential building blocks of a sustainable world society. Human health is threatened and even actually being undermined by hunger, inadequate or totally non-existent education, pollutants and a great variety of diseases, most of which are avoidable. The possible threats to health of greenhouse warming are also examined.

The disastrous consequences for the possibility of achieving sustainable development caused by the diversion of natural resources and financial means to excessive military expenditure is shown in Chapter 9, by Samuel Okoye. Expenditure on arms causes such a drain on the budgets of poor countries, already struggling with tremendous debt burdens, that education and health programmes are being sacrificed. Rediverting means now wasted on military expenditure towards such programmes would have very high efficiency in stimulating development in general, in reducing child mortality and in improving the living conditions of people.

But the problem of reaching sustainability, equity and liveability in a human society cannot be fully stated in terms of bio-physical limits, and social and political institutions. The questions of conflicting interests, examined in Chapter 10, by Jaap de Wilde, must also be confronted. The restructuring of institutions is essential, but that means there are many conflicts in the offing. These conflicts cannot be solved by platitudinous appeals to goodwill and reason. They will be decided by power politics and will have more chance of being decided in favour of sustainability, equity and liveability if at the outset it is recognized that there will be losers in the struggle. It is therefore essential to envisage methods of fair compensation so that policy debates can concentrate on the real issues. Conflict management through reasoned debate is, however, unlikely in societies in which aggressiveness and acquisitiveness have a higher social priority than cooperation and compassion. Specific ways to change social priorities and the obstacles along the road are expanded upon in Chapter 11, by Robert Hinde. The possibilities of changing society by re-education are limitless in principal, but educational processes are notoriously slow. Time is not on humanity's side. In Chapter 12, by Philip Smith and Samuel Okoye, a summary of the main arguments of the chapters is given, together with the resulting policy recommendations.

## THE ORIGINS OF THIS BOOK

At the conclusion of the thirty-eighth Pugwash Conference on Science and World Affairs, held in Dagomys on the Black Sea in the Soviet Union at the end of the summer of 1988, the Pugwash Council approved a declaration which has become known as the Dagomys Declaration. Below are quoted the parts of the declaration particularly relevant to the present book:

> *We live in an interdependent world of increasing risks. Thirty-three years ago, the Russell–Einstein Manifesto warned humanity that our survival is imperilled by the risk of nuclear war. ... in the spirit of the Russell–Einstein Manifesto we now call on all scientists to expand our concerns to a broader set of interrelated dangers: destruction of the environment on a global scale and denial of basic needs for a growing majority of humankind. ...*
>
> *Today's pattern of increasing energy use is a key link in a dangerous web of international environmental problems. Among these are the global climate change, ozone depletion, acid deposition, and water pollution. These, combined with other potentially catastrophic effects, including deforestation, soil erosion, and mass extinction of species, reduce the earth's capacity to support a growing population. ...*
>
> *To survive, we must recognize that environmental degradation weakens the security of all. The challenge is to find ways to promote sustainable development of all regions of the world while reducing both military and ecological threats. Cooperation among nations, and effective organizations at the international,*

*national, regional, and local levels, are essential to maintain earth's life-support
systems. Intense efforts must be made to foster a feeling of connectedness and
cooperation and to correct economic injustices and promote trust.*

Three years later, at the forty-first Pugwash Conference held in Beijing, China in
September 1991, a group of like-minded individuals, including most of the authors
of the present book, decided to form a study group with the object of defining
what 'sustainable development' really means and what the conditions are for its
achievement. This amounts to presenting the choice before which humankind
stands – survival or catastrophe – and elaborating on the consequences. The
authors of this introduction were asked to coordinate the activities of the study
group, and have been assisted from the start by Jaap de Wilde. A preliminary draft
of that effort was prepared for the forty-second Pugwash Conference in Berlin in
September 1992. At the conclusion of the Berlin conference the Pugwash Council
accorded the study group the status of Special Pugwash Project. The goal of the
first phase of the project, the presentation of a report to the Pugwash Council, has
been completed with this volume. Neither the Pugwash Movement, nor the Pugwash Council, is responsible for the opinions presented here. These are the viewpoints of the authors themselves.

The Crossroads study group held workshops in The Netherlands in May 1992
and again in May 1993. At the second workshop Jaap de Wilde and Priya Deshingkar were asked to join hands with Philip Smith and Samuel Okoye in a broad-
based editorial committee in charge of preparing the final manuscript. This
enterprise, because of the geographical spread of the participants, would have
been impossible without modern telecommunication systems. In the course of the
last two years there have been in total more than a thousand electronic-mail mes-
sages, telefaxes and telephone calls exchanged between the coordinators and the
other members of the group.

## ACKNOWLEDGEMENTS

The members of the study group gratefully acknowledge the financial and logistic
support of the board and the members of the Dutch Pugwash group and the Dutch
Friends of Pugwash. The work of the group was made possible by generous grants
from the Commission of the European Communities, the National Committee for
Development Education (NCO), the Royal Netherlands Academy of Arts and Sciences (KNAW) and the Algemene Loterij Nederland.

The authors of this introduction are grateful for the advice and improvements
that they have received from the other members of the editorial committee, and
from Anne Ehrlich and Hans-Peter Dürr who spent considerable time preparing
detailed criticisms. They alone are, of course, responsible for the final text. Not all of
those who have participated in the study group are to be found among the authors
of this volume. As coordinators of the project, the authors of this introduction want
to thank Raúl García and Peter Taylor, Judithe Bizot and Peggy Antrobus, Alexan-

der Ginzburg, John Shilling and Ana Maria Cetto for their efforts on behalf of this project and their contributions to it. We have learned much from them.

The accurate minutes of the workshops kept by Henny Deenen were of great value in tying the whole together. Finally we express our gratitude to Robert and Joan Hinde for their hospitality at the Master's Lodge of St John's College at Cambridge University. This made many days of fruitful work on this introduction and the final editing of the whole volume possible.

## REFERENCES

Brown, M B, *Economics of Imperialism*, Harmondsworth: Penguin Books, 1974.

Castro, Josué de, *Geopolítica da Fome*, São Paulo: Livraria Editôra da Casa do Estudante do Basil, 1953.

Daly, H E and J B Cobb, Jun, *For the Common Good*, London: The Merlin Press, 1990.

Frank, A G, *Capitalism and Underdevelopment in Latin America*, New York: Monthly Review Press, 1969.

Harrison, P, *Inside the Third World: The Anatomy of Poverty*, Harmondsworth: Penguin Books, 1979.

Keynes, J M, *The General Theory of Employment, Interest, and Money*, London: Macmillan, 1936.

Lipton, M, *Why Poor People Stay Poor: A Study of Urban Bias in World Development*, London: Temple Smith, 1979.

Myrdal, G, *An American Dilemma*, New York: Harper and Brothers, 1944.

Polanyi, K, *The Great Transformation*, Boston: Beacon Press, 1944.

UN Development Programme, *Human Development Report*, Oxford: Oxford University Press, 1990.

Wæver, O, B Buzan, M Kelstrup and P Lemaitre, *Identity, Migration and the New Security Agenda in Europe*, London: Pinter, 1993.

# I
# *FOOD AND ENERGY*

*Chapter One*

# Building a Sustainable Food System

*Anne H Ehrlich*

How many human beings can the earth support? This question is unanswerable without also defining the life-style and consumption patterns of the people in question, and the length of time that they are to be supported. Unlike other animals, human beings are capable of adjusting their levels of resource consumption enormously, largely through the use of technologies with which they can mobilize otherwise inaccessible resources and divert much of the productivity of the biosphere to their own uses (Vitousek et al, 1986). Given that the earth's daily energy income (from the sun) is limited, as is the amount of energy stored from past solar income (fossil fuels), there are ultimate constraints on the number of human beings that can be supported. Moreover, civilization is living beyond its means in so far as it depends for support on past-stored energy, reduces the fraction of current energy income made available through photosynthesis, and degrades and disperses its finite material resources. Biologists would say it has exceeded its carrying capacity (Ehrlich and Ehrlich, 1990; Daily and Ehrlich, 1992).

Carrying capacity is defined as the maximum population size of an organism that can be supported by its environment without degrading the environment's capacity to support it in the future. Human beings, like other animals, require oxygen, water, the energy and essential nutrients obtained from food, shelter and living space, a hospitable environment and contact with others of their species. But, to a far greater degree than other animals, people also use materials – resources for their technologies – to make their environments more hospitable and to facilitate access to other needed resources. They also are capable of transporting resources and products over great distances to trade for other materials locally in short supply.

The ability to use materials – minerals, inedible plant and animal products (eg wood, other fibres, natural oils and chemicals, hides, bones and teeth) – permitted a few million hunter-gatherers to expand their population by two orders of magnitude to a much larger agricultural society in a few millennia and fivefold more in the industrial era so far. This enormous increase in numbers to five-and-a-half billion in 1993 (Population Reference Bureau, 1993), accompanied by an accelerating ability to mobilize materials, has dramatically changed the earth's land surface, altered natural biogeochemical cycles (Turner et al, 1990) and launched an epidemic of biotic extinctions (Ehrlich and Ehrlich, 1981; Ehrlich and Wilson, 1991; Wilson, 1992). Now, with its population growing at a rate historically unprecedented before the middle of this century and fast approaching six billion, humanity has belatedly begun to question whether a population so large, let alone a far greater one, can be supported for long at a decent standard of living (Repetto, 1987).

## AGRICULTURE: THE UNDERPINNINGS

Of all the important elements of the earth's human-carrying capacity, food supply is probably the most critical. But maintaining food production, to say nothing of increasing it, depends on the resources and natural functions that underpin the agricultural process (Pimentel and Hall, 1989). Among these are arable land with fertile soils, adequate supplies of fresh water and the healthy functioning of the ecosystems in which the farming enterprise is embedded. Further, modern intensive agriculture has depended on a substantial subsidy from fossil fuels. The subsidy includes synthetic fertilizers and pesticides (both derived from and produced with fossil fuels), as well as power for farm machines and irrigation works, which are required to achieve high yields from specially bred crop varieties. The combination of high-yield seeds, fertilizers and pesticides is known as the green revolution (Dahlberg, 1979; Swaminathan and Sinha, 1986).

Examination of all the factors underpinning the agricultural enterprise today does not inspire confidence (Ehrlich et al, 1993). Indeed, even leading agronomists, creators of the green revolution and until recently among the most optimistic of technological optimists, have begun to issue warnings about the potential for further great expansions in food production (Walsh, 1991; IRRI, 1992). In the four decades since 1950, world food production has risen nearly threefold, while the population has increased 2.2-fold (Brown, 1988; UNFPA, 1992; USDA, 1993). But the greatest gains in food supply per capita were achieved in the first half of the period. Since 1984, global production of grains (the world's feeding base) has lagged behind population growth (Brown et al, 1991, 1993; USDA, 1993).

First among essential resources for agriculture, of course, is the need for productive land and fertile soils. The amount of land suitable for farming is clearly limited, although estimates vary on the actual amount of potentially arable land in the world, presumably because of differing standards of 'arable' and assessments of availability. Given huge deliveries of water (at a high energy and monetary cost) and other supporting activities, the central Sahara no doubt could produce crops, but such impracticalities are not seriously considered in most responsible assessments. On all continents, most of the land suitable for growing crops is already under cultivation and much that is marginal is also being cultivated. The actual land under crops therefore is a fairly good indication of what is potentially available. This amounts to about 11 per cent of the world's ice-free land surface (FAO, 1990), a portion that has risen only about 10 per cent in the last 43 years. Between 1950 and 2000, the amount of cropland per person will have shrunk by half (Brown, 1988). The huge increases in food production of the past few decades have been mainly the result of increased yields (production per hectare), not of expanded crop area.

While in some regions, especially Latin America, more rational land-use policies might make significant amounts of additional good land available for growing crops, the current distribution of wealth (including land) commonly leads to the conversion of inferior land instead (Kates and Haarmann, 1992). And, in large areas of Africa, the prevalence of human and livestock diseases prevents farming or herding on otherwise adequate land. Some potentially arable land exists in areas of unreliable rainfall. But in most regions today, new cropland can be gained only at the expense of forests, pasture land or wetland, all of which supply other valuable resources or ecosystem services to the human enterprise (Ehrlich and Ehrlich, 1991; WRI, 1992). While some new land continues to be added to the world cropland inventory each year, other land goes out of production because of degradation or other uses such as urban development, highways, airports etc (Brown et al, 1989).

As important as the quantity of farmland is its quality. Unfortunately, the quality of much of today's cropland and pasture is deteriorating rapidly. Indeed, one element in the slow rise of cultivated land world-wide is that, as new land has been put under the plough, land elsewhere has gone out of production because of excessive soil erosion or exhaustion. Annual world-wide soil losses from wind and water erosion are estimated to be some 24 billion tons (Brown and Wolfe, 1984; Brown, 1988). Land is also being taken out of production because of irrigation damage and depletion of ground water sources (Postel, 1990; WRI, 1992). A study sponsored by the United Nations Environment Programme (UNEP) has found that some 1.2 billion hectares of land have undergone moderate to extreme soil degradation since the end of the Second World War – an area roughly equal to China and India combined – as a result of human activities such as farming, overgrazing and deforestation (Oldeman et al, 1990; WRI, 1992). An additional 750 million hectares have been lightly affected and presumably are vulnerable to further damage. The study defines degradation as a process that reduces 'the current and/or future capacity of the soil to support human life'. The estimated potential for restoring moderately or more degraded land to full productivity ranges from difficult and expensive to essentially impossible.

The degraded areas comprise some 17 per cent of the planet's vegetated land surface, ranging from about 5 per cent in North America to 22–25 per cent in Africa, Europe and Central America. About 28 per cent of degraded land is cropland, another third is used as pasture, and the remainder is forests. Disturbingly, a disproportionate amount of the land affected is cropland, particularly in North America, the world's leading breadbasket. Equally worrisome is that land in some industrialized regions has suffered as much damage as that in developing countries where synthetic fertilizers and other supports of fertility have been used much less. Synthetic fertilizers can conceal the effects of soil loss and nutrient depletion for a considerable length of time (Brown, 1988), leading to unpleasant surprises when the accumulated damage can no longer be hidden.

The global extent of land degradation may be the starkest sign of how unsustainable the present agricultural system is. Enough damage has been inflicted on the world's productive land to depress the global harvest of food by a significant fraction, despite the spread of modern high-yield technologies. If so much damage to the planet's most productive land has occurred in less than two generations, what might be the prospect for the next two or three generations, when perhaps twice as many people will be depending for survival on the land's capacity to produce food?

In assessing the prospects for future food supplies, other aspects of sustainability besides land degradation also must be considered. A resource already in short supply in many regions is fresh water (Postel, 1990; Falkenmark and Widstrand, 1992; WRI, 1992; Brown et al, 1993). The leading use of water world-wide is for agriculture, with industrial and domestic uses being a distant second and third. In many areas, lack of water limits potential agricultural production as well as other kinds of development. In others, pollution is a serious problem. Acute shortages in regions such as the Middle East can even lead to conflict (Homer-Dixon et al, 1993). Water has been an extremely important factor in the green revolution's increased crop yields; without abundant water, modern crop strains cannot realize their high yields. By 1990, irrigated cropland was producing a third of the world's food, although it made up only 17 per cent of the cropland area (Postel, 1990). But irrigation also can cause land degradation through salinization and waterlogging, as well as other problems such as pollution and silting of rivers and dams. Roughly a third of the world's irrigated land has suffered such degradation. In many regions, including the US Great Plains, northern India and China, underground water sources (aquifers) are being tapped at rates far higher than natural recharge, leading to the retirement of land from cultivation when pumping becomes uneconomic (Postel, 1990; Brown et al, 1993). Since most of the areas that can easily be put under irrigation have been, future food production increases through expanded irrigation works are unlikely to match those seen in the decades before 1980. Even so, a significant increase is possible in some developing regions such as India and parts of Africa, where considerable potential remains untapped. But the net expansion of irrigated land slowed markedly in the 1980s and on a per capita basis has reversed, as more and more land is taken out of production and the rate at which new land is irrigated declines.

Agricultural production is also dependent on the health of the ecosystems in which it is embedded. Soil's fertility is a result of the activities of billions of organisms, from insects, earthworms and fungi to bacteria, that exist in every square metre of topsoil (Ehrlich and Ehrlich, 1981; Carroll et al, 1990; Hillel, 1991). Many of these organisms not only affect soil texture (and thus water absorption and retention), they also break down dead organic material, making available essential nutrients, and in some cases directly facilitating the absorption of water and nutrients by plant roots. Natural areas adjacent to farm fields also contribute to soil fertility and harbour other organisms that pollinate crops or help control pests, among other benefits (Carroll et al, 1990; Edwards et al, 1990; Pimentel et al, 1992; Soule and Piper, 1992). On a larger scale, forest or other vegetative cover in watersheds helps govern the hydrological regime, returning water to the atmosphere, and controlling runoff and the recharge of aquifers. These critical ecosystem services are usually taken for granted. In the industrial green revolution farming model, they are basically ignored. Indeed, the almost systematic elimination of adjacent natural areas in many farming regions (for instance, the ploughing up in the 1970s of many of England's hedgerows and the US grainbelt's shelterbelts) has contributed significantly to the farmland degradation recorded in recent decades.

## LIMITS TO THE GREEN REVOLUTION AND BIOTECHNOLOGY

The green revolution – the tidy technological package of high-yield seeds, fertilizers, pesticides, farm machines, and (where needed) irrigation that could be offered to farmers, and its emphasis on extensive monocultures – has been largely responsible for the remarkable surge in food production of the last four decades. But it has done so at an increasingly high cost, including accelerated soil erosion, irrigation damage, overdrawn aquifers, serious pollution of surface and underground waters, and so forth (Brown and Wolfe, 1984; Soule and Piper, 1992; WRI, 1992). In the moist tropics especially, the green revolution package has often proven both unsuccessful and environmentally damaging (Dahlberg, 1979; Goodland et al, 1984; Fearnside, 1987). Monocultures are highly vulnerable to pest attack under any circumstances; chemical fertilizers can weaken soil integrity, whereas most natural fertilizers tend to enhance it; intensive use of chemical pesticides leads to pest resistance; and heavy machinery also damages soils (Pimentel and Hall, 1989.) All these problems are intensified in the moist tropics, where soils are often fragile and thin; heavy rainfall accelerates erosion, leaches nutrients from soils, and washes out fertilizers and pesticides; and pest populations can multiply rapidly, unhindered by a marked winter or dry season (Wrigley, 1982). Furthermore, the green revolution itself is running out of steam for several reasons. First, in most regions where this technology is appropriate, it has already been adopted. In many areas, fertilizer applications have passed well beyond the point of diminishing returns; that is, additional applications of fertilizer result in little or no further increase in yield.

Most suitable areas not yet experiencing diminishing returns will reach that point before much longer (Brown, 1991). Until the early 1980s fertilizer use increased more than twice as fast as food production, reflecting the growing dependence of farmers on manufactured fertilizers for increased yields. The near levelling off of fertilizer use since 1984 reflects the widespread attainment of diminishing returns and cutbacks in some areas where fertilizers had been overused, such as the former Soviet Union (Brown et al, 1993). This is not to say that the green revolution has only been negative. Lester Brown of Worldwatch Institute has conservatively estimated that the adoption of synthetic fertilizers (and attendant increased water and pesticide inputs) has been responsible for some 40 per cent of the increase in world food production since 1950 (Brown, 1991). Quite possibly, if that intensification of food production had not been possible, even more degradation of land might have occurred because of the need to put substantially more land, most of it marginal, under cultivation. Alternatively, global food production would have increased considerably less, resulting in more hunger among the poor and higher food prices for everyone. Even so, some observers see the high and rising dependence on fertilizers derived from ultimately finite resources as a matter for concern (Smil, 1991).

Besides the limitations of fertilizers, there also seem to be biological constraints to increasing yields through genetic improvement, which plant breeders may soon reach for major crops (Bugbee and Monje, 1992). Indeed, yields of rice (the staple for nearly half the human population) already appear to have peaked in many areas (Walsh, 1991; IRRI, 1992). On the basis of these trends, Lester Brown has estimated that world food production in the 1990s might rise by an annual average of less than 1 per cent – about half the present rate of population growth (Brown, 1988). The record so far suggests that he may be right (USDA, 1993): in Africa, per capita food production has been falling since 1969; in Latin America it has failed to keep up for over a decade. On a world-wide basis, food production per person peaked in 1984 and has yet to return to that level. Meanwhile, the population has increased by some 850 million.

No technological encore that could match the multiplication of average yields of major crops produced by the green revolution over a few decades is waiting in the wings. Biotechnology, for all the hype, may make a series of useful contributions to agriculture in the next decade or two, but these will contribute more to security of production than to dramatically larger harvests (Gasser and Fraley, 1989). These contributions will include improved pest control (without killing non-target organisms and disrupting ecosystems) and the addition to crop strains of desirable characteristics such as increased pest resistance, more efficient utilization of nutrients and increased tolerance of adverse conditions such as drought or salty soils. If these innovations all pan out as hoped, the global harvest may be augmented by a few per cent and some areas that now are marginally productive at best might see significant improvements in food production.

A more promising approach is to apply green revolution yield increases to crops other than the 'big three' – wheat, rice and maize. Tropical crops, on which a large portion of the world's poor depend, have until recently been neglected by plant breeders. Biotechnology could considerably speed up the process of developing higher-yield varieties. Even so, years are required for development, and more years will be needed for field testing and distributing the seeds, and supporting inputs to farmers before new varieties can be widely adopted.

Finally, any success with biotechnology will depend on preserving the raw materials it requires: the genetic diversity contained in thousands of traditional crop varieties (NRC, 1991; Plucknett et al, 1992) and their wild relatives (Hoyt, 1988; Cohen et al, 1991). Unfortunately, despite efforts to preserve these varieties in gene banks, many are still being lost. This is an ironic result of the green revolution's success, as farmers around the world switch to the limited array of genetically uniform high-yield strains and neglect the older ones.

## THE POVERTY LINK

Despite the gains in per capita food production from 1950 to 1980, the present food system is still failing to feed all the world's people adequately. According to the World Bank, over a billion people today – nearly one in five world-wide – are undernourished in that they take in too few calories each day to support normal activity (World Bank, 1990, 1992). Other estimates, based on different criteria, are lower (Kates and Haarmann, 1992; Norse, 1992; FAO, 1992), but virtually all studies agree that a substantial portion of the human population is chronically undernourished (that is, not including the millions suffering from severe famines caused by war and political strife as in Ethiopia, Somalia and Sudan or by a sudden acute drought as in southern Africa in 1991–2). Most of the hungry people live in very poor countries. Four-fifths of them are concentrated in South Asia and Sub-Saharan Africa, where more than 40 per cent of the population is underfed. Much of the world's degraded land also is found in these regions, and a connection between extreme poverty and land deterioration has often been observed. Both may be exacerbated by rapid population growth, misguided and counterproductive development projects, or expropriation of resources by more powerful interests outside the community (Kates and Haarmann, 1992). Natural disasters, such as droughts or floods, can also precipitate a downward spiral of poverty and land degradation in an area that was relatively secure before. Such disasters in turn may result from land-use changes such as deforestation or desertification within the watershed (Ehrlich and Ehrlich, 1991; Maass and Garcia-Oliva, 1992).

Severe land degradation, as manifested in desertification processes and loss of vegetative cover, is often entwined with poverty in developing nations. In such situations, farm families may be too impoverished and powerless to protect land resources, or too needy of fuel and livestock grazing to avoid over-exploitation (Kates and Haarmann, 1992; Norse, 1992; World Bank, 1992). These are people whose lives remain untouched by agricultural modernization (Lee et al, 1988). Their plight is not the result of overindustrialized technology, but the lack of capacity to apply even basic land husbandry – the use of sufficient natural fertilizers, protective soil cover, terracing or other simple erosion control measures and avoidance of overgrazing – even when they know perfectly well what is needed.

Poverty is often accompanied by undernutrition, poor health, illiteracy and high birth rates (Lee et al, 1988; Dreze and Sen, 1991; Dasgupta, 1993). This combination leads to deepening poverty and progressive land degradation in a vicious cycle that may be extremely hard to reverse when increasing numbers of people are depending on that land for sustenance. Simultaneously improving people's well-being while restoring a deteriorating resource base to a sustainable system is doubly difficult. Even though restoration is possible, with time and much care, on lightly or moderately degraded land, restoring severely or extremely degraded land is problematic (Oldeman et al, 1990; WRI, 1992). The longer the degradation goes on, the harder restoration is to accomplish and the less likely it is to succeed.

When rapid population growth leads to intensified pressures on land, population displacement and urban migration are common responses. Poor farmers may be pushed on to marginal lands (which deteriorate even faster) or even be transferred to new areas by governments, as has happened in Brazil. Many impoverished rural people move to cities, other regions or other countries, seeking a better living. In the process, they sometimes create other social problems (Jacobson, 1988; Borrini, 1990). The mass movement of people from rural areas to cities in developing nations has several consequences for agricultural production. Although rural populations have continued to expand in most countries despite the emigration, they are growing more slowly than urban populations. Indeed, in many cases, urban growth has been extremely high – in the order of 6 to 10 per cent per year – often overwhelming the capacities of cities to provide needed services (UNFPA, 1992). This movement also may mask the increasing dependence of many developing nations on imported food to feed their populations (Brown et al, 1989, 1993). Rural populations may continue to be more or less food self-sufficient, while increasing amounts of food staples imported from other nations are delivered to and are mostly consumed in the cities.

Economic and agricultural policies can make or break the adequacy and sustainability of a nation's food supply (Lee et al, 1988; Eicher and Schaatz, 1990). Developing nations that have emphasized a strong agricultural sector with support for farm families have generally prospered in other ways as well, as witness the success of Asia's famous 'dragons' (newly industrialized countries). Even Hong Kong and Singapore, which as small city states had scant agricultural land to depend on, secured their food supply from neighbouring states early in their development history. Following the successful Japanese model, Taiwan and South Korea also made agriculture a priority, with striking results. By a different path, China too has achieved remarkable results. And it is too seldom remembered that the strength of the US was built on agriculture. Indeed, agricultural products are still among its leading exports. Elsewhere, the lack of societal investment in agriculture (along with other factors) in parts of Latin America and especially in Africa, shows up in lagging production of food for domestic consumption. Too often, investment has been funnelled into production of cash crops, frequently for export, while giving subsistence farmers little help in increasing their productivity. In many areas, the highly mechanized cash crop economy has driven poor subsistence farmers and landless workers off the land. In some areas where poor farmers have abandoned land and left it untended, deterioration has accelerated.

Agricultural and development economists tend to put great faith in the power of economic policies to increase food production: give poor people the means to generate demand for food, provide the necessary seeds and inputs to farmers, and the food will be produced (Lee et al, 1988). However, apart from persisting political and economic barriers to such changes, this view overlooks the very real biological and physical constraints that ultimately limit the amount of food that can be produced on a given piece of land (Bugbee and Monje, 1992). It also neglects the reduction, in practical terms, of potential productivity resulting from land degradation.

Changing economic policies sometimes can lead to dramatic increases in food production, but this has usually occurred in situations in which farmers previously had been given little incentive or support for maximizing their production. The results of policy changes that newly encouraged entrepreneurial farming in both China and the former Soviet Union in the 1980s are notable examples (Brown et al, 1989). Yet there are limits to the potential of such increases, however spectacular they may appear. Sometimes the increase occurs at the expense of other, less profitable crops – in China, vegetable production jumped while the rice crop declined. More important is the danger that it might lead to over-exploitation of land, with deleterious results in the long term. In short, no one can predict how much food production might be boosted by such policy changes or how sustainable the increases would be.

One further element of instability in the world food system is the extremely uneven distribution of food production and food demand. Today the majority of nations are 'food deficit' areas and depend to some degree on imported food, especially grains, for sustenance (Brown et al, 1989; WRI, 1992). How secure can a global food system be that depends on a handful of grain-exporting nations in an era of global change, including possibly drastic climate changes (Parry, 1990; Daily and Ehrlich, 1990; Ehrlich et al, 1993)? The terms of food trade and commodity prices have been hot topics of discussion in the General Agreement on Tariffs and Trade (GATT) conferences. Much has been made of the subsidized prices of exported grain, mainly by Europe but also the US, squeezing developing nations out of the international market. But little has been heard about domestic social and economic reasons for the subsidies or of the intrinsic value to any nation of supporting its agricultural and rural economy. In working out a global food trade and distribution system that is reasonably equitable and that promotes food production in sustainable agricultural systems with rational land tenure arrangements, civilization still has a long way to go (Vosti et al, 1991).

## CREATING SUSTAINABLE SYSTEMS

Given the expected medium-term expansion of the human population by roughly a billion per decade, even if strong efforts are made to curb population growth, food production must be substantially increased as well. With no improvement in distribution or average diets, harvests will have to be increased by 40 per cent in the next 20 years just to maintain today's per capita food supplies. Improving the diets of the hungriest fifth of humanity would require considerably more, unless a significant offsetting change occurred in the dietary habits of the richest fifth. Moreover, these increases would have to be accomplished while shifting towards a more sustainable world system of food production, trade and distribution. This is certainly a tall order, but fortunately much is known about how to make farming sustainable. Indeed, a movement in the US towards wider adoption of 'organic' or 'low-input' farming methods is gaining strength and attention from both scientists and farmers (NRC, 1989; Edwards et al, 1990; Soule and Piper, 1992).

These techniques, many of them based in centuries-old traditions, are much more environmentally benign and sustainable than those now viewed as conventional. The traditional agriculture of a century ago produced far lower yields than are achieved today in most temperate zone regions and in many tropical ones. But by planting modern high-yield crop varieties, while using mostly natural fertilizers along with traditional methods of fallowing, crop rotation, intercropping, biological pest control (Horn, 1988) and effective soil conservation techniques, crop yields can be achieved that are comparable to the currently favoured industrial farming methods (NRC, 1989; Edwards et al, 1990). Although yields from this approach in the US were found to be slightly lower, costs were roughly comparable and might become advantageous with higher petroleum prices. These alternative agricultural methods are more labour-intensive, but this would be a benefit in many developing regions with rapidly growing populations. Even in some developed nations, especially in times of high unemployment, labour-intensive farming could be economically beneficial. The problems of soil erosion have become serious enough to lead to changes in policies in some countries. In the US, the government has begun subsidizing farmers to protect marginal lands in conservation set-asides with permanent plantings of trees or perennial grasses. The result has been a sharp reduction in soil erosion. While total production dropped slightly, average crop yields have risen as marginal lands were retired (Brown et al, 1989, 1993).

Many European farmers have strayed less far from traditional practices than farmers in the US grain belt, although pollution problems from intensive industrial farming and livestock feeding in nations such as The Netherlands and Germany have become very serious. The extent of land degradation in Europe also has been relatively great (WRI, 1992). In Central and Eastern Europe and Russia, the policies of the Soviet Union and satellites led to inefficient farming and poor management of land resources. These problems were compounded by enormous damage inflicted in many areas by industrial pollution to crops and soils as well as to forests and surface water sources. The prime tasks there will be to abate pollution emissions, restore damaged lands and establish a more productive, sustainable food production and distribution system. Population growth is very slow or in some cases negative in most industrialized nations (UNFPA, 1992; Population Reference Bureau, 1993), so feeding a much larger domestic population is not an issue. Nor is there a need for increased production to improve diets in rich countries;

indeed, the overconsumption of industrialized countries characterizes their dietary habits as well as their use of resources. A disproportionate share (at least a third) of the grain produced world-wide is used to feed livestock. People in developed nations thus consume directly or indirectly two to three times as much grain per person as do most people in poor nations (Brown et al, 1989; Ehrlich et al, 1993).

A significant reduction in consumption of animal products, especially beef, by the rich would at least potentially release substantial amounts of grain that could be provided to improve the diets of the poor. Indeed, per capita demand is falling in some industrialized nations as people consume less meat and other animal products for health reasons. At the same time, however, the wealthier classes in developing nations are increasing their consumption of animal products, so world-wide production of meat and dairy products is still rising, often subsidized by imported grain. Demand for imported grain has also risen in poorer nations where meat consumption is hardly an issue, as population growth has outstripped local food production. Consequently, although domestic consumption may be more or less stable in the surplus grain-producing rich nations, they may feel pressure to keep expanding production because much of the world increasingly depends on their food exports. The greatest challenges will be for developing nations to develop ecologically sound and sustainable agricultural systems. This will be no small assignment, especially in regions where population growth is most rapid and resources are limited. Given the vast diversity of soils, and climatic and ecological settings in developing nations, as well as the variety of social, cultural, political and economic situations, the problems and opportunities cannot be easily summarized (Eicher and Schaatz, 1990). Some possible directions in which to seek solutions are as follows.

- Obviously, a prime task is to halt as much as possible the ubiquitous trend of land degradation. In many poor nations, this entails addressing the spiral of poverty, displacement of rural populations and the loss of local control over common property resources (Durning, 1989; Kates and Haarmann, 1992). Providing assistance to local groups while preserving their decision-making power is clearly the best way to help the poor: their 'ownership' (in several senses) of the resources at risk and of the proposed changes are necessary ingredients for success (Borrini, 1991 and Chapter 7 of this book).
- Rural development policies in many nations need to be re-examined and overhauled. Reform of land tenure may be the key in some countries to restoring land productivity and increasing food output sustainably, but it is politically almost impossible to achieve short of a revolution. Agricultural policies that do not overemphasize cash crops for export, and do provide subsistence farmers with extension services and access to credit, improved seeds and essential inputs are needed in many countries. In the poorest regions, farmers even lack the most basic infrastructure, such as roads and access to inputs and markets, which could provide incentives (and rewards) for increasing production (Lee et al, 1988). Most important is integrating direct support for agriculture with enlightened rural development policies that focus on improving the well-being,

security and empowerment of rural people (Eicher and Staatz, 1990; Vosti et al, 1991; Norse, 1992).

- In some of the poorest regions, such as much of Sub-Saharan Africa, a prime need is the empowerment of women, who do most of the farming and marketing, as well as water fetching and fuel gathering, with their children's help. Simply providing these women farmers with information, access to clean water and fuel sources (or the ability to develop and manage communal resources), and credit for purchasing improved seeds and inputs might do much to increase food production (World Bank, 1992; WRI, 1992). Such modest basic assistance could also lead to improved health and nutrition, and possibly to lower birth rates.

- Beyond changes in agricultural policy and the alleviation of extreme rural poverty, increased food production for the next few decades will depend primarily on improvements in yields of minor staple crops and on shifts to more productive farming systems (Carroll et al, 1990). Development of new farming practices is most urgently needed for moist tropical regions – the Amazon Basin, Central Africa and South-East Asia – to create sustainable systems, and avert the massive deforestation and land degradation now taking place (Goodland et al, 1984; Oldeman et al, 1990; WRI, 1992). Intensive industrial farming based on the Western model may never succeed in these areas (Sanchez, 1976; Maass and Garcia-Oliva, 1992), but other forms such as agro-forestry, intercropping or shifting agriculture might perform well (Altieri, 1983; Dover and Talbot, 1987). Another alternative is low-intensity forest exploitation, as exemplified by groups such as rubber-tappers in the Amazon and some indigenous peoples in South America, Central Africa and South-East Asia (Fearnside, 1987; Caroll et al, 1990).

- Much more experimental research on alternative forms of agriculture is needed, taking lessons from both natural ecosystems and half-forgotten farming traditions (see Chapter 5). Genetic improvement of tropical crops also could make important contributions to food supplies in poor nations.

- In many arid and semi-arid regions – especially much of Africa and South and Western Asia – lack of water obviously is a factor limiting food production. Desertification and overexploitation of natural vegetation (for fuel wood or from overgrazing) are also part of the picture. Reversing land degradation processes, improving and extending irrigation systems where feasible (without overdrawing aquifers), improving livestock productivity and alleviating poverty will all be necessary elements in putting these regions on a sustainable basis (Durning, 1989; Kates and Haarmann, 1992). Given the tight interconnections among poverty, population growth and environmental deterioration, changing the direction of development will not be easy. But here, too, experimenting with alternative practices might pay off, eg game ranching instead of herding cattle or goats and developing salt- or drought-tolerant crops (Ehrlich and Ehrlich, 1991).

- Many highland regions such as the Andes and the Himalaya also are inhabited by very poor, often hungry populations, and land degradation, especially deforestation and soil erosion, has frequently been severe (Oldeman et al, 1990; WRI, 1992). Reforestation and restoring local control over resources may be keys to making these areas more sustainable. Stabilizing highland regions both ecologically and economically could also reduce problems from floods, droughts and siltation in downstream areas (Ehrlich and Ehrlich, 1992).

■ In most developing regions an urgent task is to improve food storage and transport facilities. Post-harvest losses of foods to spoilage and pests range from 30 to 50 per cent, sometimes even higher (Greely, 1991). Reducing these losses by developing or upgrading storage facilities is one of the easiest, quickest and cheapest ways to increase food supplies significantly (Ehrlich et al, 1993).

■ Agricultural innovations in poor nations obviously cannot be brought about without significant changes in policies and, in many if not most cases, without outside assistance from the industrialized nations. Some experimentation in alternative farming and herding systems is taking place in developing nations at international or national agricultural research centres, and some is being conducted by university or private groups, but clearly much more research and more extensive field trials must be undertaken. Beyond research and development, mechanisms to impart information to farmers about new practices and systems are needed.

Most importantly, a philosophy of working with nature, learning from ecological insights and making use of traditions should be instilled in agricultural institutions everywhere. Similarly, policy makers involved in rural development need to be informed by experts in many different fields from anthropology to ecology, forestry and integrated pest management to zoology, as well as the standard agronomy and economics.

## BIODIVERSITY, ECOSYSTEM SERVICES AND AGRICULTURE

Ecosystem services are essential for preserving the health and productivity of agro-ecosystems. Many essential services are performed for humanity by natural systems (and to an unmeasured, but doubtless reduced degree, by human-controlled, simplified systems such as farms, tree plantations, pastures, gardens, parks, golf courses etc). Among these services are regulation of the gaseous composition of the atmosphere, including its 'greenhouse' qualities; modulation of regional climates, especially through the hydrological cycle, which is heavily influenced by terrestrial vegetation, thereby moderating or preventing severe floods and droughts; the cycling of essential nutrients, creation and replenishment of soils, and disposal of wastes; pollination of numerous plants (including important crops); control of the great majority of potential pests and disease vectors; and maintenance of a vast genetic library (Ehrlich and Ehrlich, 1981). That genetic library has provided the very basis of civilization: all crops, livestock species, fisheries, forest products, industrial materials and inspiration, if not the raw material, for most medicines.

Biodiversity has been succinctly defined as all the species of organisms on earth, the genetic diversity they contain and the ecosystems of which they are interdependent components. The current and accelerating epidemic of extinctions of species and populations of organisms is causing alarm among biologists for two major reasons (Wilson, 1989, 1992). First, this loss is primarily the result of converting habitats – natural ecosystems such as forests or natural grasslands – to simplified and less stable systems such as farms, pastures and urban development. The result of such conversion of any area is the local displacement and extinction of many populations of flora and fauna. When such conversion is widespread, and natural areas are reduced to small, widely scattered fragments, many species disappear entirely from the region and the population diversity of those surviving is apt to be sharply diminished, thus also lowering their chances of survival over the long term. And, of course, a species lost is lost for ever. Biologists are concerned about the loss of biodiversity for its own sake and because the losses surely will include countless potential new foods, medicines and useful materials of various sorts. But they also are concerned, for a more crucial but generally less appreciated reason: the consequences of biodiversity loss on ecosystem services, which are especially critical for agricultural productivity (Ehrlich and Wilson, 1991). The inevitable biotic impoverishment of reduced and fragmented natural ecosystems almost certainly will at some point impair their capacity to deliver ecosystem services, although the degree of loss necessary to impair services from any particular type of system remains uncertain (Ehrlich and Mooney, 1983; Ehrlich, 1993).

The reduction in extent of natural terrestrial ecosystems, the displacement of original biota and erosion of their functions are intimately connected to the degradation of land recorded on every continent except Antarctica (Oldeman et al, 1990; Turner et al, 1990; WRI, 1992), and to the reduction of net primary production on land (Vitousek et al, 1986), most of which has occurred during the last half- century due to increasing human activity. Land clearing and removal of woody vegetation, especially species-rich tropical forests, also contribute substantially to the human-caused buildup of greenhouse gases. That buildup in turn may lead to possibly unprecedentedly rapid and drastic changes in climate (Parry, 1990; Ehrlich and Ehrlich, 1991). All these trends tend to undermine the basic capacity of the planet to sustain human life.

## THE BOTTOM LINE

Even though no one can say what the earth's potential carrying capacity for humanity is, it is obvious that reducing it is not desirable. Yet we clearly are reducing it to the extent that we degrade land and lower its productivity, impoverish the planet's diversity of life, expose its surface to increased ultraviolet radiation and alter bio-geo-chemical cycles by changing vegetative cover and emitting excess greenhouse gases to the atmosphere. Meanwhile the human population is demographically committed to doubling its size, or more, in the next five to ten decades, unless much stronger efforts are made to curb its growth.

Consequently, our generation and those of our children and grandchildren face a series of immense challenges. The global community must not only double world food harvests in the next few decades, it also needs to redistribute food and other resources much more equitably. Population growth and overconsumption of resources must be brought under control, while efforts are made to enhance the quality of life for all people. Civilization must strive to halt the deterioration and loss of renewable resources (soil, fresh water, biodiversity) and, whenever possible, to reverse that deterioration. It must bend every effort to assess its carrying capacity and design a sustainable world, including a sustainable food production system. The possibilities, opportunities and challenges are boundless; it is to be hoped that the wisdom, imagination and courage to meet them can be found and mobilized.

## REFERENCES

Altieri, M, *Agroecology: The Scientific Basis of Alternative Agriculture*, Division of Biological Control, Berkeley: University of California, 1983.

Borrini, G, 'Lessons Learned in Community-based Environmental Management', International Course for Primary Health Care Managers at District Level in Developing Countries, Rome: Istituto Superiore di Sanitá, 1990.

Brown, L, 'The Changing World Food Prospect: The Nineties and Beyond', *Worldwatch Paper*, no 85, 1988.

Brown, L, 'Fertilizer Engine Losing Steam', *World Watch*, vol 4, no 5, 1991, pp 32–3.

Brown, L and E Wolfe, 'Soil Erosion: Quiet Crisis in the World Economy', *Worldwatch Paper*, no 60, 1984.

Brown, L et al, *State of the World 1989*, London: Earthscan, 1989.

Brown, L et al, *State of the World 1991*, London: Earthscan, 1991.

Brown, L et al, *State of the World 1993*, London: Earthscan, 1993.

Bugbee, B and O Monje, 'The Limits of Crop Productivity', *BioScience*, vol 42, no 7, 1992, pp 494–502.

Carroll, C, J Vandermeer, P Rosset (eds), *Agroecology*, New York: McGraw-Hill, 1990.

Cohen, J, J Williams, D Plucknett and H Shands, 'Ex Situ Conservation of Plant Genetic Resources: Global Development and Environmental Concerns', *Science*, no 253, 1991, pp 866–72.

Dahlberg, K, *Beyond the Green Revolution*, New York: Plenum, 1979.

Daily, G and P Ehrlich, 'An Exploratory Model of the Impact of Rapid Climate Change on the World Food Situation', *Proceedings of the Royal Society of London*, 1990, pp 232–44.

Daily, G and P Ehrlich, 'Population, Sustainability, and Earth's Carrying Capacity', *BioScience*, vol 42, no 10, 1992, pp 761–71.

Dasgupta, P, 'Poverty, Resources, and Fertility: The Household as a Reproductive Partnership' in P Dasgupta, *An Inquiry into Well-Being and Destitution*, Oxford: Oxford University Press, 1993 (forthcoming), Ch 11.

Dover, M and L Talbot, *To Feed the Earth: Agro-Ecology for Sustainable Development*, Washington, DC: World Resources Institute, 1987.

Dréze, J and A Sen (eds), *The Political Economy of Hunger. Vol. III: Endemic Hunger,*

Oxford: Oxford University Press, 1991.

Durning, A, 'Poverty and the Environment: Reversing the Downward Spiral', *Worldwatch Paper*, no 92, 1989.

Edwards, C, R Lal, P Madden, R Miller and G House (eds), *Sustainable Agricultural Systems*, Ankeny, IA: Soil and Water Conservation Society, 1990.

Ehrlich, P, 'Biodiversity and Ecosystem Function: Need We Know More?', foreword in E-D Schulze and H Mooney (eds), *Biodiversity and Ecosystem Function*, Berlin: Springer-Verlag, 1993.

Ehrlich, P and A Ehrlich, *Extinction: The Causes and Consequences of the Disappearance of Species*, New York: Random House, 1981.

Ehrlich, P and A Ehrlich, *The Population Explosion*, New York: Simon & Schuster, 1990.

Ehrlich, P and A Ehrlich, *Healing the Planet*, Boston: Addison-Wesley, 1991.

Ehrlich, P and A Ehrlich, 'The Value of Biodiversity', *Ambio*, vol 21, no 3, 1992, pp 219–26.

Ehrlich, P, A Ehrlich and G Daily, 'Nutritional Security, Population, and Food', *Population and Development Review*, vol 19, no 2, 1993, pp 1–32.

Ehrlich, P and H Mooney, 'Extinction, Substitution, and Ecosystem Services', *BioScience*, vol 33, 1983, pp 248–54.

Ehrlich, P and E O Wilson, 'Biodiversity Studies: Science and Policy', *Science*, no 253, 1991, pp 758–62.

Eicher, C and J Schaatz (eds), *Agricultural Development in the Third World*, Baltimore: Johns Hopkins Press, 1990.

Falkenmark, M and C Widstrand, 'Population and Water Resources: A Delicate Balance', *Population Bulletin*, vol 47, no 3, 1992, pp 1–36.

FAO (United Nations Food and Agriculture Organization), *1990 Agriculture Production Yearbook*, Rome: FAO, 1990.

FAO, *World Food Supplies and Prevalence of Chronic Undernutrition in Developing Regions as Assessed in 1992*, Rome: FAO, 1992.

Fearnside, P, 'Rethinking Continuous Cultivation in Amazonia', *BioScience*, vol 37, no 3, 1987, pp 209–14.

Gasser, C S and R T Fraley, 'Genetically Engineering Plants for Crop Improvement', *Science*, no 244, 1989, pp 1293–9.

Goodland, R, C Watson and G Ledec, *Environmental Management in Tropical Agriculture*, Boulder CO: Westview, 1984.

Greely, M, 'Postharvest Losses – the Real Picture', *International Agricultural Development*, September/October 1991, pp 9–11.

Hillel, D, *Out of the Earth: Civilization and the Life of the Soil*, New York: The Free Press (Macmillan), 1991.

Homer-Dixon, T, J Boutwell and G Rathjens, 'Environmental Change and Violent Conflict', *Scientific American*, February 1993, pp 16–25.

Horn, D, *Ecological Approach to Pest Management*, London: Elsevier, 1988.

Hoyt, E, *Conserving the Wild Relatives of Crops*, Rome and Gland: International Board for Plant Genetic Resources, International Union for the Conservation of Nature and Natural Resources (IUCN) and Worldwide Fund for Nature (WWF), 1988.

IRRI (International Rice Research Institute), 'Yield Stagnation, Yield Decline, and the Field Frontier of Irrigated Rice', *Program Report to the Board Program Committee*, 21–3 September 1992. Mimeo.

Jacobson, J, 'Environmental Refugees: A Yardstick of Habitability', *Worldwatch Paper*, no 86, 1988.

Kates, R W and V Haarmann, 'Where the Poor Live', *Environment*, vol 34, no 4, 1992, pp 4–11, 25–8.

Lee, R, W Arthur, A Kelley, G Rodgers and T Srinivasan (eds), *Population, Food, And Rural Development*, Oxford: Clarendon Press, 1988.

Maass, J and F Garcia-Oliva, 'Erosion de suelos y conservación biológica en México y Centroamérica' in R Dirzo, D Pinera and M Kalin-Arroyo (eds), *Conservación y Manejo de Recursos Naturales en América Latina*, Santiago, Chile: Red. Latinoamericana de Botánico, 1992.

Norse, D, 'A New Strategy for Feeding a Crowded Planet', *Environment*, vol 34, no 5, 1992, pp 6–11, 32–9.

NRC (National Research Council), Committee on the Role of Alternative Farming Methods in Modern Production Agriculture, *Alternative Agriculture*, Washington, DC: National Academy Press, 1989.

NRC, Board on Agriculture, *Managing Global Genetic Resources*, Washington, DC: National Academy Press, 1991.

Oldeman, L, V van Engelen and J Pulles, 'The Extent of Human-Induced Soil Degradation', Annex 5 of L Oldeman et al, *World Map of the Status of Human-Induced Soil Degradation: An Explanatory Note*, Wageningen, The Netherlands: International Soil Reference and Information Centre (ISRIC), 1990.

Parry, M, *Climate Change and World Agriculture*, London: Earthscan Publications, 1990.

Pimentel, D and C Hall (eds), *Food and Natural Resources*, San Diego, CA: Academic Press, 1989.

Pimentel, D et al, 'Conserving Biological Diversity in Agricultural/ Forestry Systems', *BioScience*, vol 42, no 5, 1992, pp 354–62.

Plucknett, D, N Smith, J Williams and N Anishetty, *Gene Banks and the World's Food*, Princeton, NJ: Princeton University Press, 1992.

Population Reference Bureau, *1993 World Population Data Sheet*, Washington, DC: Population Reference Bureau, 1993.

Postel, S, 'Water for Agriculture: Facing the Limits', *Worldwatch Paper*, no 93, 1990.

Repetto, R, 'Population, Resources, Environment: An Uncertain Future', *Population Bulletin*, vol 42, no 2, 1987.

Sanchez, P, *Properties and Management of Soils in the Tropics*, New York: Wiley-Interscience, 1976.

Smil, V, 'Population Growth and Nitrogen: An Exploration of a Critical Link', *Population and Development Review*, vol 17, no 4, 1991, pp 569–601.

Soule, J and J Piper, *Farming in Nature's Image*, Washington, DC: Island Press, 1992.

Swaminathan, M and S Sinha (eds), *Global Aspects of Food Production*, Riverton, NJ: Tycooly International, 1986.

Turner, B II, W Clark, R Kates, J Richards, J Mathews and W Meyer (eds), *The Earth as Transformed by Human Action*, Cambridge: Cambridge University Press, 1990.

UNFPA (United Nations Fund for Population Activities), *State of the World Population 1992*, New York: UNFPA, 1992.

USDA (United States Department of Agriculture), Foreign Agriculture Service, *World Agricultural Production*, WAP 2–93, February 1993.

Vitousek, P, P Ehrlich, A Ehrlich and P Matson, 'Human Appropriation of the Products of Photosynthesis', *BioScience*, vol 36, no 6, 1986, pp 368–73.

Vosti, S, T Reardon and W von Urff (eds), *Agricultural Sustainability, Growth, and Poverty Alleviation: Issues and Policies*, Feldafing, Germany: Proceedings of Conference,

23–7 September 1991 (available from Deutsche Stiftung für Internationale Entwicklung (DSE), Zentralstelle für Ernahrung und Landwirtschaft, Wielinger Str 52, D-8133 Feldafing, FRG).

Walsh, J, 'Preserving the Options: Food Production and Sustainability', *Issues in Agriculture. No 2*, Consultative Group on International Agriculture Research, October 1991.

Wilson, E O, 'Threats to Biodiversity', *Scientific American*, September 1989, pp 108–16.

Wilson, E O, *The Diversity of Life*, Cambridge, MA: Harvard University Press, 1992.

World Bank, *World Development Report 1990: Poverty*, Oxford: Oxford University Press, 1990.

World Bank, *World Development Report 1992: Development and the Environment*, Oxford: Oxford University Press, 1992.

WRI (World Resources Institute), *World Resources 1992–93*, Oxford: Oxford University Press, 1992.

Wrigley, G, *Tropical Agriculture: The Development of Production*, New York: Longman, 1982.

*Chapter Two*

# Sustainable, Equitable Economics
## The Personal Energy Budget

*Hans-Peter Dürr*

Human beings and all their activities are part of a system which is sometimes simply called 'nature'. This universal nature is more general and comprehensive in its meaning than nature in our common language, which relates to the abundant and complex phenomena on the surface of our planet (earth, water, atmosphere, plants and animals), and even more, with a somewhat romantic touch, to its virgin form before man[1] intruded on it. Defined in this more restricted sense, nature stands in contrast to culture and human civilization. Nature and culture appear as adversaries in a zero-sum-game where the flourishing of the one necessarily implies the suffering of the other. The relationship is viewed as a continuous struggle for dominance. In the past, nature was perceived as a stronger, impressive and unpredictable power to which mankind had to submit for survival. His rational abilities, however, enabled man to gather experience, to penetrate into the secrets of nature, to develop particular skills, to build up his culture. He discovered numerous ways to employ the laws of nature to his own advantage. Beginning, roughly, with the Renaissance, Western man, as the 'crown of creation' embarked on a voyage to free himself from nature and his great successes on this voyage led him to the arrogant attitude of posing as nature's master, to enslave it, to regard it merely as a big quarry for his own shortsighted benefit, rather than – what it actually is – as a foundation and the nourishing support for his own existence. It is this anthropocentric attitude which makes Western man talk of nature as 'our environment', ie nature as merely a general passive arena for his actions. The consequences of this world-view for co-existing civilisations, ie colonialism, is discussed in other chapters of this book (eg Chapter 6 by Amalric and Banuri).

It is important for the solution of the present and future problems that the artificiality of a separation between man and environment, and between culture and

---

1. The English word 'man' is used here frequently. It should be taken in the general sense as a representative of the human species, ie in the sense of the German concept 'Mensch' rather than 'Mann'. All occurrences of 'his' or 'he' should be read as 'his/her' or 'he/she'.

nature is realized. Modern physics has taught that universal nature does not proceed like a mechanical clock: the future is open, the process of creation is still going on. Hence it appears quite adequate to regard human beings as co-actors and co-creators in this continuous process. Consciously creative man does not exist outside nature or in contrast to a separate nature, but forms an integral part of it. As a consequence everything man does or does not do is, in a general sense, natural. This, however, does not mean that it is indifferent and insignificant what man does and the way he does it. What is inflicted as damage to earth does not injure nature as such, because nature presents itself in an infinite variety of forms. But it is for our own sake that we have to seek essentially to preserve that grand and unique organism on earth, 'nature around us', as we experience it. And, even more, we have to seek not only to preserve it in its present form and appearance but also to sustain its enormous potential for further evolution, its creativity and vitality, because there is no reason to believe that evolution should end with homo sapiens, except if man foolishly chooses to cut it off himself.

## DESTRUCTION AND CREATION OF DIVERSITY IN NATURAL PROCESSES

For an appropriate interpretation of nature it is important not merely to rely on a careful analysis of certain parts or aspects in accordance with our fragmenting mode of thinking and scientific investigation. The properties of the system as a whole should be considered, for the whole is more than the sum of its parts. Of course, scientific description takes this partially into account by introducing the concept of interaction between various parts and uses the concept of synergy for a more complicated interplay of many objects. But even this more sophisticated concept fails if a substantial change of character in the properties of the objects which form a joined system occurs in the process of their embedding. This is particularly evident for animated matter – dissecting a living organism leaves us, as a rule, with parts which are rather dissimilar to the corresponding pieces integrated into the organism. There is nothing strange about this observation.

Physics has discovered important laws which govern the behaviour of systems of a large number of independent objects. The most important one, perhaps, is the so-called 'second law of thermodynamics' or 'entropy law'. This states essentially that for closed systems the diversity of their structure will always decrease in time. This is connected with the fact that systems composed according to some principles of order usually represent less probable configurations than less ordered or completely disordered systems. For the lay reader, a precise mathematical definition of this principle is quite unnecessary in order to understand its consequences in daily life. The second law of thermodynamics expresses the rule that, left to itself, any ordered system such as a burning candle or a human being will tend to return to total disorder. Entropy is a measure of the disorder of a system.[2] The

---

2. The entropy of a macrosystem is expressed mathematically as the logarithm of the relative frequency of different micro-configurations constituting this system.

higher the degree of disorder, the larger the entropy, and the more probable it is (according to the second law of thermodynamics) that it will occur. Syntropy is just the opposite of entropy, ie it increases when order increases. In the following we will refer to syntropy instead of entropy.

From the second law of thermodynamics it follows that there is a continuous degradation of order in the universe on the average. This seems to contradict our daily observation of a counter-process, namely of a continual creation of intricately differentiated and highly ordered structures, as most obviously documented by the evolution of life on earth to more complex, and more highly structured and differentiated organisms. This impressive development, antagonistic to the common trend of degradation, however, is only possible because of a continuous inflow of high-temperature, unidirectional radiation from the sun, balanced by a corresponding outflow of low-temperature radiation back into space in all directions. This throughput of energy continuously 'leaves behind' a certain amount of syntropy, an order-building potential, which is the motor of essentially all net order creation on earth.

It appears appropriate and legitimate to assign positive value to the 'order' of a system as expression of its synergetic diversity, differentiation and sophistication. In this sense we could also state that in all natural processes there is, as a whole, a continuous value destruction. This continuous value degradation can only be locally halted or even reversed with the assistance of a generous sponsor like the sun or – as today in industrialized countries – by exploiting rich deposits of 'work-capable' energy or syntropy in the earth's crust. The assignment of sure values to different diversified structures cannot, however, be objectivized in general. The value of their order is only relative, in the same way that the differentiated structure of a key reveals its value only relative to the lock which it is capable of opening.

To attach an objective value to a given degree of order and to locate a system in some kind of abstract hierarchy is a very serious and delicate problem. It frustrates attempts to render reliable judgements as to whether certain active interventions will move the ecosystem up or down on such an imagined hierarchical ladder of values, or, more qualitatively, whether they do or do not jeopardize the sustainability of the ecosphere in a form in which humankind can survive. None the less, such judgements are being made continually and they must be made. Because of this uncertainty they must be made on the side of caution.

## SUSTAINABILITY

The concept of sustainability of the ecosphere appears quite frequently today in the ecological literature. For example, the Brundtland Report (WCED, 1987) emphasizes the necessity of 'sustainable growth' in the development of the national economies and the world economy as a whole. The concept of 'sustainable development' also played a dominant role at the United Nations conference on environment and development (UNCED) in Rio in 1992. Although this objective definitely signals a step forward in comparison with the simple-minded demand of 'as much economic growth as possible' and indicates our increasing awareness of the principal limitations of development in a 'finite world', it may, if too narrowly interpreted, fall fatally short of what is actually required. To realize this one has to get a clearer view of what is meant or should be meant by sustainability.

Sustainability requires more than simply securing the status quo, the substance matter of our ecosystem. Sustainability of the ecosystem has to ensure the reproductive potential and the capability for long-term survival in the present form, and beyond that sustainability has to include the preservation of vitality, the capability not only to reproduce, but to produce, to create new forms and to develop further. The productive and creative potential of nature in its characteristic features on earth is closely linked to a subtle, dynamic balance of forces and counter-forces. Contrary to the situation in a stable static equilibrium, there remains in a state of quasi-stable dynamic equilibrium a very extensive mobility, a rich opportunity for manifold and intensive interplay by which new dimensions, new alleys for the development of the system, can be opened up. As far as we know, there is no direct intention of nature, off-hand, to create certain new forms. New forms are the result of a trial-and-error procedure, of an infinite game (probably not quite like the random nature of throwing dice, but a game that involves holistic features as indicated by modern physics) with a subsequent severe selection test as to whether the (holisticly prepared) spontaneously created form fits constructively into the already established order. In this way, step by step, an increasingly complex and highly differentiated structure is built up which goes far beyond anything which could be conceived, designed and implemented off-hand by even the most imaginative mind.

This becomes apparent if we visualize the practically unlimited complexity of the ecosystem with its innumerable intertwining regulatory process cycles which equip the system with an astonishing flexibility and robustness towards changing exterior conditions. It seems to be an absolute miracle that such a highly differentiated and coordinated structure could have developed in four billion years of the earth's history. Four billion years may seem to be quite a long time. But it should be realized that the number of the possible different paths for development, among which the most promising path of evolution had to be found, is unimaginably large. This number, in fact, is so huge that in comparison to it astronomical numbers – like the number of atoms in the universe or the number of seconds that have elapsed since the Big Bang – look invisibly tiny. The task of making the most promising selection could only be successfully accomplished by a continuous process of forming certain ordered structures, of changing and differentiating them, of combining the modified forms in various new ways to compose new structures on a higher level which then, in turn, become the building blocks of the next layer and so on.

The evolution from simple to more complex structures should not be designated as 'growth'. Growth relates more to an increase in size without changing character and quality, and hence, as such, does not comprise autopoesis, the creation of new forms. To call it 'qualitative growth', as is sometimes done, can perhaps meet this objection but this is a false façade, because it disguises and underrates the fundamental difference from ordinary growth, the 'golden calf' of modern economy. Nobody would, for example, agree with the idea of calling a poem a 'qualitatively grown letter'.

Growth in the ordinary sense has the simple feature that it can be characterized by a number or a set of numbers. For example, the growth of children is indicated by the increase in their height and weight, and the growth of a national economy by the increase of its gross national product (GNP). The GNP is, indeed, very practical for an economic comparison of competitive societies because it is easy to calculate. But it is obvious that this number can hardly be, as commonly presented, a measure for the quality of life, just as the growth indicators 'height' and 'weight' of children do not indicate whether they have really grown up in the full sense of the word. A grown-up is or should be more than a bigger sized baby. We expect a grown-up to show a distinguishable individuality as expressed by particular skills, sensibilities, insights etc. These qualities prove difficult or impossible to translate into numbers. In spite of this, competitive societies are very inventive to do just this and try to assign numbers to everything they regard as being valuable. The whole hierarchical system of examinations, with more and more refined marking procedures, reflects the futile attempt to put an objective linear order into quality; to quantify it such as to know definitely, by golly, who is better or worse than the other.

Complexity of a system does not only mean complication, ie something which consists of a complicated superposition of many different aspects. In such a merely complicated case, we may by, for example, defining appropriately aggregated new qualities or by choosing a more intelligent reference frame, succeed in dramatically decreasing the apparent opacity. Complexity comprises, in addition, the intricate dynamic interplay of all components. Complexity is in a way irreducible: by trying to express it in simpler or fewer terms we deliberately mutilate the system in one way or the other. The loss caused by this procedure may be very severe, even though it is not easily noticeable.

Contrary to the goals of technology, nature under the usual changing external conditions never pushes very hard to go to the limits in one direction. No one option is maximized at the expense of others, either with respect to efficiency, productivity or 'economic' profits. Evolutionary selection leads to solutions which maximize the number of options and thereby gain maximum flexibility under changing external conditions, and establish an optimum in this extended, higher dimensional space. Nature's approach, therefore, favours long-term rather than short-term efficiency. In fact this is the wrong way to put it. Phrased more precisely, natural processes are not aimed by some divine guidance towards the creation of these absolutely miraculous organisms with their increasingly complex and extremely versatile structures, but, in trying something new, attempts just everything (or, taking the holistic dependencies into account, nearly just everything). This includes the 'stupid' and the 'wise', ie changes which eventually prove destructive as well as constructive. Actually there always will be a predominance of stupid, destructive steps because the wise, constructive choice is unknown at the outset and statistically extremely unlikely. Evolution therefore will also take full advantage of any beneficial option irrespective of others, eg by suppressing the counter-force in a dynamic equilibrium. This then leads to a destabilization of the system and, before it collapses, produces tremendous amplification effects which possibly – as can be observed in highly industrialized societies – produce short-term advantages. But because of their inflexibility these highly lop-sided solutions cannot generally prevail (except in particular ecological niches where there is little or no change of exterior conditions). They will live for a short time and disappear. Hence, these maladjusted products are hardly represented in nature. This is a direct result of their maladjustment rather than a consequence of some intentional foresight. In other words: what dominates in our natural environment has success-fully navigated a long-term test programme.

Since humankind as a species apparently has successfully passed some of the long-term survival tests of natural selection – otherwise we would not be around – it may be legitimate to assume that our physical and spiritual predisposition in all of its present variations is essentially in tune with the sustainability of the ecos-phere on which humankind vitally depends. Our reflective, intellectual capabili-ties, on the other hand, seem to be less reliable in this regard. In particular the experience of the enormous robustness and flexibility of the nature around us and the rationalization of this fortunate circumstance, has misled many of us to con-clude quite generally that everything we do will be tolerated by nature, and that nature will be infinitely patient towards our mistreating it, and extremely sub-servient if given the right orders. On the other hand, ethics – or, more specifically, moral and religious codes – in all cultures seem to contain important wisdom regarding an adequate behaviour for securing sustainability. In this respect ethics and human culture may be considered as a consequence of natural evolution rather than merely as a decoration of humankind's excellence. In particular, ethics may not primarily call for special actions, but more for moderation and also an appropriate pace in our actions to give nature a fair chance to compensate for our misjudgements.

## CYCLE VIOLATIONS IN NINETEENTH-CENTURY ECONOMICS

To secure sustainability of the ecosphere requires a profound understanding of our role as part of this complex ecosystem; the challenge it poses and the moderation it requires. It demands, on the one hand, a dramatic change in values, consciousness and way of thinking, in particular of the affluent in the industrialized countries. On the other hand it requires new instruments in order to implement the new awareness in an effective way in societies. There are many discussions about where and how to start. Obviously this is a chicken-and-egg relationship: both new consciousness and implementation are necessary, and each one will decisively support and promote the other.

To awaken a new consciousness and to attain a new thinking appears to be an extremely difficult task because it certainly requires a long learning process which probably can only be accomplished in many generations. This process, however, might proceed much faster if such a consciousness does not have to be developed anew but can be rediscovered in ourselves and recovered from our ingrained phy-logenic experience. Then perhaps only some of the recent 'debris' has to be pushed away in the minds and hearts of the great squanderers, in particular, who are so intensely focused on action rather than contemplation. Still, it is hard to judge whether such a clearing job will ever be attempted without some major catastrophes forcing us actually to do it and also whether, if it is attempted, it will catch on fast enough to meet the present urgent situation. Certainly it would be of great help if the general conditions of the 'modern life' of the affluent in the industrialized countries could be modified to fully support such a learning process and to accelerate the necessary transitions.

Yet to my mind, all attempts to secure sustainability of the earth's ecosphere will be futile without a fundamental revision of the presently accepted economic principles and practised economic rules. The economic theories advocated and implemented commonly today – whether of the socialistic type of a planned economy as exercised in the past in the East or of the capitalistic type of a free market economy as accepted in one or other form by Western countries and subsequently by most other countries – are based on nineteenth-century concepts. Under their present large-scale application they obviously prove insufficient and, in fact, highly deficient for a proper description of the actual situation. Therefore, in their practical application, they lead to undesirable consequences and initiate disastrous developments.

These economic theories perceive the environment effectively as a reservoir which serves as an infinite source of materials and energy for all human activities, and as an infinite sink for all their end-products. They ignore the obvious basic fact that, as Immler (1989) has emphasized, all real productive power derives directly or indirectly from nature. In capitalistic market economies the productivity of nature is only partially taken into account by recognizing the productive power of human beings, ie human labour, and of land. Its major part, however, the productive power of external nature, is replaced by the notion of the 'production factor' capital, because in the framework of market processes it represents the potential of transforming real physical products as produced by natural processes into objects with monetary exchange value. The organizational factor capital hence is erroneously interpreted as a production factor. Such an interpretation is justified if the notion of value is restricted to the meaning of exchange values, a notion which seems very practical and appropriate from our one-sided anthropocentric point of view. But clearly this does not reflect the internal value of surrounding nature with its highly differentiated structure.

As in the Social Revolution, which correctly recognized the synergetic, positive sum-related partnership between employer and employee, the existential dependence of human beings on their special and highly diversified environment requires new 'rules of the game' such as to recognize the superior values characterizing the joint system of man and his environment, and to optimize these values. The preservation of the full creative power of nature, based on a tremendous diversity of highly developed and intelligently interlinked and cooperating subsystems, the sustainability of the earth's ecosystem, should be regarded as such a superior value. It includes as an essential part the productive power of nature from which nearly all human 'value creation', in the restricted economic sense, derives.

Obviously the values of nature are much richer in diversity than the economically accounted values which are simply mapped and measured on a one-dimensional monetary scale. This hierarchical relationship actually demands the appropriate incorporation of economy – as a subsystem of natural activities in the general sense – into the more comprehensive system of nature, rather than the other way around of adapting the evaluation of nature to the limited exchange value system, the money price system of economy. In revising the principles of economy or in setting up a framework in which economy as a human activity can develop without violating the essential conditions of sustainability of the earth's ecosphere, it will be important not only to formulate principles which make this reconciliation possible – which may prove to be a very difficult task – but in particular to devise concrete steps which induce the system to move in the right direction or, at least, which weaken the links responsible for the present destabilizing process. As one of such initial steps a partial incorporation of nature into the monetary value system might prove instrumental because it would give the value of external nature a certain weight in the financial assessment tussle. Although such a financial assessment of external nature would be highly insufficient and inadequate, it might prove to be an important instrument for stabilizing the economy and steering it away from its present hazardous course.

Because of the diverse structure of the values of nature it is impossible to define a quantity which could serve as an objective measure for sustainability or for the creative potential of nature. But it would be very helpful if we had at least some very crude measure along this line, in order to link nature to the monetary value system of economy. It appears that something related to syntropy (negative entropy), might serve this purpose. The essential point would not be precision – this is, in principle, impossible – but some measure of nature on its own terms, which introduces its vitality as a whole into the bargaining game of economics, is needed. This would, above all, coincide with our own long-term interests, ie the welfare of our descendants.

The dynamic quasi-equilibrium on the earth which ensures stability and productivity of the earth's ecosystem uses, in general, only cyclic processes in a direct or indirect way with no real sources besides the sun, and no real sinks besides space into which waste heat is radiated. Industrial processes, in general, do not employ closed production cycles, and therefore eat up resources and pile up dumps. This imbalance will lead to severe consequences if certain limits are not observed. These limits are given by the tolerance of the environment to buffer off such cycle violations without a dramatic change of its present constitution – a change which may jeopardize humankind's existence. They do not only consist of bounds on material input or output of one kind or the other but also on the speed with which this is done. Speeding up the processes not only wastes syntropy but also because the ecosystem is not given sufficient time to go through its usual trial-and-error procedure it will not have the chance to come up with some regulatory reaction which will 'save creation', in particular a creation of which man is still a part.

Because of the very limited insight into the complex regulatory mechanism of the earth's ecosystem with which (Western) science provides us, it appears to be a good rule of thumb in human activities to aim at maximizing the number of production processes which are segments of closed cycles, ie to employ processes which do not extensively use up non-renewable resources. In this way neither do reservoirs get drained nor dumps filled. Taking this point of view seriously Northern civilizations cannot possibly serve as an example for a survival scenario of the future. It should be quite obvious that – metaphorically speaking – any economy based on a principle of 'bank robbery' where 'value creation' and 'productivity' is based on merely accounting the monetary investment for the welding equipment with which bigger and thicker safes are cracked, hardly offers an example for a future sustainable economy.

## THE ECO-BUDGET

The tormenting question is whether such bank robber societies will ever be persuaded to change their procedure before all the accessible safes are emptied or the litter and other negative side-effects following from the robbery – here a comparison with the situation in a gold rush town may be more illustrative – destroys their physical and social basis. It is hard to be optimistic here, because those who profit most from this lucrative transfer of unaccounted natural property into capital assets will be the least willing to discontinue this procedure. Because of their great wealth they will at the same time be the most powerful and decisive forces against any change. Even if some of them grasped the seriousness of the situation it is difficult to conceive that anybody would be able really to break up the intrinsic dynamics of the system which is essentially enforced and controlled by present ill-founded economic principles.

In spite of these bleak auspices efforts should be made to find paths to a sustainable development in all parts of the world. Such a development will include as an essential feature the fact that value creation in economy is more closely linked to generic productive processes in nature. These in turn are directly or indirectly connected with the continuous syntropy influx from the sun. As a consequence agricultural activities and human labour will have to regain their former dominant role. This does not imply that we have to return to the agricultural and technical activities of the past but it requires the development of new forms of activities which constructively employ our present scientific and technological know-how to meet the necessary condition of sustainability.

An automatic increase in the value of capital as reflected by interest should, from this view-point, only be possible if linked to generic natural production processes or genuine innovations of some kind without degrading the environment, rather than to the expanding exploitation of non-renewable natural resources. Such a sustainable economy will give everybody on earth a fair chance for survival because sunshine and human labour are accessible everywhere – in fact, both these factors have been the essential basis of all human civilizations up to now.

The main threat to ecological sustainability originates primarily in the unrestricted affluence and overconsumption of the people in Northern industrialized countries. Despite the fact that they constitute only about 20 per cent of the world population they use up about 80 per cent of the world's non-renewable resources and hence also produce a corresponding proportion of polluting wastes.

In view of the finite capacity and limited robustness of the terrestrial ecosystem it is quite obvious that the present standard of living of the industrialized North cannot be extended in an equitable manner to the remaining four billion people of the less developed countries without exceeding the carrying capacity of the earth and hence destroying our life-support system. It is important to note that this alarming assessment is not only a consequence of the finiteness of resources, but also and predominantly of the wastes and the speed by which human activity changes the face of the earth. Since many of us in Western society frequently and pompously proclaim, in our Sunday sermons and official speeches, liberty, equity and solidarity (to use the more modern terms) as basic goals of humanity, we had better search for life-styles compatible with these high ideals, and make serious attempts to realize them everywhere in the world and not only for a small, élite group. To many this may appear to be an impossible task because it seems to violate a general rule of historical experience that people will never voluntarily give up a high standard of living for less. Inflicting such a change by force will be even worse because of the violence and destruction it would inevitably evoke. In addition it would be rather unrealistic to expect this to happen since the most powerful people would be the least inclined to favour such changes.

Still, the situation may not be altogether hopeless because a 'high quality of life' is not so closely linked to what, in economic terms, is defined as a 'high standard of living'. More and more people realize today that the highly cherished Western standard of living requires continuous intensive activity, mostly of a rather uncreative sort, accompanied by increasing anxieties and stress, a tremendous turnover in material and energy, goods and services, producing masses of pollutants harmful to our health – all factors which are counterproductive to what people in Western societies consider 'a good life'.

To achieve the necessary change it will be important not to approach the problem by preaching solely restraint and renunciation to the affluent of the industrialized countries because they are psychologically ill-prepared to accept this message due to their present economic and social adaptation. The intrinsic dynamics of the whole process of 'development' in its modern interpretation has to be taken into account to find an appropriate access for improving the situation. Like the people in poor countries, who in an attempt to alleviate or escape their inhuman physical conditions increase the number of their children and through this on the average further seriously aggravate their detrimental conditions, people in the 'developed' countries are similarly trapped in vicious circles. An increasing lack of spiritual nourishment becomes the driving force for more individual isolation and increasing consumption, leading to a more hectic and less contemplative life-style which in turn worsens the original loss of spiritual depth. Or, even more obviously, the credo of the industrialized North is still based on the erroneous myth that only further economic growth (which is still largely material growth) will enable us to solve our present most urgent problems, although any rational extrapolation should teach us that it makes a solution meeting equitable human standards even more difficult. The point, therefore, is that people in the North should use all their imagination and ingenuity to devise life-styles which are 'better' than the present ones, without simultaneously violating the limits of their eco-budget. These limits are dictated by the finiteness of the earth and the number of people on earth with whom we want to share its fruits equitably.

In spite of the abundant historical counter-examples, I still believe in the common sense of people when enlightened by some wise women and men. These wise women and men have to demonstrate to the people the dangerous situation in which we presently find ourselves, but in a fashion relating directly to the restricted imagination of their daily routine and indicating possible paths out of it without overstraining their limited strength. For a general orientation we should perhaps start to provide a rough estimate of the human eco-budget in general and in individual terms. To give reliable numbers in this context, of course, will be extremely difficult if not impossible because such numbers cannot be objectively defined. This holds for the global assessment but even more so for the individual limits because of the great diversity in geography, culture, habits and tastes. The requirement of equity should not be interpreted to mean strict equality and uniformity. Nevertheless, we are at present so far away from any reasonable standards of equity that it should suffice to begin with to concentrate on some very coarse but reasonable and effective measures.

General considerations on the eco-budget indicate that there are a large number of factors which have to be constrained to favour sustainability. These factors, however, are intimately connected with each other. Therefore, it seems appropriate and legitimate to concentrate on a very few key factors, the control of which hopefully will also lead to effective controls of many others. One key factor is the supply of high-quality primary energy (or actually syntropy), while another one is the supply of fresh water. Here only the energy issue is discussed.

## ENERGY AS A KEY FACTOR

The primary energy supply plays a decisive role in all human activities. The possible exploitation of the immense energy reservoirs in the earth's thin crust in the form of fossil fuels – coal, petroleum and natural gas – liberated man from the continuous but rather limited, scattered and weak sun-energy, and provided him with a million times more intensive sources. The relatively simple access to these abundant energy sources was an essential factor in triggering the industrial revolution. With the technical unlocking of nuclear power during the last decades humanity got into the position of having even more energy-intensive sources available for industrial development.

As a practically unlimited energy source, in other words our continuous energy income, only the daily inflow of sun energy can be counted. This corresponds to about 178,000 terawatt (TW) (if we disregard here that the sun will soon have reached its mid-life point and in about five billion more years will have burned up its nuclear fusion fuels). About one-third of the sun radiation is reflected back into outer space by the upper layers of the atmosphere. The remaining sunlight penetrating the atmosphere and hitting the surface of the earth can be used by us either directly or indirectly as energy of the water, the winds or of biomass. Economically, sun energy is used today only to a very limited extent (world-wide biomass 12 per cent, water power 6 per cent). The dominant part (82 per cent) of the world primary energy consumption (in 1990 about 13 TW or $\frac{1}{13,700}$ of the incident sun energy) is derived from non-renewable energy resources, specifically 77 per cent from fossil fuels and about 5 per cent from nuclear fission. For general orientation, the total reserves of fossil fuels originally stored in the earth's crust amounted (before they were tapped) to an energy equivalent of only about a fortnight of incident sun radiation.

The time left before the exhaustion of the non-renewable fossil fuels follows from a comparison of the energetically accessible reserves in the earth's crust with the present and estimated future energy consumption. On the basis of the present world level of primary energy consumption and its predicted yearly increase (about 3 per cent) one estimates for the following time limits: anthracite 100 years, lignite 115 years, petroleum 45 years and natural gas 60 years. Even an effective doubling of these energy resources – eg by extensively using nuclear fuels – would only shift these time limits by less than 30 years with the present 3 per cent growth of consumption.[3] We, therefore, have to search for more dramatic means to resolve the global energy supply dilemma. But this is still not the only problem.

The main threat, at present, to survival is not a shortage of fuel but rather the general stress inflicted on the environment by the extreme intensity and acceleration of the anthropogenic energy transformation processes. The large abundance of energy reservoirs, which at first sight seemed to be a great benefit for mankind, is slowly turning into one of its main problems: the disruption of the hitherto constructive and synergetic coexistence of man with his environment.

End-products of a high consumption of energy cause serious problems, such as to call for severe restrictions on the anthropogenic energy transformations. This is well known today in connection with the production of carbon dioxide ($CO_2$) in burning of carbon fuels (in particular of coal, but also of petroleum and to lesser extent natural gas), which as a 'greenhouse gas' threatens to cause a change of climate with severe consequences for man and the biosphere. Probably this particular example only indicates the tip of an iceberg. All anthropogenic, technically applied energy flows and the accompanying matter flows act, directly or indirectly, as a potential for additional damages to the earth's ecosystem. By taking the anthropogenic loss of biodiversity as a relevant indicator for a technical-cultural over-stress of the natural environment, Ziegler (1979, 1992) promoted the interesting idea of considering the anthropogenic thermal average energy flow per unit time and area as a key indicator for the degree of environmental stress and encumbrance. For West Germany Ziegler empirically established something like a *critical anthropogenic primary energy flow per unit area and time* which cannot be surpassed without severely damaging biodiversity and hence jeopardizing ecological sustainability. Such a critical energy value can only be a very rough measure for the inflicted damage because it involves complicated "translations" of a large number of rather different damage factors caused by different pollutants and activities into

---

3. An extensive discussion of what these constraints mean for the possibility of achieving a sustainable energy supply for an equitable and liveable world is the subject of Chapter 3.

thermal energy equivalents and an extensive averaging over them.

From the anthropogenic loss of diversity Ziegler derived for Germany a critical value of about $14 \pm 2$ GJ/km²·day $\approx 160 \pm 20$ kW/km² $\approx 0.16$ W/m². This is about 0.1 per cent of the average sun energy reaching the earth's surface and about 20 per cent of average biomass formation by sun radiation in this region. This may not be accidental. This particular value of the critical energy value may just reflect the fact that the ecosystem of the earth, and in particular the bio-system, has received energy from the sun only for over four billion years. Hence it appears reasonable that energy flows of more than a very small fraction of solar energy flow (and dissimilar in density from sun energy) should cause noticeable effects and possibly corresponding damages. It should again be emphasized that the stated limitation on energy holds irrespective of the question of limited resources. It is not a resource-side (input) but a waste-side (output) restriction. Incidentally it should be noticed that this ecologically compatible anthropogenic energy flow is of a size which could be supplied by ultimately using only sun energy as energy source (which in Central Europe is about 100 W/m² average on the ground).

The critical value on the ecologically admissible anthropogenic energy flow for any given population density leads to a limitation of the energy consumption per unit time and person (excluding the direct use of sun energy). If one realizes that the present anthropogenic primary energy flow per unit time and area in Germany is more than ten times this critical value, the large-scale environmental destruction being experienced should come as no surprise. To limit the resulting damages effectively one therefore has to seek ways to reduce the energy consumption per capita and also the number of people per unit area. A reduction by a factor of ten for Germany appears, on the face of it, quite impossible, without a total restructuring of German life and society, with the attendant risk of breakdown of the civil order.

## THE PERSONAL ENERGY BUDGET: THE 1.5 KILOWATT SOCIETY

Taking 0.1 per cent of the effective sun energy incident on the ground or about 0.16 W/m² as rough measure for the admissible, ie ecologically sustainable anthropogenic primary energy consumption rate, and assuming that about 10 per cent of the earth's surface of 510 million km², ie 51 million km², can be permanently inhabited by people (the land area of the earth is about 149 million km², 91 million km² of which are to a varying degree inhabited while about 14 million km² are used for agriculture), then there is a total admissible primary energy per unit time of about 8.2 billion kW = 8.2 TW. If nature were utilized equally by the total population of about 5.4 billion people on earth today, an average energy consumption per capita (excluding use of sun energy in its natural form) of about 1.5 kW – or, more comprehensible, 1.5 kWh per hour – would result. Of course, the assumptions used here are quite uncertain and mainly presented to get some feeling about these numbers. Nevertheless, from general experience during the last decades the impression is that something of this size should be appropriate. The present world average of primary energy use per capita is about 2.4 kW and seems to be more than what can be ecologically sustained in the long term. We will just assume for the following that 1.5 kW per capita is an acceptable number in view of both the limited energy resources and the damages by waste products. This is equivalent to 36 kW hours per *day*; or 13,000 kWh, or 1300 l of gasoline, or 1.6 tonnes of hard coal, per year. If we compare this with Figure 3.7 we see that 8.2 TW is very close to the value for an acceptable scenario[4] (without $CO_2$ retention) of 20 TW (for a population of 11 billion instead of our 5.4 billion). The points of departure of the calculations of Biesiot and Mulder are totally different from the premises assumed here, yet the results agree quite reasonably.

Compare this with the almost 6 kW average primary energy consumption per unit time and per capita of Central Europeans, or the 11 kW per capita in the US, or the 150 W per capita or even less by people in the poorest countries. This would allow the poorest countries to increase the energy consumption by a factor of ten. A reduction of the energy consumption in Europe to about one-quarter of the present consumption (or to even one-seventh in the US) is not a simple matter but not an impossible task. However, to meet this goal individual goodwill and idealism will hardly suffice.

Exterior incentives are necessary to assist people in adjusting their life-styles in an ecologically compatible way. There is no reason not to use the price instrument. This was suggested quite early in the energy debate, eg in connection with nuclear energy (Dürr, 1978). Recently it was advocated in a more explicit form, in particular by Von Weizsäcker (1989). It does not seem politically impossible that in a single European country (eg Germany) or in the European Community as a whole, an appropriate special steering levy on non-renewable energy resources, such as coal, petroleum, natural gas and nuclear energy fuels can be introduced, increasing their market prices to about three or four times their current prices. Still, this only makes sense if:

- the population is comprehensively informed about the sense and purpose of this policy;
- it is done in a smooth and calculable fashion over a period of, say, 15 to 20 years (corresponding to a yearly increase of the energy price by about 7 per cent above inflation);
- the funds levied would be returned essentially integrally to the consumers in an appropriate way so as to further promote sustainability.

Regarding the last point we may consider using a small portion of these funds to subsidize scientific research and technology on the use of renewable energy sources, in particular solar energy in all forms, and also for the repair of environmental damages caused by previous excessive energy consumption. The latter would correspond to an internalization of external energy costs. In the beginning

---

4. It should not be overlooked, however, that this scenario places extremely strict constraints on the level of energy services. The 'service level' available to the populations of the industrialized countries must decrease annually by some 0.5 to 2 per cent and simultaneously the annual increase in energy efficiency must be in the same range.

prevention should be given higher priority than repair in order to reduce or stop additional damages.

## ESTABLISHING AN ECO-TRUST

Many consider the specifications of the money return from the funds to be the most critical aspect of such a measure, because it provides the state authorities with large amounts of money that may invite undesired forms for manipulations. On the other hand it should be kept in mind that the purpose of a steering levy is exactly to create the possibility of supporting preferable developments. There exists, however, widespread hesitation to hand over the full responsibility for these decisions to the state authorities. Many would rather prefer that the citizens themselves make the relevant choices. This may be achieved, for example, quite simply by a reduction of sales taxes or even better – as planned in Switzerland – by establishing a special eco-fund, the money from which is equally returned to all citizens at the end of the fiscal year as an eco-bonus. Such a sprinkler-type redistribution of the money, however, would completely sacrifice the potential of additional eco-steering. The money can be used better eg, to reduce the cost of human labour by subsidizing social security or health insurance. A more flexible arrangement is to collect the energy levy in a special eco-fund in the framework of a government-independent eco-trust which by its statutes is bound to the advancement of an ecologically sustainable economy. Such an eco-trust should be governed by a board of trustees of carefully selected people from all sections of society with special competence in ecological matters. With the assistance of a larger advisory board they should decide on the appropriate redistribution of the funds. This eco-trust could indeed play an important role in defending the rights and needs of presently non-privileged people and of future generations.

In any case, a well-balanced measure of artificially increasing the price of non-renewable energy resources might cause a decisive turning-point in the economic system. It would effect a lowering, not only of the total amount of primary energy used, but also of the turnover of material as a whole, causing a substantial reduction of pollutant emissions. Furthermore, the increase in transportation costs because of higher fuel prices would also favour a territorial decentralization of commerce and industry, which in turn would encourage the preservation and growth of relative autonomous, economic and cultural structures, with all their positive consequences for greater independence of sufficiently small-sized regions where face-to-face communication is still possible and consequently people can develop a higher quality of life (in a deeper sense).

In contrast to the optimistic view presented here, most observers consider such a price measure on energy politically infeasible, because they think that, in order to avoid competitive disadvantages, it would necessarily have to be introduced on a global scale, which is hardly achievable. But the success of a special levy on energy for its initiators is not necessarily linked to its simultaneous introduction throughout the world, because the compensating benefits from the returning money would substantially alleviate the disadvantages claimed. In addition the rapid development of intelligent power generation and utilization technologies (for many of which fully worked-out plans are already gathering dust in various drawers) would be strongly stimulated. They would open up a promising market with enormous long-term advantages to these pioneers and induce the others to follow suit sooner or later. In this way an avalanche of innovations could be set into motion which would be scientifically and technologically supported by the unfolding possibilities of the 'soft technologies' of microelectronics and informatics.

It should, however, be clear to people that these special levies are not new taxes for financing some other government expenditures, but rather a regulating instrument of incentives and disincentives with particular emphasis on the promotion of a more intelligent generation and utilization of high-quality energy. Since from an ecological point of view a more intelligent use of energy is always more favourable than the supply of additional fossil and nuclear energy, this will also result in substantial reduction in the consumption of primary energy resources. This latter statement is also economically correct if the price of energy is adjusted to account for the external costs. By responding synergetically to the ensuing price increases the 'ordinary' woman or man should on the average hardly encounter any financial hardships caused by this measure during the transition period and, in fact, will probably benefit from these in the long run.

To increase further the public acceptance of such an energy measure it would be quite important to inform everybody about his or her eco-budget and in particular his or her energy-budget. To give people further guidance on how to adhere to their limited energy-budget it would be psychologically very desirable to publish a list of common consumer goods and services exhibiting an estimate of the gross or 'embodied' energy necessary for producing these goods and rendering these services. Because the embodied energy not only includes the 'direct' energy as accounted directly by the consumer but also the 'indirect' energy as used in the whole production process 'from cradle to grave', to establish such an estimate requires, in principle, a rather complicated and cumbersome product-cycle assessment which very sensitively depends on the structure of the whole economy.[5] For our purpose, however, high precision is not necessary. Hence we should not waste too much time on the accuracy of these numbers but rather aim for fast improvements by rough estimates on the most energy-intensive products. (At a later stage it may even be arranged that, as an indicator of the 'energy quality' and for easier comparison, these numbers be explicitly printed on the various products.) An energy compilation by Greenpeace Switzerland (1992) for example, reveals that a Swiss citizen in 1991 had on average consumed 6.5 kWh per hour primary energy with the following distribution.

---

5. As difficult as they are, several large-scale projects along this line are none the less already under way (Moll, 1993).

**Table 2.1** *Distribution of energy use by Swiss citizens in 1991*

| End use of primary energy | Percentage of total energy use |
|---|---|
| Living accommodations (buildings, heating, cooling, hot water, appliances, light) | 29 |
| Transportation – personal mobility (production of vehicles, roads, private and public traffic) | 18 |
| Additional private consumption (commodities, services, insurances etc) | 27 |
| Food (production, manufacture, distribution) | 14 |
| Public consumption (schools, administration, research, culture, military etc) | 12 |

Source: Greenpeace Switzerland, 1992

Using these energy lists, people will have the chance to draw up personal 'energy menus' according to their own preferences within the limits of their average 1.5 kW energy budget. By this exercise they will learn at what point and in which way they actually live 'beyond their ecological means' and will be able to personally envisage the practical consequences in their own life in adapting to an environmentally compatible life-style. Of course, there will be disappointing surprises. A 20,000 km round trip by air from Europe to the US, for example, consumes at least the equivalent of 1300 l kerosene per passenger, corresponding to his or her total annual personal energy-budget in a '1.5 kilowatt society'.

The promotion of the idea of a 1.5 kilowatt society should not be interpreted as preparing something like an eco-dictatorship in which such limits will be strictly enforced, but rather intends to generate new standards and to contribute constructively towards creating a general ecological consciousness. Many people, in going through this exercise, may discover with some relief that the energy limitation in such a 1.5 kW society by no means requires a return to the Dark Ages, and a life in sackcloth and ashes, but would permit one to live a meaningful, pleasurable, joyous life in the best sense.

We are, indeed, highly in need of such concrete positive examples for ecologically sustainable life-styles. They would represent life-styles that everybody in the world, in principle, could strive for and adopt without jeopardizing the ecosystem of the earth. I am, of course, fully aware that the transition period to this stage may be quite difficult and painful, to say the least. Although there seem to be at present only minute chances that this can be accomplished without major catastrophes we have to make all efforts to keep these catastrophes as small as possible. The more we – and in particular the dominating élites who point the directions and set the pace – employ reason and wise foresight now, the less formidable will be the tasks of future generations in meeting this challenge.

# REFERENCES

Dürr, H-P, 'Dafür oder dagegen? Kritische Gedanken zur Kernenergiedebatte', *Phys Bl*, vol 34, no 297, 1978.

Greenpeace Schweiz und Verkehrs-Club der Schweiz (VCS), *Persönliche Energie- und CO$_2$-Bilanz, Aktion Klimaschutz*, Zurich, August 1992.

Moll, H C, *Energy Counts and Materials Matter in Models for Sustainable Development*, dissertation, Faculty of Natural Sciences, University of Groningen, Groningen: Styx, 1993.

Immler, H, *Vom Wert der Natur, zur ökologischen Reform von Wirtschaft und Gesellschaft*, Opladen: Westdeutscher Verlag, 1989.

WCED (World Commission on Environment and Development), *Our Common Future*, Oxford: Oxford University Press, 1987.

Weizsäcker, E U von, *Erdpolitik: ökologische Realpolitik an der Schwelle zum Jahrhundert der Umwelt*, Darmstadt: Wissenschaftliche Buchgesellschaft, 1989.

Ziegler, W, 'Ansatz zur Analyse der durch technisch-zivilisierte Gesellschaften verursachten Belastung von Ökosystemen', *Landwirtschaftliches Jahrbuch*, no 56, 1979, p 899.

Ziegler, W, 'Zur Tragfähigkeit ökologischer Systeme', *Wissenschaftliches Zeitschrift Technische Universität Dresden*, vol 41, 1992, p 17.

*Chapter Three*

# Energy Constraints on Sustainable Development Paths

*Wouter Biesiot and Henk Mulder*

---

Sustainability, equity and liveability are clearly terms strongly loaded with value judgements. All have to do with the distribution of goods, services and with the more qualitative aspects of living in the present generation, but also with trade-offs between the present and future generations. These terms also require specification of the desired environmental quality, of the substitutions that are allowed between environmental resources and human-made resources, and the position one takes with respect to a number of other aspects of life on earth, eg the anthropogenic acceleration of the extinction of species. The question then arises: are 'hard' constraints on sustainable development paths present or is any desired outcome realizable on the basis of the presently existing resource base, whatever value judgements are made?

This question is examined by use of a computer simulation model developed at the Center for Energy and Environment Studies (University of Groningen, The Netherlands). A number of simplifications are necessary. These are chosen conservatively. The resulting constraints are probably less severe than they would turn out to be if more detailed calculations were made, so the resulting picture may be too optimistic and the freedom of choice arrived at may be exaggerated. We specify the criteria for a sustainable, equitable and liveable world, in the energy domain, as follows: after the year 2050 every inhabitant of the earth has a right to the same level of services as every other and after a given year (2050 or 2100) these must be provided by only making use of renewable resources. The non-renewable energy resources are supposed to be consumed during the transition process at rates determined by environmental constraints. We take as the only constraint that the levels of emission of greenhouse gases are kept low enough to avoid serious effects on the world climate. It is assumed, as a further simplification, that such a transition is compatible with sufficient protection of the remaining biodiversity and cultural diversity.

The point of departure is the resource base of non-renewable and renewable resources that is still available for consumption by present and future generations. The demand and supply problems of the interaction of societal metabolism and the existing resource base are described on the basis of the greatest common denominator: energy flows. This is, of course, a drastic simplification. It is introduced in order to make simple mathematical modelling possible. The central question then becomes: what level of energy services can be made available on a sustainable basis for a growing world population, making an optimal use of the existing resource base? The answer to this question depends strongly upon assumptions regarding the growth of the world population, the distribution of energy-consuming life-styles between and within nations, and the development of efficient technologies. Many energy supply and demand forecasts simply extrapolate present trends in growth of the material standard of living and the associated demand for energy services (Bach et al, 1980; IIASA, 1981; Nordhaus and Yohe, 1983; Edmonds and Reilly, 1983; Rose et al, 1983; Holdren and Pachauri, 1991). These lead to the prediction that the world energy demand will be multiplied by a factor ranging from two to seven in the period up to 2050. Such extrapolations assume no fundamental change in the unsustainable characteristics of the present world economy. Given the asymmetric distribution in, for example, energy and raw material consumption (20 per cent of the world population consumes 80 per cent of the resources), such development scenarios do not satisfy our criteria for a sustainable, equitable and liveable world. Other forecasts assume quite different social and technological development, and arrive at much lower energy demands (Lovins et al, 1981; Goldemberg et al, 1985; Johansson et al, 1993; Lazarus et al, 1993). These studies, however, do not address the transition issue fully.

## BACKCASTING

Forecasting studies require detailed research into the complex relations of economic growth, development, demographic trends and access to resources, including nutrition (Arizpe et al, 1991). The results hinge crucially on assumptions over the future trends in these relations and developments. It is therefore not surprising that the predictions for energy use differ by more than a factor of ten between different forecasts. For this reason we have chosen to study the problem from another perspective, ie a backcasting approach. The starting point is a sustainable, equitable and liveable world at some point in the future. The requirements for the transition to and the maintenance of that state of affairs can be studied and compared with the present day capabilities in terms of stocks of material and human resources. This provides insights into the constraints that are inherently present or that must be removed on the road to the desired state. The approach does not aim at prediction, but at discovering constraints on the different paths that can be followed.

The time span available for such a transition can be determined as follows. Over 85 per cent of the primary energy used nowadays stems from fossil fuels. The proven non-renewable reserves will, under present trends and with proven technology, be depleted within a century. If the demand continues to rise, this depletion period will be even shorter. The present annual energy consumption of non-renewable energy resources amounts to 350–400 exajoules ($1EJ = 10^{18}$ joules), while the proven reserves add up to about 35,000–45,000 EJ (Shell, 1991 and 1992), giving at most a century of leeway. At an annual growth rate of 4 per cent, ten times these reserves would be exhausted in less than a century. The time span available for the transition can thus be estimated to be some 50–100 years, ending in the second half of the twenty-first century, say.

The central issue is illustrated in Figure 3.1. It shows an arbitrarily chosen development of the annual world energy demand during the transition to a sustainable state in the next century. Initially the annual demand rises sharply because the non-OECD nations get access to energy services. After the world population stabilizes (see Figure 3.2), the continuing development of energy efficient technologies becomes the dominant factor and the energy obtained from non-renewable resources decreases. In the mean time the contribution from renewable resources expands, finally leading to a phase-out of the non-renewable energy sources. In Figure 3.1 the amount of energy produced from non-renewable resources is represented by the vertical distance between the curves and is seen to diminish to zero at the end of the transition period. The area between the two curves corresponds to the cumulative demand of fossil fuels. It is clear that a chosen transition scenario cannot be realized if that area is larger than the presently existing stocks of non-renewable resources.

If the world embarks on a route directed towards a sustainable, equitable and liveable state of affairs, the question then is what physical constraints will be met in terms of:

- limited availability of fossil fuels of adequate quality (the area between the curves in Figure 3.1);
- limited supply of renewable energy sources (the maximum height of the end point of the curves in Figure 3.1); and
- limitations to be imposed by greenhouse gas emissions (limiting the permissible rate of increase of the area between the curves in Figure 3.1 and thus constraining growth rates).

These constraints can be translated into the levels of energy services that can finally be delivered on a sustainable basis to every inhabitant of the globe. The constraints which are found are complementary to those found by Hans-Peter Dürr (see Chapter 2) and, although arrived at by quite a different line of reasoning, they are in good agreement with his conclusions.

## THE MODEL USED IN THE SCENARIOS

### *Definitions and scenario families*

There are two conditions placed on the end point in this backcasting study. The first is that of an equitable and liveable world, defined here simply as an equal distribution over the globe by the year 2050 of access to the energy services needed to satisfy at a comfortable level the requirements for housing, lighting, transportation, food etc. We assume that due to the continuing development of new technologies the energy requirements per service will decrease. In this study this is modelled by

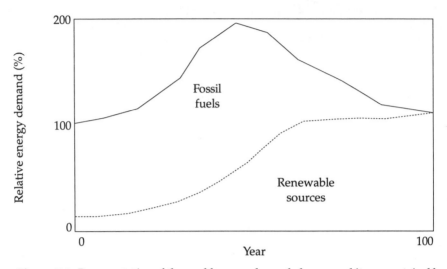

**Figure 3.1** *Representation of the world energy demand along an arbitrary sustainable development path. Over this period renewable sources replace fossil fuels, starting from the present 15 per cent contribution*

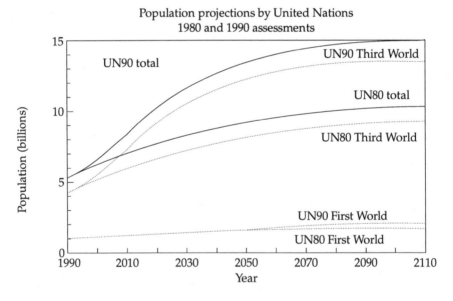

**Figure 3.2** *Two scenarios for the increase of the world population over the period 1990–2100, specified for the First World and the Third World, taken from the United Nations 1980 and 1990 long-term projections*

assuming a given yearly percentage improvement in efficiency. The yearly percentage efficiency improvement is one of the two adjustable parameters in the calculations. New technologies are supposed to diffuse instantaneously all over the globe. The availability of services is the other parameter. This is also taken to change by a given (adjustable) percentage per year, ranging from greatly increasing to severely shrinking.

The second condition on the end point, that of sustainability, demands a transition from fossil fuels to renewable energy sources (hereafter denoted renewables). Out of the infinite number of paths that such a transition could follow, we have chosen two. In the first path the transition takes place in the period 2000–2050 through an ingrowth of renewables at a rate which increases exponentially up to the end, ie the rate of buildup of the capital plant is proportional to the plant that exists at every moment. This is not unreasonable since infrastructure and experience feed upon themselves. The path is, however, doubly difficult, since it makes the transition take place in the same period as that in which the achievement of an equitable world has been postulated. The second path has the transition occur in the period 2050–2100, ie after an equitable world has been achieved.

We assume that the necessary technology and infrastructure have been built up in the previous period, and therefore choose a linear function for the phasing out of non-renewables (ie a constant rate of replacement of fossil fuel sources by renewables). There are thus two families of scenarios, denoted early (E-type) and late (L-type) transformations, respectively. The first path is exponential (and early) and the second linear (and late). In the remainder of this chapter the first will be called an E-type and the second an L-type transition. Both paths assume a phase-out of fossil fuels in five decades and both require an annual multi-gigawatt increase of renewables, the amount depending on the values of the other parameters chosen (see below). The cumulative fossil fuel requirements over the period 2000–2100 of the two sets of scenarios differ appreciably, the L-type requiring significantly more fossil fuel. In the L-type transition both fossil fuels and renewables contribute to satisfy total energy requirements in the period from 2050 to 2100. Since for the E-type the transition to renewables is assumed to have been completed in the first half of the twenty-first century, all energy requirements in the second half of the century are provided by renewables. Most other feasible scenarios for the transformation of the energy system will result in fossil fuel requirements that lie between these extremes.

Most scenario studies project a stable world population in the range of 10–15 billion people. In this study two different demographic scenarios have been used for the calculations, derived from the United Nations 1980 and 1990 long-range world population projections (leading to a stable world population of almost 11 and 15 billion people in 2100, respectively) (UN, 1983, 1991). In our scenarios only the categories First and Third World are distinguished. We have split the regions of what was the Second World between these two on the basis of prospects for future development.

## Parameters of the scenarios

The energy requirements in the year *t* can be calculated by adding the demands from the First and the Third World using the simple formula:

Equation 1 (Eq 1)
total energy demand = number of people ×
service level per capita (SLC) × energy required per service per year (ERS)

in which an average over different services is used for the service level per capita (SLC) and the energy requirement per service (ERS). These are used as parameters in the calculation of the cumulative energy requirements. The energy units used are gigajoules (GJ), so that ERS has the dimensions of GJ per service per year, henceforth referred to as an ERS-unit.

The ERS and SLC parameters have been disaggregated into First and Third World values. (When the year is not relevant these will be referred to as SLC1 or SLC3 and ERS1 or ERS3.) The SLC value of the First World in 1990, denoted as SLC(1,1990), is normalized to unity. Taking this normalization of SLC(1,1990) into account, from data on population and energy consumption in the First World, ERS(1,1990), can be estimated at 200 ERS-units. At present the energy efficiency is considerably lower in the developing world than in the industrialized countries and therefore the ERS value for the Third World in 1990, ERS(3,1990) is set to 400 ERS-units; twice as high as ERS(1,1990), in agreement with most estimates. Given this value for ERS(3,1990), and data on population and energy consumption in the Third World, SLC(3,1990) is calculated to be 0.083. The ERS can be reduced by investments in energy efficiency in industry and in energy conservation programmes. In this backcasting study it is assumed that ERS3 will catch up with the First World value in 2050 and be equal to ERS1 from then on. This assumes an almost instantaneous adaptation and integration of newly developed (dominantly First World) processes and procedures in the developing world, and therefore leads most certainly to an underestimate of the energy requirements in the Second and Third World. It also requires a huge investment in research, development and training in order to realize as much as possible of this assumption. No changes in ERS are modelled for the period 2050–2100. In accordance with the expressed goal of this study, that of modelling an equitable world, the service levels in the First and Third Worlds, SLC1 and SLC3, are assumed to become equal by the year 2050 and to remain constant thereafter. It is assumed that SLC3 rises exponentially to meet this equity requirement.

The assumptions specified above relate Third World values of ERS and SLC to the corresponding values for the First World over the entire scenario period (1990–2100). It is therefore only necessary, given a population scenario, to specify the way in which these two (First World) parameters vary to determine the yearly and cumulative energy requirements of the whole world. In the different variants the efficiency of energy use is assumed to increase by 0, 1 or 2 per cent annually. Note that the higher the efficiency, the lower ERS will be, meaning it will decrease by 0, 1 or 2 per cent, annually. The actual average value of this parameter will depend critically on policy decisions, as well as on technological achievability. For each of these variants the service level in the First World, SLC1, is assumed to change annually by +3, +2, +1, 0, –1, or –2 per cent, ie ranging from a high rate of increasing luxury (an increase of services up to six times the present average level in 2050) down to a severe austerity (a reduction of services down to 30 per cent of the present average level in 2050). There are thus 18 scenarios (three assumptions concerning ERS1 multiplied by six assumptions for SLC1), for each chosen population scenario. In addition the choice of either an E-type or an L-type doubles the number of variants. The actual constraints applied are specified in the following section. The constraints of fossil fuel reserves and of permissible $CO_2$ emissions render most of these scenarios impossible.

## Constraints

According to recent estimates (eg Shell, 1991 and 1992) the world reserves of economically recoverable fossil fuels amount to 4800 EJ of natural gas, 5700 EJ of crude oil, 25,200 EJ of coal equivalent (hard coal and lignite), totalling to about 36,000 EJ. Speculative coal reserves amount to about 74,000 EJ. Total coal resources not considered recoverable under current or anticipated local economic conditions are estimated at 150,000 EJ. These data are used as constraints in the discussion of the scenario outcomes.

Limitation of $CO_2$ emissions in the twenty-first century to about 300 Gton C or about 1100 Gton $CO_2$ may be sufficient to reduce global warming due to anthropogenic greenhouse gases to 1.5–4.5°C (Bolin, 1991; Krause, Bach and Koomey, 1989). This value is also used as a constraint. For each scenario calculation the cumulative energy requirements have been translated into $CO_2$ emissions based on the fossil fuel mix of 1990 with the associated $CO_2$ emission factors. We assume $CO_2$ emissions due to deforestation (now responsible for 20 per cent of the anthropogenic $CO_2$ emissions) will stop in the near future, since deforestation is incompatible with our hypothesis of sustainability. We also assume that $CO_2$ emissions unrelated to energy production in agriculture and industrial processes (amounting to 10 per cent of all anthropogenic $CO_2$ emissions) will follow the same trend as the emissions from the use of fossil energy. If in a scenario calculation the total $CO_2$ emissions exceed the given limit (depending on the use of renewables and nuclear energy), that excess is thought to be retained (be it dumped into deep sea and/or emptied gas wells or sequestered via reforestation). In this way a retention percentage is calculated that can be compared to present day technologies for $CO_2$ removal (retention percentages of over 90 per cent are claimed to be feasible for stationary sources, while for mobile sources a conversion to $H_2$ or electricity is thought to be the appropriate route; see Blok et al, 1992). The $CO_2$ removal technology is not yet commercially available and deep sea storage may even be ecologically dangerous. In this study an average value of 50 per cent retention is considered to be a high estimate for the twenty-first century.

The supply from renewables is limited for various reasons (see IIASA, 1981; WEC, 1983; SERI, 1989; Veziroglu and Barbir, 1991; Johansson et al, 1993). The wind-energy potential is limited due to the scarcity of wind-rich areas and for hydro power specific geographical conditions must be met. The production of biomass for energy purposes is limited due to land use and mineral circulation constraints. Solar energy (heat and electricity) is often mentioned as the candidate for unlimited energy supply, but here also constraints appear in the material and land use requirements (Bryson, 1989; Moll et al, 1991). Large-scale applications of photovoltaic solar cells, for instance, are based on the relatively low-efficiency silicon systems, while the high yield solar cells require relatively scarce elements, such as arsenic and cadmium.

Estimates of the total realizable potential of renewables vary between 10 and 1000 TW of installed capacity (Sørensen, 1991; Turkenburg, 1992; Mulder et al, 1993). The higher estimates rely strongly on massive contributions from solar and biomass energy sources. The lower estimates are based on constraints of the type described in Chapter 2 by Hans-Peter Dürr. In this study silicon-based photovoltaic cells are supposed to be the supplier of renewable energy, delivering the energy not produced by fossil fuels, nuclear power or the 'traditional' renewables. This is a conservative approach in comparison with other scenario studies in which a significant contribution for biomass is projected. The output per unit of area is higher for solar cells than for biomass and solar energy does not compete the way biomass does with other land use requirements. It is estimated that about 35 per cent of the energy output of such devices will be needed for buildup and maintenance of a solar energy park. The energy required for energy value (ERE) for such parks is expected to fall from 48 per cent at present to 35 per cent by the year 2015. This adds an extra energy demand term on the right-hand side of Eq 1. The results of the scenario calculations are screened for possible constraints arising from this additional demand term.

To construct the scenarios it was necessary to assign values to the contribution of hydro power and biomass. For the L-type, nuclear power is assumed to double in the period 1990–2020 – a net annual expansion of 20 GW(electric) for 30 years – and remain constant thereafter. Nuclear power (with presently known technology) will then have depleted the presently known recoverable reserves of uranium by 2050 and in the process have replaced the consumption of 4000 EJ of fossil fuels. In the E-type variants no nuclear power expansion is assumed, as all (human and material) energy investments will be required for the massive buildup of genuine renewables (including distribution and storage systems etc). The influence of this assumption on the results can be assessed from the figure of 4000 EJ as the total contribution of nuclear power. For both the E-type and the L-type variants the total contribution of renewables (other than solar) is taken to increase, in the period 1990–2020, to a value three times the present output of hydro power and remain constant thereafter (delivering about 7,000 EJ in the period 1990–2100).

## RESULTS

### *Sustainable, equitable and liveable world-energy scenarios*

A typical picture of the annual world energy requirements is shown in Figure 3.3. It clearly indicates the rise in consumption in the Third World and the reduction in the First World (in this case principally because of the assumption of an annual

2 per cent improvement in ERS). After 2050 total demand still rises slightly as the result of the (small) increases in population.

For each combination of scenario parameters outcomes like Figure 3.3 can be generated. These give little insight, however, into the constraints which form the main subject of this chapter. Therefore a different representation is chosen, illustrated in Figures 3.4 and 3.5. Each such diagram covers the whole range of assumed annual SLC1 variations for a given combination of population scenario (UN 1980, 1990), energy system transformation (E or L) and annual energy efficiency improvement (0, 1 or 2 per cent). The cumulative fossil fuel requirements are plotted against the $CO_2$ retention percentage that is necessary in order to stay within the $CO_2$ limit assumed. As mentioned above, an average of 50 per cent retention is considered an upper limit for the twenty-first century. In these figures this level is indicated by a horizontal dashed line. The points based on the (consensus) value of permissible annual emission of 300 Gton C are indicated by circles. In order to study the sensitivity of the calculations for deviations from this value the results of a more stringent limit of 150 Gton C and a less strict limitation of 600 Gton C are indicated by triangles and diamonds, respectively. The annual percentage change in SLC is shown next to each of those lines. In each diagram vertical dotted lines correspond to reserve estimates, ie 36,000 EJ (proven reserves), 110,000 EJ (proven + speculative reserves) and 260,000 EJ (sum of all categories). The last only appears in Figure 3.5.

The advantage of this representation is that one sees immediately what is possible and what is not. If a point lies either to the right of the vertical dotted line giv-

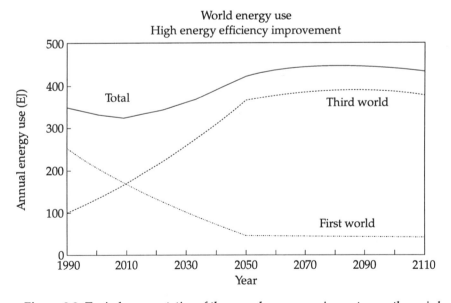

**Figure 3.3** *Typical representation of the annual energy requirements over the period 1990–2100 that results from the calculations described in the text*

ing the total stocks present or above the dotted line giving the presupposed limit on $CO_2$ retention, the scenario is not realizable.

Realizability is, however, not determined in any absolute way, but is dependent on the optimism (or pessimism) of the assumptions made concerning both the stocks and the possibilities of $CO_2$ retention. One can choose to regard the proven reserves, the proven plus speculative reserves or the total of all categories (including the possibly not recoverable reserves) as the constraint. Assumptions concerning the possibilities of applying the not-yet tested technologies of $CO_2$ retention are even more arbitrary. Besides the value of SLC change per annum, the effect of the assumption regarding permissible emissions (ie permissible with respect to tolerable world climate changes) can be important. If the $CO_2$ ceiling must be lowered to only 150 Gton C, only scenarios with decreasing SLC levels are feasible, whereas if the emission of 600 Gton C is permissible, a slightly increasing SLC could be possible.

In Figures 3.4 and 3.5 the diagrams corresponding to a 1 per cent annual growth of the energy efficiency (a formidable requirement) are shown as typical examples. From the first (an example of the E-type) it can be concluded that scenarios allowing more than zero growth rates of SLC in the First World are only realizable if very high values of $CO_2$ retention turn out to be possible and are realized, and speculative stocks turn out to exist and to be exploitable. The constraints are, of course, more severe in case of the late energy transformation (the L variant, Figure

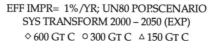

EFF IMPR= 1%/YR; UN80 POP.SCENARIO
SYS TRANSFORM 2000 – 2050 (EXP)
◇ 600 GT C   ○ 300 GT C   △ 150 GT C

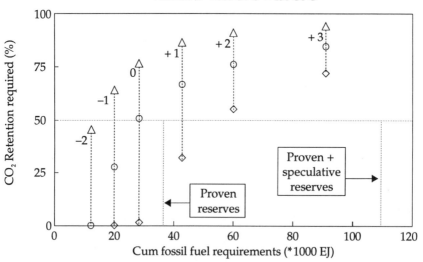

**Figure 3.4** *Cumulative fossil fuel requirements versus the retention percentage needed to keep the corresponding $CO_2$ emissions below the specified levels. The annual percentage change of SLC1 is indicated (see text)*

3.5). Note that the horizontal scale is greatly extended compared to Figure 3.4. Comparison of the diagrams shows that the reduction in fossil fuel consumption by shifting from an L-type to an E-type transformation varies from a factor of 1.5 (for the left side of the diagram) to 3 (for the right side). Only moderate changes are found, however, in terms of $CO_2$ retention constraints, if regarded as percentages (in absolute amounts naturally the E-type causes much lower $CO_2$ emissions).

In the E variant for the transformation of the energy system from fossil fuels to renewables the ingrowth of renewables starts in 2000 and is completed in 2050. The annual growth percentages in total energy consumption may be as high as 7 per cent for the period 2000–2050, producing a serious strain on the production of the required photovoltaic devices and the associated materials production facilities (and on competing applications of these materials).

Nuclear power does not contribute significantly to the resolution of the problems encountered in the high annual SLC increase scenarios. More can be expected at the other side of the range of annual SLC changes: in scenarios characterized by a decrease of SLC in the industrialized world, nuclear power can significantly reduce the $CO_2$ retention requirements (the 4000 EJ nuclear contribution forms a significant fraction of the total energy requirements in those variants).

Increasing the annual energy efficiency improvement to 2 per cent does not change these conclusions significantly. The points in Figures 3.4 and 3.5 are shifted somewhat towards the lower left corner. Still, all scenarios with a positive annual

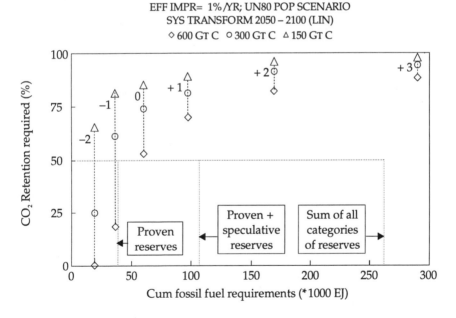

**Figure 3.5** *The same as Figure 3.4 (but with a much larger range on the horizontal scale), for a transformation of the energy system in the period 2050–2100 (L-type)*

increase in SLC for the industrialized world will meet the same constraints as the ones discussed above. Zero average improvement of the energy efficiency produces, of course, the opposite effect: the points shift towards the upper right corner of the diagrams.

The calculations summarized in Figures 3.4 and 3.5 are based on the 1980 UN population projection. Corresponding analyses on the basis of the UN 1990 population estimates have also been made. The cumulative fossil fuel requirements of such scenarios are some 20–25 per cent higher than those corresponding to the 1980 population estimate. Likewise, a development path ending with only some eight billion world inhabitants would require cumulative fossil fuel consumption 15–20 per cent lower. Given the differences in the scenario results and the uncertainties involved, such changes are of minor importance at the upper right side of the diagrams while of more significance at the lower left part.

The required installed solar capacity in the year 2050 varies greatly: from 6 terawatts ($1TW = 10^{12}$ watts) for extreme conservation scenarios to over 600 TW for extreme growth scenarios. These values should be compared to the 1990 value of about 11 TW total annual energy use, and indicate the type and magnitude of the problems in the conversion from fossil fuels to renewables. For scenarios with zero growth in the SLC of the First World the required capacity in 2050 is a factor three to ten higher than the present value, which may be at the high end of the range of the realizable potential from renewables. And for scenarios with a positive SLC growth in the First World this value becomes certainly unrealistically high. In the latter cases solar capacity has to increase up to 22 per cent annually in an E-type transition or, in an L-type transition, up to over 1000 GW new renewable energy capacity that must be installed annually (for comparison, at present only a total of about 1200 GW hydro capacity and only a few GW of photovoltaic cells have been installed).

## Non-equity scenarios and corrections for the rising energy costs of materials

The scenario calculations have been extended: first, by the supposition that development strategies directed towards equity will fail, and that the gap between poor and rich will remain 'frozen' at the present ratio of approximately 0.083; second, by correcting for the rising energy costs of materials. This correction takes into account the possibility that certain materials will become scarce (that is, the quality of some mineral ores will become lower). As a consequence more energy will be required to extract and process these minerals. In some cases even so-called back-stop technologies will have to be used. These are very energy intensive (in the ultimate case extraction of minerals from sea water). Thus, in the future the energy demand per service may increase, instead of decreasing as we have assumed. This correction is not made by changing the ERS value, but by adding an extra term on the right-hand side of Eq 1 (see Eq 2), representing the energy requirements for the supply of materials. A quantitative approximation is made in Mulder et al (1993), with the energy 'gains' resulting from optimized reuse of materials taken into account. From that analysis it is concluded that, in the absence of recycling, the energy requirements per unit of materials supply output will double after the cumulative use of about 400 times the materials used during the year 1990.[1] On the other hand, this energy requirement per unit of materials would go down to half the 1990 value if recycling is optimized and scarcity is not taken into account.[2] It is also assumed that the material intensity of services decreases proportionally to the decrease in ERS. This means that future services will take less materials (in case of a decreasing ERS), but that these materials may or may not require more energy for their production, depending on which effect exerts the greatest influence; recycling or scarcity.

> Equation 2 (Eq 2)
> total energy demand = number of people
> × service level per capita × energy required per service per year
> ± energy costs for materials.

The influence of both of these modifications is illustrated in Figure 3.6 (UN 1980 population scenario, 1 per cent annual decrease in ERS and 1 per cent annual increase in SLC). The solid vertical lines are modifications of Figure 3.4 (E-type energy transition) and the dotted vertical lines are modifications of Figure 3.5 (L-type). The two on the far left show the consequences for the cumulative fossil fuel consumption on the assumption of no change in the welfare gap. For these calculations the extra energy cost of materials is not taken into account. The vertical lines second from left (solid and dotted) are the same as the lines for 1 per cent annual increase in SLC in Figures 3.4 and 3.5, ie equity in 2050 and no extra energy costs for materials. It is evident that equity requires at least twice the amount of fossil fuels as a continuation of the present inequality. The E and L lines on the far right show the effect on fossil fuel requirements if equity is assumed and the energy cost of materials is taken into account; the energy requirements rise another 2.5–4 per cent. A number of such comparisons lead to the conclusion that in high growth and L-type scenarios the materials effect is more pronounced, and that in scenarios with negative annual changes in both ERS and SLC recycling can effectively counteract scarcity.[3]

---

1. The GER (gross energy requirement) values will increase: ferro with 50 per cent, most non-ferro with 100 per cent, other minerals with 20 per cent. A small fraction of non-ferro will need high-energy, intensive backstop technologies, giving a further GER increase.
2. The following maximum recycling percentages are assumed: ferro 80 per cent; non-ferro 60 per cent; plastics and other minerals 50 per cent. The rate of optimizing is coupled to the change in ERS. Optimizing is assumed to go on after 2050 (even if ERS values are taken to be constant thereafter). Due to scarcity effects recycling might become increasingly attractive. This is once more a conservative approach.
3. An additional 15–20 per cent is needed for equity scenarios with a 3 per cent annual increase in SLC; if SLC decreases with 3 per cent annually there is even about 0.5 per cent energy profit, due to recycling (and the absence of scarcity problems). The L-type scenarios require more fossil fuels to counteract scarcity of materials, since the transition to renewables has not yet been made when this problem arises. In E-type scenarios extra energy for materials comes mostly from renewables.

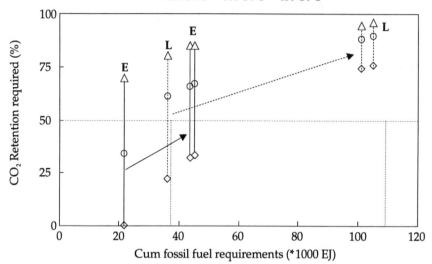

**Figure 3.6** *Modifications brought about in the scenario results depicted in Figures 3.4 and 3.5 for the case of a 1 per cent annual increase of SLC by a 'non-equity' variant and an 'equity plus materials cost' variant (see text)*

## Overall picture

For the UN 1980 and UN 1990 population scenarios the combined transition constraints (including the energy for materials effect) are shown in Figures 3.7 and 3.8, respectively in the form of boundary lines for either 0 per cent $CO_2$ retention or 50 per cent $CO_2$ retention as the maximum. In these figures only scenarios lying to the left of the lines are feasible. Figure 3.7 leads to the conclusion that no sustainable development scenarios are feasible with an annual change in SLC higher than +1 per cent, even under extreme energy conservation programmes combined with 50 per cent $CO_2$ retention (which as mentioned above may not be achievable). More realistic scenarios (annual change in ERS1 of –0.5 to –1 per cent for 50 years; $CO_2$ retention of 0–50 per cent) require an annual change in SLC of –1 to –2 per cent. The total generating capacity to be installed from renewable resources then remains within feasible ranges (10–50 TW). If the world population develops according to the UN 1990 scenario, more severe constraints will be met, as is shown in Figure 3.8. In both figures the total necessary solar capacity in 2100 is shown as a rough approximation.[4]

---

4. If we assume recycling optimization does stop in 2050 (see footnote 2), about 1 to 5 per cent extra capacity would be needed. Effects on cumulative fossil fuel use turn out to be negligible.

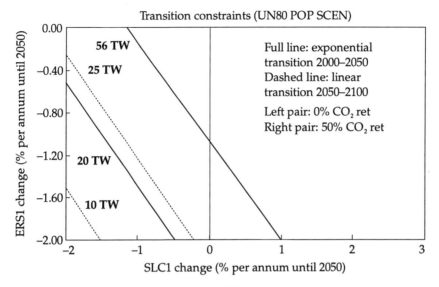

**Figure 3.7** *Transition constraints for the UN80 population scenario. Scenario variants in the lower left region as defined by the diagonal lines are feasible under the $CO_2$ constraints indicated*

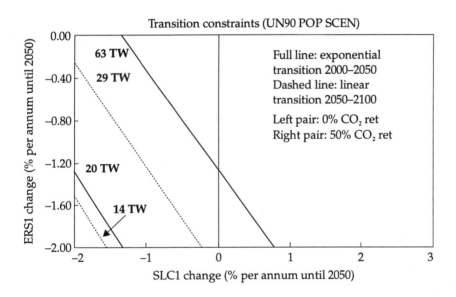

**Figure 3.8** *Transition constraints as presented in Figure 3.7, but now for the UN90 population scenario*

## *Discussion*

The results described above are derived from a simple model, based on coarse approximations. More in-depth studies could be done by means of detailed research using ECCO-type models (Slesser, 1987).[5] Also, some dynamic problems have been omitted at this stage, eg the energy requirements for food and fresh water.

With present-day technologies a major disruption of environmental resources (clean air, water, soil, biodiversity) can be expected with increasing levels of production, distribution and consumption of material goods (see eg Glasby, 1988). The consequences thereof in terms of additional constraints on sustainability, equity and liveability are not discussed in this chapter.

The results suggest the existence of a sustainable development dilemma. If the trends in the growth of population, service level and energy efficiency improvement are chosen as is done in the positive SLC growth scenarios presented here, the transition to sustainable states implies the depletion of fossil fuel resources to such an extent that greenhouse issues become much more serious and the requirements for renewables become almost unsurmountable. Such problems seem only avoidable at the expense of maintaining the gap between rich and poor for another century. Neither solution can simultaneously be termed as sustainable, equitable and liveable.

Every delay in changing present-day trends towards increasing SLC with little or no decrease in ERS will narrow the solution space because the energy consumption levels will grow, low target values for SLC will be more difficult to reach and more fossil fuels are burned, so less will be available for the transition. This means that public policy action is necessary immediately, even though the resource depletion problems will not be visible in daily life for decades to come.

There are many expectations of, and speculations about, the possible contribution of nuclear fusion and nuclear fission breeder reactors to the energy supply in the next century. Large-scale commercial application of these technologies are not expected much earlier than 2050, so that they, in any case, cannot play a role in phasing out fossil fuels in E-type transitions. In high-growth scenarios the required capacities in 2050 are so high that it is doubtful whether these new technologies will be able to contribute significantly, even in L-type scenarios. Only extreme enhancement of energy efficiency will lead to a required capacity in 2050 low enough so that 'inherently safe' fission and fusion will be able to contribute significantly to the phasing out of fossil fuels.

Obviously, a number of implementation issues are associated with these conclusions. Present-day market mechanisms may contribute to the implementation of new energy-efficient technologies and life-styles if an adequate pricing system can be created (converting the environmental externalities into the realm of the market

---

5. In an ECCO model the economy is represented in physical (energy) flows rather than in terms of money flows. This allows the study of restrictions on the rate of formation of new capital (capital goods, infrastructure, services) that follow from physical conservation laws.

system). The scale of the required transformation processes is nevertheless so enormous that it must be doubted whether such so-called optimal allocation mechanisms can contribute to the solution of the equity problem: how can we allocate eg only 50 per cent of the proven fossil fuel reserves to the First World for use in the transition period until 2100 (about 100 EJ per year on the average in the next century, while the present level is 200–50 EJ), preserving the remainder for the developing world? How can we realize a non-growing SLC in the rich world? How can we control the processes accompanying a fast increase in the material standard of living in the developing world? Nevertheless, in several fields (industrial energy use, household appliances etc), enough knowledge and skills are already available for a start with the necessary transition (Keepin, 1988; Jackson and Roberts, 1989; RMI, 1991). The extension to a rationalization on all levels can thus build on partly existing equipment and knowledge.

The calculations have been made in order to assess the impact of fossil fuel depletion on sustainable development paths. This is not meant to imply that the specific Western world market systems and cultures are the solution for the development problems in other parts of the world. The results point out that intergenerational and intragenerational solidarity (protecting options outside the present First World) may require limitation of fossil fuel consumption in the First World to levels much lower than would be the case under free market relative scarcity conditions.

The rise of energy consumption in the Third World can be limited in a sustainable way only if local conditions of preservation of biodiversity and cultural diversity are integrated with efficient technologies, and with sustainable yield from renewables. The improvement of the energy efficiency in the industrialized world and the reintegration of renewables in their energy supply system is also quite a challenge because it must be carried out under conditions of sustainability. The analysis presented here sheds only a faint light on these problems.

The model used can be refined in terms of development stages of (groups of) nations, delays in transfer and absorption of new technologies, changes in lifestyles, etc. The assumptions of the present model have nevertheless been chosen to be conservative: (most) probably a more detailed calculation would yield world energy requirements with more stringent constraints than the ones presented here. This is especially so if service levels in the Third World rise without simultaneous improvement in energy efficiency. Unfortunately, this is what is happening in the rapidly developing Asian economies today.

If the calculations presented had been made some 40–50 years ago, the dilemma most certainly would not have emerged in the present form. If, for instance, the world population was then estimated to grow to some five to ten billion people, with a service level per capita of five to ten times the 1950 level in the First World, such a sustainable, equitable and liveable state could have been reached without serious fossil fuel depletion problems. At that time a $CO_2$ problem was not yet perceived to exist. It is only since the post-war explosion of material standards of living in the First World and fast increase of the world population to the 1980–90 values that possible constraints on sustainable development paths have increasingly become visible, and have become the object of research and public policy.

# CONCLUSIONS

A simple and transparent model for the development of the world energy demand for the period 1990–2100 has been used in a backcasting study in order to identify possible (physical) constraints that will be met if the world embarks on a route towards sustainability, equity and liveability. Three constraints have been applied to the scenarios: depletion of fossil fuel reserves; $CO_2$ emission maxima due to greenhouse gas problems; and maximum supply from renewables. The latter two turn out to be the most stringent.

These conclusions must be examined in detail in future research in order to assess how conservative the approach has been. It would also be of interest to study these issues more in-depth with ECCO-type models.

Scenarios with a positive service level growth in the industrialized world are most probably incompatible with the simple equity criterion (equity in service level per capita by the year 2050) that has been defined here as a milestone on the road towards a sustainable world. Only a decreasing SLC in the developed world will result in acceptable $CO_2$ emissions and in feasible requirements for renewables. In those cases the following conditions must be met.

- The energy efficiency must be improved in the developed world in an unprecedented way: at least 1 per cent and preferably 2 per cent per year for at least 50 years. The same goes for recycling optimization.
- New technologies must quickly be adapted for local conditions and must be assimilated in a sustainable way all over the world.
- As no room is available for quantitative growth in the energy service level of the industrialized world, other perspectives offering qualitative growth must be found and introduced into people's lives in order to acquire public support for this strategy. It should be emphasized that 'economic growth' need not be the same as growth in energy services.
- Development of renewable energy conversion processes must also be stimulated on an unprecedented scale. This challenge is even greater than in previous major (dominantly technological) forecasting studies, as the overall goal must be reached along a sustainable path.
- In most scenarios $CO_2$ retention must be applied in order to reduce the greenhouse warming to several degrees Celsius in the twenty-first century. This implies the development of efficient industrial removal processes and/or large scale reforestation schemes in order to reach an overall 10–50 per cent $CO_2$ retention as the average value for the twenty-first century.
- Societal structures and processes (including the education system) must be reoriented in order to provide solutions for the tensions that may arise and to secure effective citizen participation in the decision-making processes (see Part II of this book).
- All goals (stabilization of population, energy efficiency improvement, lowering of the energy intensity of goods and services, rapid transfer of technology, construction of high sustainable yield renewables, new economic and political instruments, etc) need to be reached simultaneously. So, a huge demand for

new knowledge, skills and financial resources will have to be confronted.

Answers to the challenges formulated above will require international agreements which, considering the history of international decision making, will be difficult to reach. If they are reached the impacts on human culture and on nature will be significant. Denial of the problems may lead to even greater impacts.

# REFERENCES

Arizpe, L, R Constanza and W Lutz, 'Primary Factors Affecting Population and Natural Resource Use', paper presented at the International Conference on an Agenda of Science for Environment and Development into the 21st Century, Vienna, Austria, November 1991.

Bach, W, J Pankrath and J Williams (eds), *Interactions of Energy and Climate*, proceedings of an International Workshop, Münster: Reidel Publ Co, March 1980.

Blok, K, W C Turkenburg, C A Hendriks and M Steinberg (eds), 'Proceedings of the First International Conference on Carbon Dioxide Removal, Amsterdam, March 1992', *The Journal of Energy Conversion and Management*, vol 33, no 5–8, 1992.

Bolin, B, 'Man-induced Global Change of Climate, the IPCC Findings and Continuing Uncertainty Regarding Preventive Action', *Environmental Conservation*, vol 18, no 4, winter 1991, pp 297–303.

Bryson, R A, 'Environmental Opportunities and Limits for Development', *Environmental Conservation*, vol 16, no. 4, winter 1989, pp 299–305.

Edmonds, J and J Reilly, 'Global Energy and $CO_2$ to the Year 2050', *Energy Journal*, vol 44, no 3, 1983, pp 21–47.

Glasby, G P, 'Entropy, Pollution and Environmental Degradation', *Ambio*, vol 17, no 5, 1988, pp 330–5.

Goldemberg, J et al, 'An End-use Oriented Global Energy Strategy', *Annual Review of Energy*, vol 10, 1985, pp 649–710.

Holdren, J P and R K Pachauri, 'Energy', paper presented at the International Conference on an Agenda of Science for Environment and Development into the 21st Century, Vienna, Austria, November 1991.

IIASA (International Institute of Applied Systems Analysis), *Energy in a Finite World, a Global Systems Analysis*, Cambridge, MA: Ballinger, 1981.

Jackson, T and S Roberts, *Getting out of the Greenhouse, an Agenda for UK Action on Energy Policy*, London: Friends of the Earth, December 1989.

Johansson, T B, H Kelly, A K N Reddy and R H Williams, *Renewable Energy (Sources for Fuels and Electricity)*, London: Earthscan Publications, 1993.

Keepin, B and G Kats, 'Greenhouse Warming, Comparative Analysis of Nuclear and Efficiency Abatement Strategies', *Energy Policy*, December 1988, pp 538–61.

Krause, F, W Bach and J Koomey, *Energy Policy in the Greenhouse*, vol 1, El Cerrito, CA: IPSEP, September 1989.

Lazarus, M, et al, *Towards a Fossil Free Energy Future (The Next Energy Transition)*, Boston: Stockholm Environmental Institute – Boston Center, 1993.

Lovins, A B, L H Lovins, F Krause and W Bach, *Least-cost Energy, Solving the $CO_2$ Problem*, Andover, MA: Brick House, 1981.

Moll, H C, K Vringer, W Biesiot and A J Schilstra, 'Sustainable Use of Solar Cells: Is it

Possible and Desirable?', paper presented at the International J D van der Waals Conference on Thin Layer Technology, Eindhoven, The Netherlands, November 1991.

Mulder, H A J, W Biesiot, H C Moll and G M van Elburg, *De transitie naar duurzaamheid in de 21ste eeuw*, IVEM, University of Groningen, 1993.

Nordhaus, W D and G Yohe, *Future Paths of Energy and Carbon Dioxide Emissions, Changing Climate*, Washington, DC: NAS, 1983.

RMI, Lovins, A B et al, *COMPETITEK, an information service of RMI (Rocky Mountain Institute)*, Snowmass, CO: RMI, 1991.

Rose, D J, M M Miller and C Agnew, *Global Energy Futures and CO₂-induced Climate Change*, MITEL 83-015, Cambridge, MA: MIT Energy Laboratory, 1984.

SERI, Solar Energy Research Institute, *The Potential of Renewable Energy*, 1989.

Shell, *Energy in Profile*, London: Shell, 1991.

Shell, *Energy in Profile*, London: Shell, 1992.

Slesser, M, *The Use of Resource Accounting in Development Planning Using a Dynamic Simulation Model: ECCO*, Edinburgh: Centre for Human Ecology, University of Edinburgh, 1987.

Sørenson, B, 'Renewable Energy. A Technical Overview', *Energy Policy*, vol 19, no 5, 1991, pp 386–91.

Turkenburg, W C, 'A Survey of World Energy Problems' in J Weerdenburg (ed), *Kernenergie: Bron van energie of bron van problemen?*, Studium Generale, University of Utrecht, 1992.

United Nations, *Long Range World Population Projections, as assessed in 1980*, New York: UN Population Bureau, 1983.

United Nations, *Long Range World Population Projections, as assessed in 1990*, New York: UN Population Bureau, 1991.

Veziroglu, T N and F Barbir, 'Solar-Hydrogen Energy Systems: The Choice of the Future', *Environmental Conservation*, vol 18, no 4, winter 1991, pp 304–12.

WEC (World Energy Conference), *Energy 2000–2020, World Prospects and Regional Stresses*, London: Graham and Trotman, 1983.

*Chapter Four*

# Understanding Biofuel Dynamics in Developing Countries

## The Need for the Local Context

*Omar Masera and Priya Deshingkar*

Biofuels remain a globally important source of energy second only to fossil fuels in their scale of use. Nearly 2 billion people rely almost exclusively on biofuels (wood, charcoal, dung and crop residues) for their energy needs (Tolba and Goodman, 1990). Some statistics are appropriate to better understand the dimensions of fuelwood use. Biofuels account for 14 per cent of the world's total energy use; 35 per cent of energy use in developing countries; and an average of 75 per cent of energy use in rural areas of these latter countries (Smith, 1991). In many African countries fuelwood may account for as much as 90 per cent of total energy use.

The large amounts of fuelwood consumed, together with the poor prospects for a rapid and massive switching to the so-called 'modern' fuels, present important energy, social and environmental concerns. It is mainly the poor in rural as well as urban areas who are forced to rely on biofuels for cooking, water heating, space heating and, in many cases, process heating for home-based enterprises (pottery workshops, bakeries etc). In several regions access to biofuels has become a problem: people have to walk long distances in search of fuel, cooking times are cut down which may affect nutrition and undesirable fuels may be used with adverse effects on the health of the user. When harvested in a non-sustainable basis, biofuels are associated with several environmental impacts, contributing to soil erosion, forest degradation and to emissions of greenhouse gases, among other effects.

Adequately managed, however, biofuels – including the modern forms of biomass energy conversion – represent a sound energy source, and have the potential to cover a significant share of future world energy needs (see Chapter 3). Confronted with the problems of the current patterns of use, the central concern is to assure sustainable supplies of adequate quantities of biofuels, beginning with the most disadvantaged segments of society. The biofuel problem must therefore be incorporated into the more general analysis of strategies for assuring sustainable, equitable and liveable livelihoods. A central element of these strategies is the search for approaches that help improve the conditions of biofuel supply and use for the poorest households in the short term, at the same time facilitating the building of the social, economic and technical conditions for a gradual transition to more efficient forms of use (eg gasified and liquid fuels) in the mid and long term.

Approaches to the biofuel problem (or 'biofuel trap') have varied. Early analyses concentrated on the technical dimensions of biofuel use and proposed standard packages that were weak in dealing with the complexity and variability of fuel-wood dynamics. The first attempt to understand the biofuel problem, influenced by the world oil crisis of the early 1970s, 'discovered' the so-called 'other energy crisis' (Eckholm, 1980) wherein it was argued that people in developing countries were facing a fuelwood crisis similar to the oil crisis being experienced by the North. This was followed by the rather alarmist 'gap theory' (CEC, 1985; Shell, 1980) which used highly aggregated and inaccurate figures on supply and demand. The theory says that biofuel reserves were being destroyed because of gaps between supply and demand of biofuels. More recently fuelwood use has been studied in connection with health issues ('indoor air pollution'; Smith, 1987) and for its potential contribution to climate change (Ahuja, 1990; Smith et al, 1991). Sociologists have also stressed the class and gender specificity of fuelwood use – naming fuelwood scarcity as the poor woman's problem (Hoskins, 1981).

Experience to date has shown that many projects based on simplistic analysis have failed, so much so that wood scarcity is now worse than 20 years before in many critical areas (Agarwal, 1986; Leach and Mearns, 1988). Far from a straight-forward 'energy' problem with relatively simple 'technical' solutions, understanding biofuel use dynamics and relieving biofuel scarcity has thus proven a formidable challenge. Against mounting empirical evidence, and notwithstanding repeated project failures, aggregate, simplistic explanations about biofuel scarcity are still the conventional wisdom, particularly within influential circles of natural scientists (Myers, 1992).

In this chapter the dangers of using simplistic aggregate models describing the relationship between biofuel use, people and the environment are shown. The nature and evolution of biofuel use patterns and biofuel scarcity is determined by complex interactions between local production systems, biophysical conditions of the associated natural resource base, the local socio-cultural setting and technology, as well as wider socio-economic structures. Which social, political and economic factors determine access to biofuel resources and end-use devices? A clear understanding of indigenous land-use management strategies, household priorities (particularly women's priorities) and constraints is critical for the correct identification of problems related to biofuel dynamics. (Compare Deshingkar, 1989; Morse et al, 1984; Tinker, 1987.)

The biofuel problem has implications at the local, regional, national and global levels. There is therefore a need to analyse biofuel dynamics in the broader context of natural resource management strategies and rural development policies. Such analysis has received some attention before but it is still under-represented in the literature (see eg Agarwal, 1986; Cecelski, 1985; Leach and Mearns, 1988; Soussan et al, 1992a).

This chapter begins with a description of conventional wisdom about biofuel use dynamics. The main premises, policy implications and shortcomings of the approach are shown. The second section discusses the main factors that may induce or reduce biofuel scarcity. The discussion about the theoretical approaches to biofuel dynamics is relevant because, on the one hand, the way the problem is framed has profound consequences on the type of policies and interventions designed to solve it; and, on the other hand, because biofuel issues may serve as a case study that illustrates the dangers of using aggregate models to describe the broader relationship between people and environmental degradation.

In the third section the theoretical and practical aspects that have proved important in order to effectively exit the 'biofuel trap' are described. The concluding remarks regard the opportunities and challenges for improving the conditions of biofuel use in developing countries.

## CONVENTIONAL WISDOM ON BIOFUEL USE DYNAMICS

The most influential explanation of biofuel use dynamics in developing countries has been the 'gap theory' (Shell, 1980; FAO, 1981; CEC, 1985). Developed in the context of the energy crisis of the 1970s, the model uses a Malthusian approach by which population-driven biofuel demand leads to extensive depletion of forest resources. In this model, aggregate biofuel demand is estimated by multiplying consumption per capita by total population. Supply is calculated using official statistics on the mean annual increment of forests (eg FAO, 1981; World Bank, 1985). The resulting difference between supply and demand – the 'biofuel gap' – is used to determine whether a region has a biofuel 'surplus' or 'deficit'. Future biofuel demand is estimated using current per capita biofuel consumption levels and population growth rates (Dewees, 1989), while future biofuel supply is assumed to be declining due to agricultural expansion and over-cutting of trees (OTA, 1991).

Not surprisingly, this model leads invariably to catastrophic predictions about biofuel shortages. For example, using this methodology the FAO (1981) determined that 1.3 billion people live in wood deficit areas and that 3 billion people would be suffering acute wood shortages by the year 2000 (see also Anderson, 1986, for the case of Africa). Biofuel deficits are equated to deforestation due to over-harvesting and biofuel scarcity is assumed to lead to increasing use of crop residues and dung, compounding the environmental impacts. Following this logic, the predicted effects of wood shortages were stated by Eckholm (1980, p 60) as 'one of the most profound ecological challenges of the twentieth century'. Social consequences are also predicted to be severe as biofuel scarcity is also assumed to lead automatically to rocketing wood prices and increases in wood collection time. A logical consequence of the model is the creation of a 'biofuel trap' from which, in the absence of external intervention, escape is only possible by reducing local population growth rates (see Figure 4.1).

Policy recommendations arising from the model focused on the need of huge reforestation programmes (particularly fuelwood plantations) and energy centred measures to reduce biofuel use (dissemination of improved wood stoves and

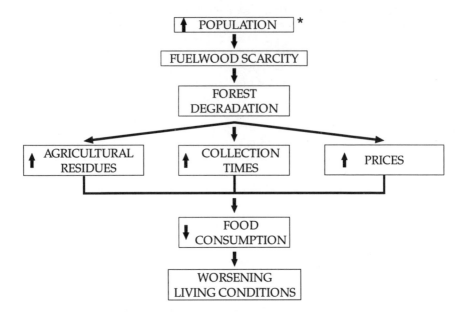

**Figure 4.1** *Fuelwood trap created by the 'gap' approach. The postulated source of stress is indicated by the asterisk\**

switching to modern fuels). Since solutions to biofuel scarcity were perceived to be so obvious, most projects followed a top-down approach, reducing local people's participation to merely implementing already designed programmes. Reality proved more difficult to cope with. Most of these early programmes failed to ameliorate shortages experienced by poor households. Also, and despite its alarming predictions on biofuel scarcity, programmes based on the model assumptions failed to capture situations where acute biofuel scarcity was present in spite of overall supplies of biofuel being adequate to meet the demand of the local population.

## BEYOND CONVENTIONAL WISDOM

The underlying assumptions of the 'gap' model are as follows:

- fuelwood consumption per capita is fixed, ie biofuel demand is inelastic (Wallace, 1988);
- biofuel demand increases at the same rate as population growth;
- biofuel supply is well characterized by commercial wood supply;
- increases in biofuel prices and change in fuels (eg from wood to dung) are a direct cause of biofuel scarcity;
- average physical fuel scarcity (ie total resources divided by total population) is a

good measure of individual household or village scarcity;
- wood resources are open access (ie in principle everybody can have access to existing forest resources).

These assumptions have been increasingly questioned by empirical research, at least as far as their universality is concerned.

Below we review critically the factors that have been identified (either by the 'gap' model or by other approaches) as most influential for the creation – or the relief – of biofuel scarcity. We also briefly review the problems in establishing a simple link between biofuel scarcity and environmental degradation. The discussion will help provide insights towards providing more adequate explanations of biofuel use dynamics and, therefore, towards the implementation of more successful projects.

## Variability of per capita biofuel consumption
Per capita biofuel use, far from fixed, has been shown to be fairly elastic, depending on:

- physical conditions of the rural setting, such as climate, physical availability of biomass resources, type of fuel burned;
- demographic variables, like household size and age composition;
- cooking habits and practices (eg type of pots used for cooking and diet);
- technical characteristics of the end-use device as expressed by its energy efficiency (Islam et al, 1984; Evans, 1987; Leach, 1988; Munslow et al, 1988);
- women's time that is available for cooking (Tinker, 1987).

Also, it has been seen that households respond to increasing biofuel scarcity by reducing their biofuel use per capita (Agarwal, 1986; Leach and Mearns, 1988; Soussan et al, 1991), even when using the same end-use device (for example, through more careful fire tending, better management of residual heat, changes in cooking practices or the amount and type of food intake). Finally, interfuel substitution (particularly in urban areas) and multiple fuel cooking also reduce average biofuel consumption per capita (Cline-Cole et al, 1990a and 1990b).

The variations in per capita biofuel use, either because of differences in the socio-cultural and physical conditions of biofuel use, or by people's adaptations to increased biofuel scarcity, may span more than an order of magnitude – from 2.4 GJ/cap/yr in arid regions with acute biofuel scarcity to 59.2 GJ/cap/yr in villages with abundant forest resources in cold climates (Leach, 1988). Under these conditions, regional or national estimates on biofuel consumption based on data from a small number of villages are usually severely biased.

## Population growth
A growing population certainly induces stresses on available biofuel supplies. However, given the elasticity of biofuel use, either as a result of people's adaptations to scarcity and the large variation in local socio-cultural and physical conditions, or because of biofuel switching, biofuel consumption does not necessarily increase at the same rate as population growth. Thus, the relationship between people, biofuel

and the environment is no longer a question of simple multiplication.

There is no doubt that in many circumstances the increase in population has had a negative impact on biofuel resources, particularly in the burgeoning urban areas of some African countries and densely populated parts of South Asia. It is also true that increasing numbers of biofuel users constitute an important source of stress on the biofuel system that tend to increase biofuel scarcity. However, the link between population growth and environmental degradation from biofuel over-cutting has proven more elusive in the real world. Comprehensive research in some of the most critical areas of Nigeria show, for example, that people react to biofuel scarcity by increasing the woody biomass in their farms or home gardens (Cline-Cole et al, 1990a and 1990b). Similarly the results of a ten-year study on the fuelwood crisis in Kenya have shown that, contrary to popular opinion, the amount of woody biomass cultivated on farms actually increased as population density grew and farms were subdivided into smaller units (Bradley, 1991; Bradley and Huby, 1993). Research in other parts of Kenya has also identified positive effects of increasing population density. In the Machakos district population increases led to beneficial changes in the management of drylands and diversification of the economy which outweighed any negative effects associated with population growth (Tiffen, 1992).

## Urban versus rural biofuel consumption
Urban and rural biofuel demand have very different patterns and therefore need to be analysed separately. Whereas rural people use a variety of biofuels, urban fuelwood is usually solid wood which comes from felling live trees. Therefore, even if in absolute terms rural biofuel use might be larger, the environmental impacts of biofuel are more linked to urban demand. Also, in many cases, the increase of urban biofuel demand has worsened biofuel scarcity in local villages because the selling of firewood represents a source of income for local households. As household monetary incomes are higher and alternative fuels more readily available in urban areas, fuels tend to be commercialized compared to the rural sector where most biofuel is still collected. The distinction between rural and urban biofuel demand is therefore also crucial for the type of approaches and interventions to be promoted.

## The characteristics of biofuel supply
Local biofuel supplies (from home gardens, shrubs, agricultural plots, living fences etc) are considerably larger than commercial biofuel supplies from forests (Agarwal, 1986; Morse et al, 1984). Besides that, domestic biofuel is mostly from tree species and parts that are considered non-commercial. Rural people tend to use twigs, branches and dead wood rather than whole trees. Biofuel harvesting methods have environmental consequences very different from those of commercial tree logging. It should be noted too that, in many countries, even commercial wood supply is very uncertain. For example, the United Nations Food and Agriculture Organization estimates about production of forest products from African countries for the early 1980s relied in 73 per cent of the countries on 'unofficial sources or estimates' rather than on national surveys. This percentage reached

88 per cent for statistics on fuelwood and charcoal use (Laar, 1991).

Under these conditions, the calculations of supply based on the commercial mean annual increment (which only accounts for the stem volume of wood from commercial tree species) and biofuel consumption lack any empirical validity. Before concluding that there exist biofuel deficits and/or surpluses, future studies must incorporate the diversity of sources of biofuel supply and the intraregional variations in biofuel demand and must discern between the different categories of biofuel (ie the differing demand on different tree species, part of trees and living or dead wood). This poses difficult research challenges, given the poor data on production of woody biomass in local ecosystems.

## *The methods and intensity of fuelwood harvesting*

Although biofuel gathering accounts for the largest share of biomass use in developing countries, it is seldom the principal cause of deforestation. In terms of scale, clear felling of forested land for agriculture, timber production and beef ranching cause far more damage to the environment than the collection of twigs, dead branches and forest litter. It is now widely accepted that extensive deforestation has been mainly a result of macroeconomic policies which have favoured certain economic activities, such as cash crop cultivation and cattle rearing over forestry (Cecelski, 1985; Dewees, 1989; Leach, 1988; Repetto and Gillis, 1988; Hurst and Barnett, 1990). In this regard, it should be noted that biofuel shortages are usually more the outcome rather than the cause of extensive deforestation.

The environmental impact of biofuel collection depends mainly on the method and intensity of harvesting. At moderate levels biofuel harvesting provides several benefits to local forests, such as the reduction in the probability of forest fires, reduction in forest pests and diseases, and even the acceleration of tree growth (in the manner of selective pruning). In many regions, farmers also plant trees when facing acute biofuel shortages (Cline-Cole et al, 1990a and 1990b; Soussan et al, 1991; Dewees, 1989). Over-harvesting of biofuel, on the other hand, leads to a wide range of local to global environmental impacts, including forest degradation, soil erosion, changes in nutrient cycles and emissions of greenhouse gases. Even when there is over-cutting of wood resources, biofuel use leads more often to forest degradation than to extensive deforestation.

Finally, it must also be mentioned in this context that there is no clear-cut downwards substitution from wood to crop residues and dung in situations of wood scarcity. It is commonly assumed that a direct consequence of wood scarcity is increased levels of crop residue and dung consumption. However, in some cases the use of agricultural residues has been customary for centuries (Alcántara et al, 1985; Dewees, 1989). In other cases crop residues are actually preferred over wood (Ernst, 1978) or were as difficult to procure as wood (Deshingkar, 1992). The negative impact of the use of agricultural residues also depends strongly on the particular residues used, the quantity removed from the fields etc (Laar, 1991). Some residues, like stalks of millet and sorghum, have little fertilizer value, are difficult to recycle and are often burned on the fields. Again, no simple connection between the use of residues and environmental degradation can be stated.

## Access and fuel entitlements – beyond simple demand-supply calculations

Another popular belief which must be challenged is the assumption that there is a direct relationship between the physical supplies of biofuels and the quantity that a person is able to consume. There is strong evidence that the relationship between the resource and the consumer is not straightforward. In other words, simply the fact that there are enough trees in an area to satisfy local fuel demands does not guarantee that everybody in that region will be able to obtain enough fuel.

People's ability to obtain fuel or their 'entitlement' to biofuels depends on a number of social, economic and political factors, such as ownership of land, income levels, traditional rights to private and common property resources, and commercialization of the resource in question (Deshingkar, 1993).[1] Access to biofuels is rarely a function of supply levels alone and reliance on whole population 'average' figures regarding patterns of biofuel dynamics is clearly fraught with problems.

The ability of people to use or benefit from biofuel resources depends more on the particular configuration of the patterns of resource ownership, control, local rules and institutional arrangements, rather than on the physical quantity of resources present. Therefore the entitlements to biofuels of a landless labourer may be significantly different from that of, say, a rich landlord. The fact that the type and amount of fuel consumed shows significant variation according to socio-economic status and gender has been documented (Briscoe, 1979; Cecelski, 1985; Alcántara et al, 1985; Masera et al, 1989). In Tables 4.1 and 4.2 the importance of taking social differences into account is illustrated by the results of case studies in Mexico and India.

**Table 4.1** *Social differences in fuelwood consumption patterns: Cheranatzicurin Village, Mexico*

(A) Labour and fuel use

| Income group[b] | Percentage village households | Household activities[c] (hr/cap/day) | Wood collection (hr/cap/day) | % total activ | Fuelwood use (kg/cap/day) | Liquefied petroleum gas use (% hh) |
|---|---|---|---|---|---|---|
| I | 12% | 4.9 | 1.3 | 27% | 1.8 | 0% |
| II | 61% | 5.1 | 1.3 | 25% | 1.6 | 0% |
| III | 10% | 2.8 | 0.7 | 25% | 1.9 | 0% |
| IV | 10% | 4.0 | 1.0 | 25% | 1.6 | 5% |
| V | 5% | 2.4 | 0.7 | 29% | 1.6 | 20% |
| VI | 2% | 2.0 | 0.4 | 20% | 3.8 | 50% |

Header spanning "Labour Use" over Wood collection, % total activ, Fuelwood use.

1. For a definition of common property resources, and the causes and effects of their degradation, see Jodha, 1986 and Ostrom, 1990.

*Omar Masera and Priya Deshingkar*

(B) Ways of obtaining fuel, and fuel type[d]

| Income group | Collected | | | Purchased | | Fuel use by type | |
|---|---|---|---|---|---|---|---|
| | Men w/ animals | Men w/ trucks | Women and children | % households[e] | % income[f] | Only pine and oak | Various |
| I | 0% | 0% | 100% | 0% | – | 0% | 100% |
| II | 0% | 0% | 66% | 34% | 10% | 34% | 66% |
| III | 100% | 0% | 0% | 0% | 10% | 100% | 0% |
| IV | 34% | 33% | 0% | 33% | 5% | 66% | 34% |
| V | 17% | 33% | 33% | 17% | 3% | 66% | 34% |
| VI | 0% | 100% | 0% | 0% | 2% | 100% | 0% |

Source: Masera, 1990
(Notes: [a] From Masera (1990). Data taken from a sample of 22 families; figures correspond to the year 1987. [b] Higher Roman numeral indicates higher household income. [c] Includes water and fuelwood collection, clothes washing, and tortilla making. [d] All figures are percentage of total households in each income group. [e] Includes households that purchase biofuel on a non-systematic basis. [f] Refers to the percentage of household income devoted to biofuel purchases in households that regularly buy fuelwood.)

**Table 4.2** *Annual fuel use according to type of fuel and landholding size: Rampur Village, India (GJ/yr/hh)*

| | Landless | Small and marginal | Medium and large |
|---|---|---|---|
| Sugarcane (stalks and roots) | 24.3% | 22.9% | 6.8% |
| Dung (cakes) | 2.0% | 5.5% | 1.1% |
| Shrubs (Ipomoea) | 41.0% | 7.4% | 7.1% |
| Wood | 19.2% | 30.2% | 21.3% |
| Twigs | 1.2% | 3.9% | 1.6% |
| Kerosene | 2.0% | 5.2% | 3.6% |
| Liquefied petroleum gas | 1.6% | 5.4% | 6.4% |
| Biogas | – | 19.4% | 53.7% |
| Total (GJ) | 24.40 | 30.94 | 56.42 |

(Notes: From Deshingkar (1993). Data collected through actual measurements from a sample of 94 households in a village with 334 households. Figures correspond to the year 1988–9.)

Processes which negatively affect any of the elements which determine a person's entitlements – such as a decrease in income, the deterioration of common property resources or erosion of traditional rights – will have a differential impact across social groups, even if the physical amount of woody resources remains the same. This explains the persistence of fuel deprivation in poor families living in areas with an abundance of biomass (Deshingkar, 1993). Landless agricultural labourers, poor female-headed households and marginal farmers are particularly susceptible to biofuel deprivation (Cecelski, 1985; compare Table 4.1). Figure 4.2 shows a scheme of the overall relationship between the type of fuel used, gender, access to common property resources and social groups.

### The macro-economic context

Finally, the conditions of biofuel use and access at the local level are also influenced by national policies regarding land-use management and ownership, public investment in rural and urban deprived areas, and the evolution of rural and urban real wages (Leach and Mearns, 1988). In general, macropolicies that spread poverty (eg that result in a reduction of real wages or the underpricing of peasant products) and

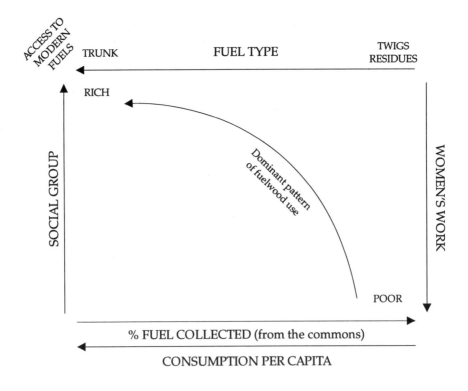

**Figure 4.2** *Social and ecological dynamics of fuelwood use*

induce deforestation (eg subsidizing alternative land uses like cattle ranching or agriculture – Cecelski, 1985) are likely to exacerbate biofuel scarcity. Other policies with negative impact on biofuel availability include those that induce the breaking down of collective institutions for the management of local resources (for example, through legislation that facilitates the erosion of traditional resource distribution mechanisms), insecure land tenure and the deterioration of tenure rights, the privatization and/or nationalization of common property resources (which, in the first case, usually preclude the poorest households' access to woody resources and, in the second case, may create 'open access' conditions to forest resources). On the other hand, social investment to improve the reliability of supply of alternative fuels, policies that favour increases in real incomes and employment generation in low income areas, and that secure land tenure rights for the poorest households, will usually help ameliorate biofuel scarcity.

## EXITING THE BIOFUEL TRAP

The discussion above shows the dangers of applying simplistic analysis to understand and solve the biofuel problem in developing countries. The diversity of conditions and problems at the local level imply that a variety of approaches and interventions is needed. Little can be said at the general level that is applicable everywhere.

In contrast with the 'biofuel trap' assumed by the 'gap theory', where the dynamics is centred in the population/environmental degradation loop, there are multiple conditions of 'stress' inducing changes in biofuel demand and supply. The term 'stress' is used here to indicate factors that either put more pressure on fuelwood resources and use (eg increased competition for fuelwood) or release that pressure (eg fuel switching). These stresses can be local (like a forest plague or struggles for political control of the village leading to forest degradation) or national (because of new legislation regarding the land tenure system). They can be demand-driven, for example, through population increase, or improved access to alternative fuels, or supply-driven, through deforestation from commercial logging. Or they can be a combination of all these. The response of households can be progressive (improving efficiency of biofuel use) or regressive (reducing food consumption) and will typically have differing impacts by gender, age and social group (or caste), as is shown in Figure 4.3. In these circumstances, the particular configuration of the multiple conditions of stress to the biofuel system acting at the local level, rather than any 'universal process', will determine whether a biofuel 'trap' or a 'non-problem' situation arises.

Studies of biofuel use need to identify the main sources of stress to the local biofuel system, and analyse the way households respond to these stresses according to different household strategies and social groups. In this manner, the associated environmental and social consequences of the process can be documented, and the potential feedback between environmental and social processes can also be identified (eg biofuel scarcity leading to conflicts over resource use which accelerate depletion of biofuel resources and increase biofuel scarcity).

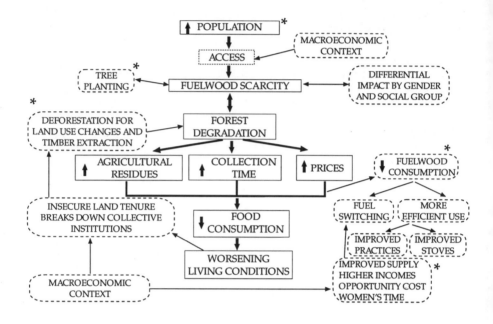

**Figure 4.3** *Alternative model of the dynamics of fuelwood scarcity. The different sources of stress are indicated by the asterisks (\*)*
*Source: Masera, 1993a*

Programmes are more likely to succeed if they are based on a better understanding of the dynamics of rural energy use, the character of driving forces which cause the particular stresses to the biofuel system and the behavioural responses by people affected by biofuel shortages (De Laar, 1991). Such understanding will enable projects to be designed which can protect people's biofuel entitlements as well as minimize negative impacts on the environment.

In recent years a whole range of experiences have been accumulated illustrating innovative schemes to solve biofuel problems. The experiences range from the successful dissemination of improved wood stoves in rural and, particularly, urban areas, to integrated agro-forestry schemes with multipurpose trees to increase biofuel supply in rural areas. (For reviews of these experiences, see eg Leach and Mearns, 1988; Munslow et al, 1988; Joseph et al, 1990; and Bradley, 1991.) Some factors can be singled out that have proved important for the success of the different projects. Some interesting guidelines towards such an identification of 'common themes' regarding fuelwood situations in developing countries is provided by Soussan et al, 1992b. These authors construct a typology that attempts to resolve the tension between achieving a level of generalization needed for policy formulation, and the need to capture the specifics of fuelwood production and use at the local level. The typology is based on a series of criteria, including the characteristics of the biomass resource potential in the area under study; socio-economic structure at the local level (access to fuelwood resources, population densities and settlement forms); factors inducing the export of fuelwood resources out of the area; and the major structural changes affecting the fuelwood situation (like urbanization, colonization projects etc). Still, as has been emphasized throughout this chapter, generalization of methods and approaches is very difficult. The following, therefore, highlights important issues, rather than providing recipes for action.

## Giving people a share in the management of biofuel resources

There is strong evidence that, given the right circumstances, people will conserve and manage resources to provide sustainable supplies of biomass and protect livelihoods. The thesis that people invariably treat natural resources which do not exclusively belong to them as open access resources is now widely discredited. One of the most important conditions for ensuring the success of natural management schemes has been to give people a genuine stake in the management of the resource. 'Participatory' projects span a whole spectrum of arrangements from those with outside funding and government support to those which are completely independently managed by the concerned groups of people.

The Forest Protection Committees (FPCs) of West Bengal in India are a good example of participatory management of resources with state support. FPCs were first established in 1973 as a joint venture between the Indian Forest Department and the people. A group of unemployed or underemployed villagers and landless or marginal farmers was given a block of degraded public land for planting trees. Members of the group were not given ownership of the land but were given usufruct rights to the land, and ownership of the trees they had planted and protected. Besides access to thinning residues, fallen twigs, grass, fruit, seeds and flowers, the participants were also given 25 per cent of the proceeds from the sale of the forest produce. The biofuel entitlements of the villagers were therefore enhanced through the generation of employment, cash incomes and biomass products from the projects. Over a period of 20 years FPCs have taken over some 237,000 hectares for management. This experiment was so successful that the Indian government has issued an order supporting joint management of degraded forests all over India.

## Understanding people's priorities and concerns

Procuring adequate quantities of fuel is only one of many concerns in most households. Household decisions regarding biofuel use are made within complex and holistic perspectives on the entire land-use and household economy (Morse et al, 1984). These decisions are based on and constrained by fundamental issues such as the distribution of land holdings, security of tenure, changes in control and access to lands, and the environmental conditions that govern the productive potential of land (Agarwal, 1983; Leach and Mearns, 1988). Thus, very often biofuel savings are not at the top of people's priorities. Indirect approaches to the biofuel problem, that encourage farm and agro-forestry for multipurpose products and services, and aim at improving the conditions of biofuel use at the end-use following people's own ranking of priorities (eg improving sanitary conditions in the kitchen or saving cooking time rather than saving biofuel) have a much larger probability of success than single targeted technical packages.

## Building on indigenous knowledge of wood production systems and biofuel end-use practices and technologies

Rather than relying on technical solutions designed by foreign experts, successful projects have been built on a good understanding of indigenous knowledge and traditional solutions to the biofuel problem. This objective can only be reached through effective participatory approaches, which encourage dialogue between villagers, technicians and/or government officials (NES-WRI, 1990). Achieving a synthesis between local knowledge, and modern science and technology, while difficult, is usually important as both local people and the different agencies can mutually benefit from their strengths and weaknesses (Altieri, 1988). The ceramic 'jiko' stove programme in Kenya, in which the new stoves were designed and disseminated in close cooperation with local artisans, provides a good example of the successful combination of modern and traditional knowledge (Karekezi and Walubengo, 1989).

## Identify target groups, paying attention to different fuel entitlements by social group and gender

The biofuel problem is felt differently by distinct social groups. The design of alternatives needs to take into consideration these differences in access and control over biofuel resources. Approaches that acknowledge these differences and design solutions accordingly have been more successful. In the case of the Dhanusha district in Nepal, for instance, different alternatives were developed according to the characteristics of the settlement (urban/rural), its biofuel endowments and social group (Soussan et al, 1991). These alternatives ranged from the establishment of 'buffer plantations' of fast-growing fodder and biofuel shrubs and agro-forestry schemes managed by local communities to the encouraging of fuel switching.

## Provide the correct policy context at the macro level for the effective empowerment of local communities

This is the most difficult requirement but the one that ultimately determines the long-term viability of the local interventions and initiatives. Basically it entails a reversal of the progressive alienation of the poor from the natural resource base and their environment. Rather than viewing people as the enemy which must be kept away from nature, governments can help people with environmental conservation through legislation which facilitates management at the grass roots level. People's empowerment can be supported through the securing of land tenure rights, the reduction of anti-agrarian policies (like the underpricing of peasants' products), investing in basic infrastructure and education in rural areas, and other policies that help reduce poverty.

## CONCLUSION

Biofuels are and will remain a very important energy source for a large number of households in developing countries for many years to come. In many regions biofuel scarcity at the household level worsened during the 1980s. Urgent measures are needed to improve the situation, which is already critical for millions of the poorest in developing countries.

In the search for solutions, aggregate approaches, based on simplistic assumptions about the relationship between people, biofuel use and environmental degradation (like the 'gap approach') are of little practical value. Interventions guided by these assumptions have led to drastic failures and even to worsening the biofuel situation.

Alternative approaches should begin by acknowledging that the dynamics of biofuel use and biofuel scarcity in developing countries is complex and extremely diverse. Solutions are more likely to be found through flexible, decentralized approaches that start from an understanding of the local context, and are integrated into national and international levels. A significant number of experiments based on these premises show how the biofuel problem might be eased. The need now is to have the courage to challenge conventional wisdom and help effectively to promote sustainable development from the bottom up.

## REFERENCES

Agarwal, B, 'Diffusion of Rural Innovations: Some Analytical Issues and the Case of Wood-burning Stoves', World Development, vol 11, no 4, 1983, pp 359–76.

Agarwal, B, Cold Hearths and Barren Slopes, Riverdale: The Riverdale Company, 1986.

Anderson, C, 'Declining Tree Stocks in African Countries', World Development, vol 14, no 7, 1986, pp 853–63.

Ahuja, D, 'Research Needs for Improving Biofuel Burning Cookstove Technologies', Natural Resources Forum, May 1990, pp 125–34.

Alcántara, E, M de la Peña, M Abuhadba and D Flores, 'Crisis de Energía Rural y Trabajo Femenino en Tres Areas Ecológicas del Perú', Geneva: ILO Working Paper, September 1985.

Altieri, M, 'Sistemas Agroecológicos Alternativos para la Producción Campesina' in Desarrollo Agrícola y Participación Campesina, Santiago de Chile: CEPAL, 1988, pp 263–76.

Bradley, P, Woodfuel, Women and Woodlots, volume 1: The foundations of a woodfuel development strategy for East Africa, London: Macmillan, 1991.

Bradley, P and M Huby, Woodfuel, Women and Woodlots, volume 2: The Kenya Woodfuel Development Programme, London: Macmillan, 1993.

Briscoe, J, 'Energy Use and Social Structures in a Bangladesh Village', Population and Development Review, vol 5, no 4, 1979, pp 615–41.

Cecelski, E, 'The Rural Energy Crisis, Women's Work and Basic Needs: Perspectives and Approaches to Action', Geneva: ILO Rural Employment Policy Research Programme Technical Cooperation Report, 1985.

Cline-Cole, R et al, 'On Biofuel Consumption, Population Dynamics and Deforestation in Africa', *World Development*, vol 18, 1990a, pp 513–27.

Cline-Cole, R et al, *Wood Fuel in Kano*, Hong Kong: United Nations University Press, 1990b.

CEC (Commission of European Communities), 'Dossier: La Crise du Bois de Feu', *Le Courrier*, no 95, 1985.

Deshingkar, P, *Markets, Natural Resource Mobility, and the Rural Poor: Crop Resources in South Gujarat*, occasional paper no 5, Surat: Centre for Social Studies, 1989.

Deshingkar, P, 'Biomass Entitlements and Rural Poverty in India: A Village Study of Crop Residues in South Gujarat', (PhD thesis) Institute of Development Studies, University of Sussex, 1992.

Deshingkar, P, 'Biomass Entitlements: The Determinants of Access to Biofuels in Developing Countries', Helsinki: Report to WIDER, April 1993.

Dewees, P, 'The Woodfuel Crisis Reconsidered: Observations on the Dynamics of Abundance and Scarcity', *World Development*, vol 17, no 8, 1989, pp 1159–72.

Eckholm, E P, 'The Other Energy Crisis: Firewood' in V Smil and W Knowland (eds), *Energy in the Developing World*, Oxford/New York: Oxford University Press, 1980, pp 63–71.

Ernst, E, 'Fuel Consumption among Rural Families in Upper Volta, West Africa', paper presented at Eighth World Forestry Congress, Jakarta, 16–28 October 1978.

Evans, M, 'Stoves Programmes in the Framework of Improved Cooking Practices: A Change in Focus with Special Reference to Latin America', Geneva: ILO Working Paper, 1987.

FAO (United Nations Food and Agriculture Organization), *Map of the Fuelwood Situation in Developing Countries*, Rome: FAO, 1981.

Hoskins, M, 'Women in Forestry for Local Community Development: A Programming Guide' in B C Lewis (ed), *Invisible Farmers: Women and the Crisis of Agriculture*, Washington, DC: AID Report (AID/OTR-C-147-35), 1981.

Hurst, C and A Barnett, *The Energy Dimension*, London: Intermediate Technology Publications, 1990.

Islam, M Nurul, R Morse and M H Soestastro (eds), *Rural Energy to Meet Development Needs: Asian Village Approaches*, Boulder, CO: Westview Press, 1984.

Jodha, N S, 'Common Property Resources and Rural Poor in Dry Regions of India', *Economic and Political Weekly*, vol 21, no 27, 1986, pp 1169–81.

Joseph, S, K Krishna Prasad and H B van der Zaan (eds), *Bringing Stoves to the People*, Foundation for Woodstove Dissemination, 1990.

Karekezi, S and D Walubengo, 'Household Stoves in Kenya: The Case of the Kenya Ceramic Jiko', Nairobi: KENGO, 1989.

Laar, A van de, 'The Rural Energy Problem in Developing Countries: Diagnosis and Policy Approaches. Major Issues', The Hague: Institute of Social Studies, Working Paper 98, 1991.

Leach, G and R Mearns, *Beyond the Woodfuel Crisis*, London: Earthscan, 1988.

Leach, G, 'Residential Energy in the Third World', *Annual Review of Energy*, vol 13, 1988, pp 47–65.

Masera, O R, R S Almeida, J Cervantes, J F Garza, C Juárez, M A Martinez and C Sheinbaum, 'Energy Use Patterns and Social Differences: A Mexican Village Case Study', Ottawa: International Development Research Center (IDRC), manuscripts reports no IDRC-MR 215e, 1989.

Masera, O R, 'Sustainable Energy Scenarios for Rural Mexico: An Integrated Evaluation Framework for Cooking Stoves', (MSc thesis) Energy and Resources Group, UC Berkeley, May 1990, 93 pp.

Masera, O R, 'Sustainable Fuelwood Use in Rural Mexico, Volume I: Current Patterns of Resource Use', Berkeley, CA: Energy and Environment Division, Lawrence Berkeley Laboratory, (forthcoming, 1993).

Masera, O R, 'Socioeconomic and Environmental Implications of Fuelwood Use in Rural Mexico', PhD dissertation, Berkeley: Energy and Resources Group, University of California at Berkeley, 1993a.

Morse, R et al, 'Organizing Current Information for Rural Energy and Development Planning' in Islam et al, op cit, 1984, pp 473–519.

Munslow, B, Y Katerere, A Ferf and P O'Keefe, *The Fuelwood Trap*, London: Earthscan, 1988.

Myers, N, 'Population/Environment Linkages: Discontinuities Ahead', *Ambio*, vol 21, no 1, 1992, pp 116–18.

NES (National Environment Secretariat), WRI (World Resources Institute), *Participatory Rural Appraisal Handbook*, Washington, DC: NES-WRI, 1990.

Ostrom, E, *Governing the Commons: The Evolution of Institutions for Collective Action*, Cambridge: Cambridge University Press, 1990.

OTA (United States Office of Technology Assessment), *Energy in Developing Countries*, Washington, DC: OTA, 1991.

Pandey, M, K Smith, J Boleij and E Wafula, 'Indoor Air Pollution in Developing Countries and Acute Respiratory Infection in Children', *The Lancet*, 25 February 1989, pp 427–9.

Repetto, R C and M Gillis (eds), *Public Policies and the Misuse of Forest Resources*, New York: Cambridge University Press, 1988.

Shell Briefing Service, 'Energy in Developing Countries', London: Shell, January 1980.

Smith, K, R A Rasmussen, F Manegdeg and M Apte, 'Greenhouse Gases from Small-Scale Combustion in Developing Countries: A Pilot Study in Manila', Washington, DC: Office of Research and Development, Environmental Protection Agency Report (EPA-600-R-92-005), 1991.

Smith, K, *Biofuels Air Pollution and Health: A Global Review*, New York: Plenum, 1987.

Soussan, J, E Gevers, K Ghimire and P O'Keefe, 'Planning for Sustainability: Access to Fuelwood in Dhanusha District, Nepal', *World Development*, vol 19, no 10, 1991, pp 1299–314.

Soussan, J, P O'Keefe and D Mercer, 'Finding Local Answers to Fuelwood Problems: A Typological Approach', *Natural Resources Forum*, vol 16, no 2, 1992a, pp 91–101.

Soussan, J, D Mercer and P O'Keefe, 'Fuelwood Policies for the 1990s', *Energy Policy*, vol 20, no 2, 1992b, pp 137–44.

Tiffen, M, *Productivity and Environmental Conservation under Rapid Population Growth: A Case Study of Machakos District*, London: Overseas Development Institute, 1992.

Tinker, I, 'The Real Rural Energy Crisis: Women's Time', *The Energy Journal*, no 8 (special LDC issue), 1987, pp 125–46.

Tolba, M and G Goodman, 'Foreword' in J Pasztor and L A Kristoferson (eds), *Bioenergy and the Environment*, Boulder, CO: Westview Press, 1990.

Wallace, M, 'Forest Degradation in Nepal: Institutional Context and Policy Alternatives', HGM-AID-GTZ-IDRC-FORD-WINROCK Project Strengthening Institutional Capacity in the Food and Agricultural Sector in Nepal, report no 6, March 1988.

World Bank, 'The Fuelwood Crisis in Tropical West Africa', Washington, DC: World Bank, 1985.

*Chapter Five*

# The Value of Indigenous Knowledge

## The Case of Water and Soil Conservation Ecosystems in Sri Lanka

### *D L O Mendis*

Sri Lanka is an island lying between 6 and 8 degrees north latitude, about 30 km south-east of southern India across the Palk Strait. It receives rainfall from two monsoons, each blowing for about half the year: the north-east monsoon from about October to March; and the south-west monsoon from about April to September. Due to a south-central massif rising to over 2500 m, the south-west quadrant of the island receives more than 2500 mm of rainfall from each monsoon and is known as the wet zone. The dry zone receives less than 1900 mm of rainfall annually, mainly from the north-east monsoon, while an intermediate zone receives between 1900 and 2500 mm of rain each year (Figure 5.1).

In ancient times a system of irrigation works, now recognized as water and soil conservation ecosystems, had been built in stages, mainly in the dry zone. These works consisted of river diversion systems, and small, medium and large storage reservoirs. They were the basis for a hydraulic civilization that had flourished from about the fifth century BC to the beginning of the thirteenth century AD. The evolution and development of the ancient irrigation systems, their stability, productivity and sustainability through a period of over 17 centuries, and the reasons for their final decline have yet to be completely researched by multidisciplinary scholars rather than by narrow specialists. It is known that there were a number of contributing causes, including invasions, internecine strife, occupation of the northern regions by invaders, elimination of the class of persons, called *kulinas*, traditionally entrusted with maintenance and operation of the systems, the advent of malaria and decline of foreign trade (Indrapala, 1971). However, research in depth has been eschewed in favour of the facile assumption that the ancient systems were

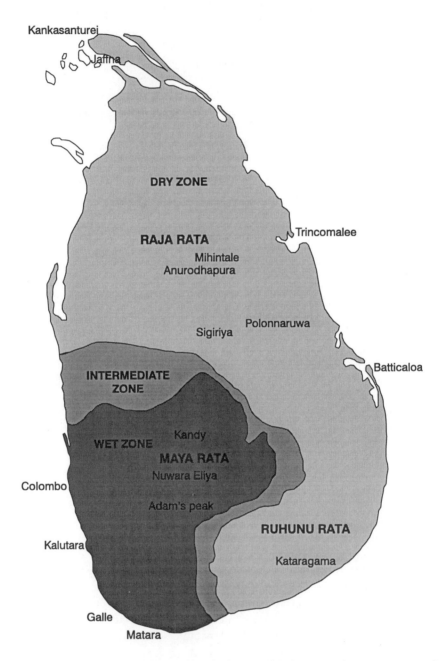

**Figure 5.1** An outline map of the island of Sri Lanka showing climatic zones and ancient kingdoms

'inefficient' and should be replaced by new large-scale centralized systems. Various problems, discussed below, have arisen on new projects based on this hypothesis and built in large part with transferred technology. Restoration of the ancient systems based on a correct understanding of their functions, even at this late stage, would contribute to both environmental and socio-political stability in the island.

## THE ANCIENT SYSTEMS

Wittfogel (1957), taking the example of ancient China, surmised that ancient hydraulic societies came into existence simultaneously with the growth of the extensive bureaucratic organization that managed it. Leach (1959) discounted this with the example of ancient Sri Lanka where a system of taxation in kind called *rajakariya* or king's labour, which he called *corvee labour*, had been used. Leach however made some serious mistakes concerning the ancient irrigation systems (Mendis, 1990).

In ancient Sri Lanka there were three main regions, Rajarata and Ruhunurata, together covering the dry zone, and Maya rata covering most of the wet zone. These had been ruled at times as separate kingdoms or as principalities under satraps owing allegiance to a single king. There were three kingdoms, in Kandy, Kotte and Jaffna, when the Portuguese arrived in 1505. They occupied the maritime provinces from 1505 to 1658, until they were displaced by the Dutch, who in turn yielded these provinces to the British in 1795. The British captured the Kandyan kingdom in the central hills in 1815 and ruled over the whole country until 1948.

A comprehensive topographical survey of the island completed by the British in the early twentieth century (Skinner, 1960), and plotted on a scale of 1 mile to 1 inch, show the remains of the ancient irrigation works in detail. These maps have been used by historians, surveyors and engineers researching the ancient systems. R L Brohier's *Ancient Irrigation Works in Ceylon* (1934) remains the best example of such research work to the present day. Brohier (1937) showed that all the large reservoirs in the ancient Rajarata were interconnected by means of large channels, some of them trans-basin channels, built as far back as the fifth century, if not earlier. He also showed, with the example of the Kalaweva, that these interconnected large reservoirs and channels supplemented the small village tanks which were the heart of the village settlements in ancient times (ibid, p 70). In contrast to this system in Rajarata, there was a noticeable paucity of interconnected large reservoirs and channels in the southern area, which was part of the ancient Ruhunurata. On the other hand a large number of small village tanks are shown in this area on modern topographical survey maps. Historical sources indicate that at one time some 20,000 of these small tanks may have been functioning in the ancient Ruhunurata alone (Geiger, 1960).

Viewed from a biotic perspective (as against a hydraulic engineering perspective) the ancient irrigation works are seen as water and soil conservation ecosystems. It has been argued that the evolution and development of these systems took place in the following seven stages (Mendis, 1986):

1  rain-fed agriculture;
2  temporary river diversion and inundation irrigation on river banks;
3  permanent river diversion and channel irrigation systems;
4  development of weirs and spillways on diversion channels;
5  invention of the sluice;
6  construction of reservoirs equipped with sluices;
7  damming a perennial river.

Six types of water and soil conservation ecosystems may be identified in Sri Lanka from this hypothesis, of which all but the first are irrigation ecosystems:

1  rain-fed agriculture ecosystems of two types – traditional *haen govithan* (also described as swidden agriculture) and permanent tree crops of which the Kandyan forest garden is the best example (Knox, 1965);
2  flood or inundation irrigation ecosystems;
3  channel irrigation ecosystems;
4  a micro-irrigation ecosystem below a small tank with a sluice;
5  a macro-irrigation ecosystem with one or more micro-irrigation ecosystems of types 2, 3 or 4 in its command area;
6  a complex of macro-irrigation ecosystems consisting of a number of interconnected macro-irrigation ecosystems, as in the ancient Rajarata.

The purpose of the large number of small tanks shown on the topographical survey sheets of the southern area (in the ancient Ruhunurata) remained an enigma until detailed engineering surveys were done in the Walawe ganga (*ganga* means a perennial river) basin. These surveys revealed that the ends of the small earth embankments called bunds, apparently forming small tanks, were all curved in the downstream direction and that they had been built in echelon at corresponding elevations along the small non-perennial streams. These streams are called *oya* or *ara* (Tamil *aru*), to distinguish them from a *ganga*.

The discovery of the curved ends of the earth bunds, together with the already known fact that none of these bunds was equipped with a sluice, made clear that these were not the bunds of conventional small tanks, which are meant for the storage of water. They were in fact earth diversion structures, referred to by traditional farmers as *vetiya*, different from the traditional diversion structure, the *amuna*, made of stone masonry. The function of the *vetiya* was to raise water in the *oya* above the low humic gley rice soils in the valley bottom and divert it into channels on either side, in the less impermeable, reddish-brown earth soils in the valley shoulders, during the monsoon rain season. This must have made it possible to cultivate seasonally what are now described as 'other field crops', together with permanent tree crops, in the reddish-brown earth soils of the valley shoulders. This resulted in a unique rain-fed agriculture ecosystem, irrigated during the monsoon rain season.

The high productive potential of such a system, as it probably existed in ancient times, has been demonstrated under the Hambantota Integrated Rural Development Program funded by the Norwegian aid agency NORAD (*Daily News*, 26 January 1993). However, the actual carrying capacity of the system must await a study of the type carried out in Peru, where an ancient technique is again being used for cultivation (Erickson, 1988). Meanwhile a tentative assessment of the direct carrying capacity indicates that it was between 4.5 and 7.3 persons per irrigated hectare (Goonesekera, 1991).

## THE ROLE OF ENGINEERS

In British colonial times, engineers did some pioneering investigative work on the ancient irrigation works and other engineering structures, such as roads and buildings, and especially religious structures, of which the *stupa* is the best known (Paranavitana, 1960). Henry Parker's *Ancient Ceylon* (1909) contains useful information about ancient bricks and also the first definitive statement about the invention of the sluice in ancient Sri Lanka (Parker, 1909, p 379):

> Since about the middle of the last century, open wells, called 'valve-pits' when they stand clear of the embankment, and 'valve-towers' when they are on it, have been built on numerous reservoirs in Europe. Their duty is to hold the valves, and the lifting gear for working them, by means of which the outward flow of the water is regulated or totally stopped. Such also was the function of the bisokotuwa of the Sinhalese engineers; they were the first inventors of the valve-pit, more than 2100 years ago.

The word *bisokotuwa*, which means 'indraught enclosure' (Geiger, 1960), describes the valve-tower or valve-pit of the sluice. The Sinhala word for sluice is *sorowwa*. The invention of the *sorowwa* with its *bisokotuwa* in about the third century BC enabled construction of true storage reservoirs in ancient Sri Lanka, with this device for control and issue of irrigation water.

In 1900, the irrigation department of Sri Lanka was set up by hiving off the irrigation branch from the public works department. The new department undertook restoration of ancient large reservoirs and channels, most of them in the ancient Rajarata, while small tanks came under the purview of government agents. Small tanks were therefore given less attention and the function of the small bund, the *vetiya*, was not understood at all by the irrigation department's hydraulic engineers and their perception, now seen as a 'hydraulic engineering' approach, was dominant.

In 1923 the failure of a chain of small tanks (often described as a cascade of tanks) in the dry zone resulted in an official study of the small tanks by the irrigation department and a landmark paper was published by J S Kennedy, who later became director of irrigation. He stated, inter alia, 'The small village tanks, like the village cattle, are too numerous for efficiency' (Kennedy, 1934, p 132). This statement led to the conviction among irrigation engineers that the small tank was 'inefficient' and had to be replaced by large reservoirs. Their arithmetic was correct, but probably little else besides.

This error also led to a wrong interpretation of the evolution of the ancient irrigation systems in Sri Lanka as having taken place in four successive stages (Figure 5.2). The small earth bund, whether tank or *vetiya*, was mistakenly assumed to be an

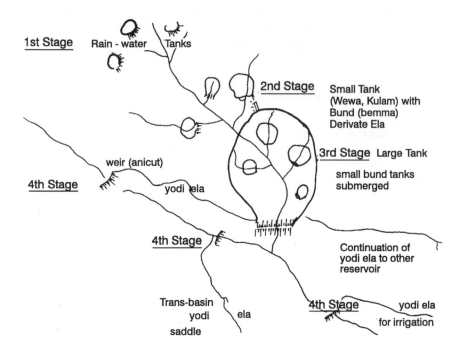

**Figure 5.2** The ancient irrigation system according to Brohier's hypothesis
Source: Needham, Wang Ling and Lu Gwei Djin, 1971, p 369

early stage in the evolution and development of large reservoirs that were thought to have been built later, submerging the small bunds which had become obsolete. Brohier (1956) unfortunately placed the seal of his undoubted authority on this erroneous hypothesis of the hydraulic engineers. This hypothesis was also adopted by Joseph Needham (Needham, Wang Ling and Lu Gwei Djin, 1971), although he acknowledged later that Brohier's interpretation was incorrect (Needham, 1989).

The four-stage hypothesis also incorrectly assumed that construction of storage reservoirs preceded river diversion systems. River diversion irrigation was practised in the river valleys of the Tigris and Euphrates, the Nile, the Indus and the rivers in China, long before construction of storage reservoirs which depended on the invention of the sluice. River diversion represents water management in space, while storage represents water management in time. The former is a much earlier achievement in human history than the latter.

In the dominant view of hydraulic engineers in Sri Lanka, water is seen as inanimate and active, as is generally the case in the study of hydraulics (Ven Te Chow, 1959). A bio-scientist, however, sees water in exactly the opposite terms, as animate and passive, due to its role as a solvent for nutrients in the root zone of soils and as a facilitating agent in nature's bio-geochemical cycles, for example in fixing carbon from atmospheric carbon dioxide in photosynthesis.

A map described as the Water Resources Development Plan of Ceylon was prepared by hydraulic engineers and published in 1959, based on the four-stage hypothesis. This map shows suitable sites for construction of large reservoirs, most of which submerge ancient small earth bunds. The best examples are the Uda Walawe reservoir on the Walawe ganga and the Lunuganvehera reservoir across the Kirindi oya in the south-east dry zone. Both reservoirs were built without investigating much better alternative sites, each about 20 km upstream of the selected site, because of the authority of the Water Resources Development Plan.

New agricultural development projects are based on these new large reservoirs. It has been argued that a contributory cause for civil commotion and riot in the southern area of Sri Lanka in recent times has been the incorrect location of these reservoirs, and the wrong designs based on purely hydraulic engineering, ie hard technology principles, of the irrigation systems under these new reservoirs (Mendis, 1990, 1992a, 1992b, 1993a, 1993b).

This type of exercise in hydraulic engineering (in which water is treated as inanimate and active) assumes that the ancient water conservation systems have no intrinsic worth. This is well illustrated in the following statement from a feasibility report for another large reservoir selected from the Water Resources Development Plan of Ceylon, the Heda oya reservoir, in the south-east dry zone area further east from Kirindi oya, which, however, has never been constructed (Irrigation Department, 1950: 5):

> *The development of Heda oya is recommended as it compares very favourably, from technical and financial viewpoints, with other major schemes already undertaken by government. There does not exist any doubt as to the need to achieve self-sufficiency in food. This is an achievement that cannot be realized by spending large sums of money on tiny village tanks which do not have the staying power in a drought, nor can a better standard of living be taken to a people depending on them. Vagaries of the monsoons and resulting destitution can be fought only by spending public funds on large schemes and not by creating little evaporating pans and relief works. The age of the village pond has passed away and the time has come to embark on large projects like the scheme under review.*

## THE ROLE OF MODERN EDUCATION

There can be no real justification for this approach to the ancient systems, based as it is on ignorance of the biotic nature of water's function in crop production, especially its role as a facilitating agent in nature's bio-geochemical cycles. It is therefore important to understand how this attitude came about, by taking a look at the modern education system in Sri Lanka.

In British colonial times, state and missionary schools were set up, displacing the school system that had been in existence since ancient times (Ruberu, 1962). Students from the new schools had the best opportunities for higher education and employment in the public and private sectors. With few exceptions, education in the English medium was biased towards Western cultural values and the study of indigenous traditions was neglected. This resulted in the emergence of a Western-oriented and privileged class of élites.

On the positive side, the high level of literacy resulted in the introduction of universal adult franchise under the Donoughmore constitution in 1931, well before any other colonial country. In turn parliamentary democracy on the Westminster model became firmly established in the country. A tradition of free and fair elections prevailed up to and including the general elections in 1977.

On the negative side, well before the present ethnic and non-ethnic conflicts started in Sri Lanka, a group of these privileged élites attempted to stage a coup against the democratically elected government in 1962. Those élites who occupied high positions in the administration, especially in the police and armed services, were largely from ethnic and religious minorities (Horowitz, 1980). This was a result of the educational and employment advantages made available to minorities under the colonial policy of *divide et impera*.

Today, at secondary school level, students are routed into science and arts streams for the GCE O level examinations. The science stream is directed into a physical science stream and a biological science stream for the A level examinations. Until very recently engineering graduates in the physical sciences stream were never exposed to biosciences. Consequently those who became irrigation engineers quite naturally adopted a hydraulic engineering attitude towards the ancient irrigation systems. This was not the case at Indian universities, where irrigation engineering was taught as a subject. In the 1940s and 1950s a few technical assistants and engineering assistants from Sri Lanka were sent to these universities to qualify as engineering graduates, but that practice was stopped after the Faculty of Engineering of the University of Ceylon was set up in 1950.

In any case, even in the irrigation department the dominant influence was that of the Western trained engineers, especially those from the prestigious Oxbridge universities, of which there were a select few who wielded considerable influence. It would seem that their foreign education had consolidated their faith in Western scientific methods, at the cost of any sympathy for, or understanding of, the intrinsic value inherent in traditional knowledge systems (Goonetilake, 1983). This is of course understandable in the context of the period.

## THE ROLE OF FOREIGN AID AND FOREIGN AGENCIES

In Sri Lanka in the 1990s, the expenditure necessary for operation and maintenance of existing services exceeds revenue. Consequently any capital expenditure has to be met with foreign assistance (Central Bank of Ceylon, *Annual Report 1992, 1993*). All national development projects today are funded by what is euphemistically called foreign aid. In practice this omnibus term embraces everything from outright grants to ordinary commercial credits. The result is a situation fraught with danger to national economic sovereignty (Jayawardena, 1969). This potentially dangerous situation was further compounded in 1977 by the abolition of the Ministry of Planning and Economic Affairs. The national planning function is

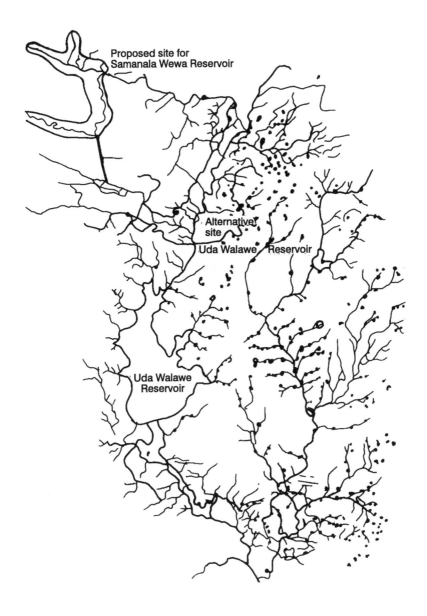

**Figure 5.3** The Walawe basin showing the ancient, dispersed small-scale system
replaced by a modern, centralized large-scale system

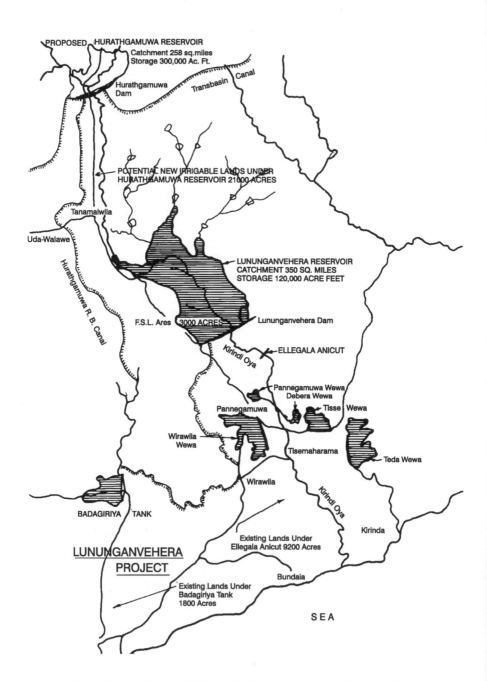

**Figure 5.4** As Figure 5.3, but the Lununganvehera basin project

today exercised by the Ministry of Finance and Planning, which publishes an annual rolling plan. Foreign aided projects virtually determine the plan each year.

An important project launched in 1989, allegedly against the advice of the World Bank and the IMF, was the Janasaviya or Poverty Alleviation Programme. It consisted of the social welfare measures necessary to support the poorest of the poor after previous welfare facilities had been removed by the new government that came into power in July 1977. The programme was a personal endeavour near and dear to the heart of the then president of the country, Ranesinghe Premadasa, who was assassinated in May 1993. Its future is now in doubt.

The welfare measures that were discontinued in 1977 included a subsidy on the staple food, rice. Sri Lanka at that time had acquired an enviable reputation as a poor Third World country that had achieved an extraordinarily high physical quality of life index (PQLI) of 82 and had very low military expenditure. The following figures speak for themselves in this context:

|  | *1977* | *1987* |
| --- | --- | --- |
| Percentage of GNP spent on: | | |
| rice subsidy | 5.0% | 0.7% |
| military expenditure | 0.07% | 5.0% |

Source: World Institute for Development Economics Research (WIDER, 1990)

Achievement of self-sufficiency in rice has long been a major objective of government in Sri Lanka. Before independence, the colonial government started so-called colonization schemes based on restoration of large ancient reservoirs in the dry zone and resettlement of pioneer peasant colonists. This was continued after independence by successive governments (Farmer, 1956). A new major irrigation and settlement project was started after independence in 1948, for which preliminary investigations had commenced many years earlier. This was the Gal oya project in the eastern dry zone, based on the model of the Tennessee Valley Authority (one of the major schemes in President Franklin D Roosevelt's 'New Deal' in the early 1930s). In this scheme a very large new reservoir, the Senanayake samudra, named after the first prime minster D S Senanayake, was built. This gigantic new reservoir provided supplementary (assured) irrigation water for some 14,000 hectares of existing irrigated lands and also irrigated about 34,000 hectares of new land in its command area.

In effect a macro-irrigation ecosystem was being created (by accident, not by design) with a number of micro-irrigation ecosystems, based on small tanks and river diversion *amunas*, within its command area. This could have resulted in a stable and sustainable system, but for the fact that irrigation facilities for the new lands (34,000 hectares) were designed on the hydraulic engineering model. Consequently, this scheme, too, has been faced with irrigation difficulties in recent times.

In the irrigation subsector of the agriculture sector of the economy, a number of foreign funded projects have been launched since 1977, of which the Accelerated Mahaweli Development Project (AMDP) is by far the largest. To date the cost of the AMDP is in excess of 60 billion rupees (about US$1.25 billion). The AMDP has been criticized by local engineers for the high proportion of foreign exchange cost in the total cost due to the large number of foreign consultants and contractors that have been employed on projects funded by foreign agencies in this programme.

Employment of foreign consultants on the AMDP has further aggravated the situation where new designs are imposed on existing ancient water conservation ecosystems, as if they did not exist. The major objectives of the AMDP were the construction of six new headworks, which have now been completed and the introduction of modern agribusiness in the downstream development areas. This latter objective was more or less surreptitious in the beginning, but is now gathering momentum through foreign aid and foreign expertise.

Outside the AMDP a number of foreign funded programs have been undertaken in the irrigation subsector, many of them described as 'rehabilitation' or 'modernization' projects. Examples are the Village Irrigation Works Rehabilitation Project (VIRP), the Major Irrigation Works Rehabilitation Project (MIRP), the National Irrigation Rehabilitation Project (NIRP) and the Uda Walawe Rehabilitation Project. In addition to these projects, there are a number of Integrated Rural Development Programmes (IRDP) in administrative districts, in which rehabilitation of small village tanks is a major component.

Rehabilitation work under the Uda Walawe project with financial assistance from the Asian Development Bank, started in the early 1970s, well before downstream development and settlement work was completed. The need for rehabilitation soon after or during construction, can only be due to bad construction or inherent defects in the underlying design. At Uda Walawe there was no doubt that the prime cause was the latter – there were basic conceptual errors in the design and layout of the modern hydraulic engineering design superimposed on the ancient man-made ecosystems in the area (Figure 5.3), but they were never recognized as such.

Recognition of these basic errors would have required revolutionary changes in the attitudes of Western trained and Western oriented engineers using a hydraulic engineering approach to design (Mendis, 1968). This was unthinkable at the time, and is still not easy to achieve among older engineers and decision makers who are quite unsympathetic to the concept of water and soil conservation ecosystems, since this requires an appreciation of biosciences.

In Uda Walawe there had already been resistance, in the late 1960s and early 1970s, from traditional peasant cultivators in the area, to the land alienation work consisting of acquisition of existing lands under minor irrigation schemes (described in this chapter as 'micro-irrigation ecosystems'), re-blocking out and resettlement. This was commented on much later as follows:

> *The blocking out and land alienation did not actually take place. The purana villagers infuriated by the coming of outsiders, forcefully and disorderly occupied the land.*
> *Dvroey and Shanmugaratnam, 1984, p 85*

This is an unwarranted slander on the old (purana) villagers who had tried to resist what they saw as an attempt to destroy their traditional irrigation ecosystems, in the name of development. This became quite apparent, some years later in the mid 1970s when the same thing happened again in Mahaweli System H area, below the great ancient tank Kalaweva, considered by most Sri Lankans to be the heart of the ancient irrigation systems of the Rajarata. Purana villagers resisted the blocking out of their lands for reallocation under the Mahaweli scheme.

The then chairman of Mahaweli lived in the area for a month to find out for himself why the old villagers were protesting against the blocking out of their existing lands irrigated under ancient small tanks systems, when they were being promised an assured water supply under the new major scheme. He learnt from them that the small tank is a necessary complement to the large interconnected system of large reservoirs and channels in the ancient Rajarata, and gave orders that as many as possible of these small tanks should be incorporated in the new designs. Sadly, the chairman died just two years later, and the Mahaweli designs once again came under the sway of hydraulic engineers who would rather follow the foreign engineers than discuss these issues with, and learn from, the ancient wisdom of local farmers, about the *vetiya, amuna* and *weva* (Mendis and Tennakoon, 1993).

## A SOUTHERN AREA PLAN BASED ON 'SOFT TECHNOLOGY'

Restoration of the ancient irrigation works on a piecemeal basis started by the British (who restored Kalaweva in 1883 for example) was continued after independence in 1948. The grand leitmotiv of the ancient system of interconnected large reservoirs and channels in the Rajarata and the complementary system made up of the small village tanks, and small diversion structures (*amunas* and *vetiyas*, see above) was lost in the course of this piecemeal restoration. Consequently later commentators, like Leach, did not even know of its existence (Leach, 1959).

Modern development in the malaria-stricken dry zone took the form of colonization schemes based on this piecemeal restoration of large reservoirs and channels. In the process, irrigation engineers who played the dominant role focused attention only on the visible aspects of the schemes, neglecting the intangible features. A recent comment sums this up:

> *The supposed causal relation between gravity flow irrigation and socio-economic differentiation is, in the Sri Lanka case, illusory and deceptive. The appearance is created and becomes convincing, only to the extent that observers adopt a highly restricted definition of technology, a technology that includes only the hardware of irrigation (such as dams, pumps and canals). As scholars in the history of technology frequently argue, a more useful definition of technology would certainly include cultural values and social behaviour, which are, after all, vital to the operation and maintenance of a technical system... The question ... is not why Sri Lanka's modern irrigation technology creates socio-economic differentiation; on the contrary, the question is why the schemes' social design omitted the customs and behaviours that could have mitigated the differentiation process.*
>
> *Pfaffenberger, 1990, p 364*

By analogy with Amory Lovins's concept of soft and hard energy paths (Lovins,

1977), the hydraulic engineering approach may be described as a hard technology and the ecosystems approach as a soft technology. The hard technology approach described by Pfaffenberger is the one used by irrigation engineers in Sri Lanka. The soft technology approach that would avoid many of the problems he describes would be an ecosystems approach, based on a correct understanding of the ancient water and soil conservation ecosystems.

The Southern Area Plan that was proposed in the late 1960s by M S M de Silva (Mendis, 1971) was also originally based on a hard technology approach. It has now been restructured by this author (Mendis, 1993b) in terms of the soft technology ecosystems approach. In its modified form this could be the basis for a stable and sustainable system for irrigated agriculture over the long term. However, this proposal has still not been accepted due to the obstacles arising from a lack of awareness of traditional agricultural systems on the part of Western trained and Western oriented modern irrigation engineers.

An example that illustrates the hard technology approach now practised is the present design of the development area in the south. Wildlife reservations have been demarcated in the catchment areas immediately above the two large new reservoirs, Uda Walawe and Lunuganvehera, and these two reservations have been joined together by another reservation. The new reservation has also been connected up with the large reservation in the southern area, the Yala sanctuary. A state sugar plantation has cultivated land immediately below this reservation (see Figure 5.5).

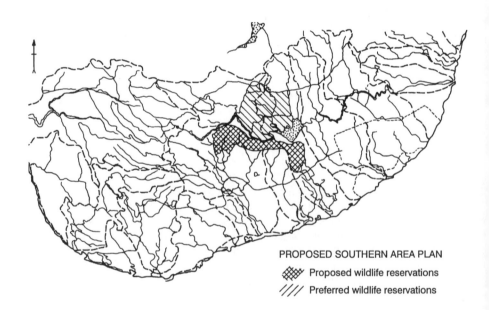

PROPOSED SOUTHERN AREA PLAN

Proposed wildlife reservations

Preferred wildlife reservations

**Figure 5.5** *The proposed Southern Area Plan showing wildlife reservation and the suggested alternative location*

The boundary between the wildlife reservation and the sugar plantation now has a live electric fence, allegedly to keep wild elephants from trespassing into the sugar plantation. But this fence also serves to warn people not to trespass into the new reservation, which was prime agricultural land in ancient times and which the new settlers in the state settlement schemes often try to cultivate illegally. It will become increasingly difficult to enforce the no trespassing rule as time passes. The hard technology method that starts with electric fences will soon progress to firearms. This will further aggravate rather than resolve the conflict between human and human, and between human and beast.

If the soft technology approach to the Southern Area Plan mentioned above were to be carried out, there would be two new large reservoirs in locations each about 24 km above the present Uda Walawe and Lunuganvehera reservoirs, and these two new reservoirs will be connected by a transbasin channel (Figures 5.3, 5.4, 5.5). The new wildlife reservation will be located above this channel, well above the agricultural land and therefore safe for wildlife for the foreseeable future.

This proposal can be implemented in stages by local endeavour rather than with massive lump-sum foreign aid, but the main problem is to make the administrative machine accept the reality of the situation. This means agreeing that the already constructed two large reservoirs, Uda Walawe and Lunuganvehera, will have to be abandoned as 'sunken capital', while the ancient micro-irrigation ecosystems that were submerged under these reservoirs will be resurrected as the new centres of human settlements. In short, this means creation of two new modern macro-irrigation ecosystems to replace two unsuccessful hydraulic engineering projects.

A referendum among the southern farmers could be a way to decide the issue if the government were prepared to hold one without intimidating the voters. In today's context in Sri Lanka, this does not seem likely.

## CONCLUSION

What has been discussed in this chapter is the situation prevailing in southern Sri Lanka due to the use of hydraulic engineering models for modern irrigation projects. These projects were built on the remains of traditional water and soil conservation ecosystems that had flourished for many centuries, until their decline about seven centuries ago. Whereas hydraulic engineering models are part and parcel of temperate zone agribusiness systems – designed for summer-winter cropping cycles on temperate-zone soils – traditional agricultural ecosystems on tropical soils had evolved down the ages in a wet season/dry season cycle.

The transfer of this inappropriate technology from the West took place because the evolution and development in stages, from pre-Christian times, of ancient water and soil conservation ecosystems in Sri Lanka, had been wrongly understood by hydraulic engineers. Although they were quite ignorant of traditional agriculture, hydraulic engineers succeeded in convincing policy makers of the correctness of their interpretation of the history of the ancient irrigation systems. That wrong interpretation became the basis for modern water resources development planning in Sri Lanka.

Apart from ignorance of traditional culture and their own history, a contributory cause for neglect of traditional knowledge in agriculture by decision makers in Sri Lanka has been the social distance between them and traditional farmers. The potential of the ancient systems for sustainable and stable crop production is known to the latter who, given the opportunity, still live by practising it, but is quite unknown to the former.

Incomplete knowledge of the reasons for the decline of the ancient irrigation systems after about the twelfth century AD may also have led decision makers to believe that these systems were intrinsically unsustainable. As mentioned above this decline has yet to be adequately studied. Another contributory cause of this decline may possibly be added to the list given above (Indrapala, 1971), namely the impact of hydraulic engineering after the well-known Parakrama Bahu era (1153–87). This may sound blasphemous to some who honour that king for having 'accelerated' development during his reign (Geiger, 1959). However, it is possible that in the process of promoting rapid development he introduced hydraulic engineering concepts which for the first time superseded age-old concepts of water and soil conservation ecosystems, thereby destabilizing those systems for the first time in history.

Among Western trained and Western oriented modern scientists and technologists, an awareness of the stable and sustainable potential of ancient water and soil conservation ecosystems that had evolved down the ages is comparatively recent. Assessment of their full potential has yet to be done by means of full-scale field trials. Meanwhile, as mentioned above, there is mounting evidence that the instability and lack of sustainability of the modern systems has been a contributory cause of civil commotion and attempted insurrection in southern Sri Lanka.

## REFERENCES

Brohier, R L, *Ancient Irrigation Works in Ceylon*, 3 vols, Colombo: Ceylon Government Press, 1934. Brohier, R L, 'Inter-relation of Groups of Ancient Reservoirs and Channels in Ceylon', *Journal of the Royal Asiatic Society, Ceylon Branch*, vol 34, no 90, 1937, pp 64–85.

Brohier, R L, 'Some Structural Features of the Ancient Irrigation Works in Ceylon', Presidential Address, Engineering Association of Ceylon, 1956.

Central Bank of Ceylon, *Annual Report 1992*, Colombo: Central Bank, 1993.

*Daily News*, 'Hambantota IRDP a Success', Colombo, 26 January 1993.

Dvroey, M and K Shanmugaratnam, *Peasant Resettlement in Ceylon*, London: Tri-continental, 1984.

Erickson, C L, 'Raised-Field Agriculture in the Lake Titicaca Basin', *Expedition*, vol 30, no 3, 1988, pp 8–16.

Farmer, B F, *Pioneer Peasant Colonization*, Cambridge: Cambridge University Press, 1956.

Geiger, W, *Culture of Ceylon in Medieval Times*, Wiesbaden: Otto-Harrosowitz, 1960.

Geiger, W, *Culavamsa*, Colombo: Ceylon Government Press, 1958.

Goonesekera, K, 'Ancient Irrigation Systems in the Walawe Basin: Are they Sustainable?', Institution of Engineers, Sri Lanka, 1991 (mimeo).

Goonetilake, S, *Crippled Minds*, New Delhi: Vikas, 1983.

Goonetilake, S, *The Evolution of Information: Lineages in Gene, Culture and Artefact,* New Delhi: CBS Publishers and Distributors, 1991.

Horowitz, D L, *Coup Theory and Officers' Motives: Sri Lanka in Comparative Perspective,* Princeton, NJ: Princeton University Press, 1980.

Indrapala, K (ed), *The Decline of the Rajarata Civilization and the Drift to the Southwest,* Peradeniya: Ceylon Studies Seminar, 1971.

Irrigation Department, *Feasibility Study on Heda oya Project,* Colombo, 1950, (mimeo).

Jayawardena, L R, 'National Economic Sovereignty and the World Bank', *Proceedings of the Ceylon Association for the Advancement of Science,* Colombo: SLAAS, 1969, pp 237–54.

Kennedy, J S, 'Evolution of Scientific Development of Village Irrigation Works in Ceylon', *Transactions of the Engineering Association of Ceylon,* Colombo: 1934, pp 229–320.

Knox, R, *An Historical Relation of Ceylon,* Colombo: Tisara Prakasayo, 1960.

Leach, E R, 'Hydraulic Society in Ceylon', *Past and Present,* April 1959.

Lovins, A, *Soft Energy Paths,* Harmondsworth: Penguin books, 1977.

Mendis, D L O, 'Some Observations on the Designs for Uda Walawe Headworks', *Transactions of the Institution of Engineers, Ceylon 1968,* Colombo, vol 1, 1968, pp 131–71.

Mendis, D L O 'The Southern Area Plan', *Transactions of the Institution of Engineers, Ceylon,* 1971, Colombo, vol 1, 1971, pp 71–101.

Mendis, D L O 'Evolution and Development of Irrigation Ecosystems and Social Formations in Ancient Sri Lanka', *Transactions of the Institution of Engineers, Sri Lanka 1986,* Colombo, vol 1, 1986, pp 13–29.

Mendis, D L O, 'Theory, Paradigm and Crisis in Understanding the History of Irrigation Systems in Sri Lanka', International Association of Historians of Asia, 11th Conference, August 1988, Colombo (mimeo).

Mendis, D L O, 'Irrigation Development and Underdevelopment in Southern Sri Lanka', *Economic Review,* December 1990, pp 11–9.

Mendis, D L O, 'How Hydraulic Engineering Underdeveloped Southern Sri Lanka', *Transactions of the Institution of Engineers, Sri Lanka, 1992,* vol 1, 1992a, pp 221–37.

Mendis, D L O, 'The Water Resources Development Plan of Ceylon, 1959', *Engineer, Journal of the Institution of Engineers, Sri Lanka, 1992,* vol XX, 1992b, pp 44–50.

Mendis, D L O, 'Non-Ethnic Causes of Violent Conflict in Sri Lanka: Environmental Degradation on Account of Destruction of Ancient Irrigation Ecosystems by the Impact of Hydraulic Engineering', *Proceedings of the 41st Pugwash Conference on Science and World Affairs, Beijing, China,* Singapore: Continental Press, 1993a, pp 698–709.

Mendis, D L O, 'Irrigation Systems in the Walawe Ganga Basin in the South-East Dry Zone of Sri Lanka – an Overview', *Proceedings of a Seminar,* Colombo, Agrarian Research and Training Institute, 1993b.

Mendis, D L O and M Tennekoon, 'Vetiya, Amuna and Weva', Colombo, Proceedings of a Seminar of the Ministry of Environmental Affairs, 1993, (mimeo).

Needham, J, Wang Ling and Lu Gwei Djin, *Science and Civilization in China,* vol 4, part 3, Cambridge: Cambridge University Press, 1971, pp 221–389.

Needham, J, (personal communication, unpublished), 12 May, 1989.

Pfaffenberger, B, 'The Harsh Facts of Hydraulics: Technology and Society in Sri Lanka's Traditional Colonization Schemes', *Technology and Culture,* July 1990, pp 361–97.

Paranavitana, S, *The Stupa in Ceylon,* Colombo: Gunasena Press, 1960.

Parker, H W, *Ancient Ceylon,* London: Lusacs, 1909.

Ruberu, R, *Education in Ancient Ceylon*, Kandy: Kandy Printers Ltd, 1962.
Skinner, T, *Fifty Years in Ceylon*, Colombo: Tisara Prakasayo, 1960.
Ven Te Chow, *Open Channel Hydraulics*, New York: McGraw Hill, 1959.
WIDER (World Institute for Development Economics Research), Helsinki: *Occasional Publications No 1*, 1990.
Wittfogel, K, *Oriental Despotism*, New Haven, CT: Yale University Press, 1957.

# II
# POLITICS AND SOCIETY

*Chapter Six*

# THE ROOTS OF UNSUSTAINABILITY

## COLONIZATION IN SPACE AND TIME

*Franck Amalric and Tariq Banuri*

---

Manfred Max-Neef (1982) once posed the paradoxical question to Ecuador's politicians, whether the rich or the poor were more important for the functioning of a society. If the rich were to disappear he asked, what would be the effect on the lives of the poor? Surely quite small. But what if the poor disappeared? Then the whole functioning of society would break down. Analogously, one could argue that if the poor were to disappear, the effect on the environmental crisis would be quite limited, but if the rich were to disappear, the very basis of global unsustainability might also vanish. While in this chapter we do not suggest anything as extreme, we do argue that the roots of global unsustainability lie in the behaviour of the rich not the poor. As a consequence, we doubt that the current global discussions will lead to sustainability, exactly because they ignore this fundamental point.

In making this argument, we rely on a useful metaphor provided by Alain Lipietz (1992), who described the UNCED process as a global 'enclosures movement' through which rights to the global commons are being allocated. We use this metaphor to argue that this assignment of rights has three problems: political, institutional and conceptual. The political problem is that today's allocation, as was the case of the earlier enclosures movement, might turn out to be inequitable and unjust, and therefore become a focus of opposition and resistance. The institutional problem is that, even if rights could be assigned fairly and democratically, not enough attention is being devoted to the creation and strengthening of institutions that can enable democratic communities to monitor and regulate the rights so created. The conceptual problem is that, even when rights to every inch of the land have been allocated, there still remains the future; and today's political problems are in part being solved, or rather being veiled, by making optimistic assumptions about the future – in effect allocating rights over more resources than can be used sustainably.

To return to North–South issues, sustainability considerations dictate on the one hand a reduction in Northern consumption levels – to make them compatible with the carrying capacity of the planet – and on the other hand an increase in per capita consumption in the South. The latter is needed not only on equity grounds but also because poverty itself is a major cause of environmental distress. The political question is whether there can be agreement over an allocation of rights that produces this outcome. The institutional question is whether, even with the optimal allocation of rights, the outcome can be guaranteed by the existing system of rules; note especially that global macroeconomic relations are such that reduction in Northern economic activity will lead directly to an equal or even deeper reduction in Southern consumption levels. The conceptual question is that while the historical evolution of rights over the global commons took the form of a progressive 'colonization' of space, the trend today is towards what can analogously be called the 'colonization of time'.

The problem of unsustainability can be traced back to this process of colonization. The rights and behaviour patterns created by this process have been neither socially nor environmentally sustainable. Furthermore, the process must necessarily create the problem of survival for marginal populations and this too feeds back to the problem of sustainability. The required global compact can be seen simply as something that will stop the process of colonization and therefore of growing unsustainability. In other words, both sustainability and survival will remain elusive targets unless this issue of global rights is met head on.

## UNSUSTAINABLE DEVELOPMENT: THE REAL TRAGEDY OF THE COMMONS

The unsustainability of current modes of production and consumption is directly related to the treatment of the commons. By 'commons' we mean any area with 'fuzzy' rights of ownership or usufruct – village and town commons, regions inhabited by conquered and colonized populations, mineral and natural resources, and such free resources as rivers, oceans, forests, air and the atmosphere. The colonization of the commons has taken many forms. In most cases, customary rights of usage were usurped (or 'colonized') by individuals, states (whether colonial or indigenous) or other organized groups. The global commons, on the other hand, were probably genuinely free (and therefore without customary rights or restraints) until the recent scarcity, created by the pressure of growing consumption, led to a move towards their colonization, too. It must be noted here that this new process of colonization is not being driven by population expansion, as argued by Garrett Hardin (1968), but by allowing free rein to the push towards domination of nature and human beings.

In Southern countries, the degradation of natural resources – land, water, air – is directly related to their transformation from community to state property. This has, on the one hand, led to the erosion of participation and cooperation of the population in regulating use, and on the other hand to the transfer of rights to an agency (ie the state) that has often been unable or unwilling to compensate for this loss of regulation. The erosion of cooperation takes place partly because of the denial of local participation and partly because legislation transforming common property into state property often alienates local populations by denying many customary rights of usage. This has been documented most extensively in the case of forests where (presumably because of difficulties of regulation) local populations were abruptly forbidden to exercise their customary rights to graze their animals, and collect fuelwood and fodder, as well as edible roots. Thus, almost overnight the guardians of the forests were transformed into poachers and destroyers. Many writers, see eg Chapter 7, claim that local restoration of sustainability will be impossible without the restoration of local rights in the commons.

At the global level, the problem is somewhat different. The 'global commons' (atmosphere, oceans) are characterized by the absence of customary rights and restraints. Until very recently, as mentioned above, these have been viewed as free goods. Here, the problem is not to restore some set of customary rights, but to establish rights and responsibilities over a diminishing resource. However, these will have to be both enforceable and legitimate.

The transformation of the commons can be divided into three stages: 'colonization', 'enclosures' and 'legitimization'. Historically, such resources or areas were governed by customary rules of behaviour, but often not by formal laws. The first step in the process of transformation is generally the erosion of these customary restraints on usage and the increased exploitation of the commons, usually by outsiders. This would correspond, for example, to the entry of colonial powers into Asia, Africa and the Americas.

In the second phase, when the conflict between potential new users becomes too costly, 'legal' rights vested in these users begin to emerge, often accompanied by the formal expropriation of the usage rights of the customary (ie old) users. The classic example is the 'enclosures' movement in England, which would not have been possible without the disenfranchisement of the peasant population. Similarly colonizing powers made implicit or explicit agreements respecting each other's areas of control. Similar too is the transformation, in the post-colonial period, of local common property into national or state property in the Second as well as the Third World. Paradoxically, the creation of explicit property rights may hasten the colonization of the commons, because as property rights in more and more areas become explicit, the pressure to find new 'soft' frontiers becomes more intense.

Be that as it may. On the other side of the fence, this process has been accompanied by what has been described elsewhere as the deresponsibilization of local populations (Amalric and Banuri, 1992) or as the 'learned helplessness of developing societies' (Zaman and Zaman, 1991). Only when the consequent non-cooperation and resistance of those whose usage rights have been expropriated becomes too problematic, does one observe the gradual emergence of a search for legitimacy, usually by redefining and extending rights of usage, and returning areas or countries to local control (ie decolonization), but in such a manner as to maintain, as much as possible, the open access of the ex-colonial powers to the natural resources.

The recounting of this history, albeit in such a heuristic form, demonstrates three points. First, the discovery that there is no such thing as a free resource must lead to the invention of ways of imposing self-restraint upon use. In other words, since history is one of exploiting soft frontiers, mechanisms have to be created that place limits upon such exploitation. Secondly, in the case of local resources, these limits would be neither feasible nor acceptable without the cooperation and participation of local populations. And thirdly, in general an allocation of rights and limits that is not viewed as fair and equitable will not be socially and politically sustainable.

## UNCED AS A 'GLOBAL ENCLOSURES MOVEMENT'

In the metaphor of Lipietz (1992) the UNCED represents a global enclosures movement, seeking to establish rights over the global commons – the atmosphere, the forests, biological diversity. The parallel to the original enclosures movement is even stronger. This has been pointed out forcefully by Agarwal and Narain (1991). Since the discussions take existing use patterns as the norm, the resulting agreement must necessarily confer more legal rights precisely to those countries (ie the North) that have overused the global commons. The interest of sustainability lies in ensuring that the allocation of rights is both legitimate and equitable. Another way of stating this is that at the global level the second phase of colonization, that of 'enclosures', has been reached. But this will not be sustainable unless it takes into account the question of legitimacy and justice.

This last requirement runs against mainstream economic theory. In a seminal article, Nobel Laureate Ronald Coase (1960) argued that the failure of the market to regulate the production of public (or common) goods arises from the absence of property rights to the good or the resource. Coase's solution is to create explicit property rights. As long as these are explicit, it does not matter in whom the rights are vested. However, there are three reasons why Coase's solution may not be applicable to a dynamic world and why it would matter whether the rights are vested in an individual, a community or a state. First, if the rights are not viewed as legitimate and equitable, they will not be politically sustainable. Not only would there be an absence of the acquiescence of local populations that is necessary for the enforcement of rights, but there would also be an incentive for affected groups or countries to oppose and transform the situation.

Secondly, if the social interest lies in ensuring that natural resources are not degraded, it is essential that rights are vested in those who share this concern. This is the main reason why writers on scientific forestry (eg Fernow, 1902) argued in the nineteenth century that control of forests should be vested in governments or perpetual corporations, ie in entities with a sufficiently long time horizon. While the individual's incentive may be to, say, cut down a forest and invest the money in a better paying financial instrument, this will generally not be in the social interest.

Thirdly, it is important to ensure that whoever has rights over a resource also has the capacity to manage and protect the resource. In the absence of this capacity, individuals will be tempted to transform the resource into a form (eg a financial asset) that they are capable of managing. These considerations may lead us to rule out individual ownership of public goods; they may also disqualify most Southern governments. More importantly, they may lead to the necessity of creating some form of effective collective organization, one that will be legitimate, have a sufficiently long time horizon and have the ability to manage the resources.

The upshot is that the discussion of global sustainability must begin with the explicit treatment and analysis of rights, empowerment and legitimacy. Neglecting to bring these issues into the discussion is tantamount to acquiescing in the 'Enclosures Movement circa 1992'. At the global level, there is a need to talk about the allocation of rights over the global commons in a manner that is equitable and socially sustainable. At local levels, it means the restoration of community rights over the local commons. More generally, it means that we have to think of a way of preventing the spread of colonization.

It was possible to have soft frontiers as long as the avidity of individuals, states or other organized groups could be kept in check through customary or legal restraints. Once these checks become ineffective, it makes sense to clarify and establish rights over every single inch of territory so to speak. However, even when every inch has been allocated problems will still remain. The first problem is that if the allocation is not legitimate or just, it will not be socially sustainable. The second problem is that if the allocation is not followed by the evolution of appropriate institutions of resource management, it will not be environmentally sustainable. The danger is that environmentally and socially unsustainable allocations will be legitimized by invoking yet another soft frontier: time.

## THE COLONIZATION OF THE FUTURE

Unlike spatial frontiers, the time frontier is intrinsically soft. It is not limited by physical or political boundaries, but depends in essence on people's conception of the future. Hence, unlike spatial frontiers which are embedded in the reality of the present world, the time frontier is defined in an imaginary world, whose shape depends crucially on how optimistic people are about the future, especially about the progress of science and on how much people need to be optimistic.

The crux of the matter is that the use of time cannot follow the same transformation as the other commons. The enclosure of time as advocated by some authors is crucially confronted with two problems.[1] First, since future generations cannot be empowered, it is impossible to construct a political solution based on the sharing of rights. Secondly, given the uncertainty surrounding the global crisis, it is also impossible to construct a technocratic solution. Unlike local environmental degradation (which is often highly visible and the consequences of which can be assessed, monetized and taken into account through cost/benefit analysis) the consequences

---

1. The current debate on the issue has focused on the question of how much the present should take into account the future, hence on the definition of the frontier. If one requirement of sustainable development is that 'the current generation should not prosper at the expense of the next generation', it is also noted that if the sacrifice to be made for the present generation to follow a sustainable path is large, 'then it is wholly legitimate to look at the "trade-off" between present and future and decide on the best evidence available' (Pearce, 1991: 13).

of global stress on the environment – greenhouse effect, depletion of the ozone layer, loss of biodiversity – are to a large degree uncertain and therefore cannot be subjected to a cost/benefit analysis (Marglin, 1991; Lipietz, ibid). This makes it virtually impossible to arrive at a technocratic consensus. Even if some broad agreement on the enclosure of time could be reached (for example an agreement on global emissions of $CO_2$), speaking of legitimacy of such an agreement, which is the necessary condition for sustainability, would clearly be devoid of meaning. The only viable solution that remains is to live in the presence of a soft frontier while avoiding trespassing it. But for this to be possible, the right conditions must be met.

One could compare economic growth to a means of transportation, which would take society from a state characterized by scarcity to one in which the 'economic problem may be solved' (Keynes, 1963: 366). The classic metaphor was provided by Walt Rostow (1960), who implicitly compared economic growth to an aeroplane, which would take off towards self-sustained development under the right conditions. However, one particularity of a plane is that, unlike other means of transportation, it cannot cruise at just any speed. A plane flies only above a minimum speed. Reduce the speed and it will crash. There is, of course, the old idea, known as Kondratieff's cycles, that crashes are inherent to capitalism and that, in the long run, they may have a beneficial effect. Needless to say the price of a crash today would certainly be beyond anything we can imagine; let us remember that the last crash found its regeneration in the Second World War. But there is today a fundamental difference, which is that we are not dealing here with the sustainability of capitalism as such, but with the sustainability of capitalism within the biosphere. Unlike Kondratieff's crashes, which destroy one plane so as to permit building a new and even bigger one, what may be destroyed now is the very possibility of building not only planes, but even any alternative to planes.

Hence, although a take off first evokes a flight, it also creates the necessity of thinking about a landing. That a landing will eventually have to take place is evident: anyone having any notion of exponential functions will agree that a steady growth rate (of let's say 1 per cent) during an infinite time in a finite world is just a ridiculous idea. Hence economic growth, as we experience it today, will stop, be it tomorrow, or in a century or more. Convinced modernists will argue that the necessity of more growth is so urgent that it would be a waste of time to start thinking about the landing; just as one does not expect a ten-year-old child to worry about retiring. This is clearly the view taken by the Brundtland Commission (WECD, 1987). There are others, however, who see in environmental constants or in social disruptions signs that it is high time to think about the end of the growth era (Meadows, 1972; Meadows, 1992; Hirsch, 1977; Daly and Cobb, 1990). In this view the realization of long-term objectives for sustainable development will necessitate the creation of favourable conditions for a transition between the unfettered economic growth experienced today and something more sustainable. In other words, conditions for a safe landing must be created, at least so that a 'landing' can be thinkable. Most of the chapters of this book are concerned with creating these conditions.

It is not economic growth per se that we view as the central issue. The problem is that modern societies have become enslaved to economic growth; thus people's perception of the future and of the environmental burden transmitted to future generations is biased by the need to be optimistic.

## CREATING CONDITIONS FOR A SAFE 'LANDING'

The point is quite simple: the different prescriptions for sustainable development (see eg WCED, 1987) are not mutually compatible in the present institutional setting. For instance, the long-run objective of reducing the level of consumption in the North (and thus a slowdown of economic growth) poses two types of problems. First, it would lead immediately to a reduction of consumption in the South, which would contradict other objectives of sustainable development. Secondly, the slowdown of economic activity in the North would jeopardize some existing institutions, the efficiency of which depends crucially on the persistence of economic growth. Hence, these institutions would be in conflict with the political will needed for sustainable development.

The path towards sustainable development needs, therefore, not only new institutions to cope with global crises (as is one of the objectives of the UNCED process), but also an assessment of the compatibility of existing institutions with the long-run objectives. However, in contrast to a large body of literature focused on institution building in the South (eg Banuri, 1992; Banuri and Holmberg, 1992), we wish to focus mainly on the need for a transformation of institutions in the North. Just as it is argued that new institutions are needed in the South to cope with population growth, that is for people's desire for large families, we argue that Northern people's 'hunger for more' (Shames, 1986) is in part due to inadequate institutions. This approach is quite similar to the 'regulation' school of which the basic hypothesis is that 'economic adjustments cannot be disentangled from social relationships and values, political and economic rules of the game, and more generally the web of interrelated institutions' (Boyer, 1992: 12). But whereas the 'regulation' school focuses on the lack of institutions as a constraint to economic development, we see in the existence of pro-growth institutions the main impediment to a reduction of consumption in the North.

### Example 1: Labour institutions

It is Keynes's major contribution to have argued that equilibrium in the labour market depends on the level of investment, which in turn depends on subjective factors. Expectations of a higher demand due to economic growth leads to investment, which in turn leads to economic growth and the fulfilment of prior expectations.

The point is that labour institutions have been designed around the expectation of economic growth and therefore around two central principles. First, that economic growth will lead to full employment, and thus solve the possible conflict between the employed and the unemployed; and secondly, that economic growth will benefit everyone, thereby alleviating the conflict inside the firm between profits and wages.

The first principle applies more readily to countries which emphasize static efficiency (fluidity in the labour market, eg the US, Canada, and the UK (Boyer, ibid). By contrast, countries emphasizing dynamic efficiency (some rigidities with the risk of high levels of unemployment, eg Japan, Germany) rely more on social consensus grounded in the second assumption. Reliance on growth, however, plays the same role in the two cases. In the former, it is the potentiality of 'extensive' growth (or growth in a spatial sense) that gives it legitimacy; in the latter case, it is the belief in 'intensive' growth (growth through technical improvement and gains in competitiveness) that legitimizes wage rigidities and higher levels of long-run unemployment. This difference is hardly surprising since in the US, Canada or even the UK, development has historically taken the form of expansion in space. In contrast, in continental Europe and in Japan (especially in Germany and Japan after their defeat in the Second World War) space was soon perceived as limited, and technical innovation had replaced it as the favoured direction for further expansion.

The German or Japanese models may seem attractive in a time when spatial growth reaches its limits, but one can doubt the replicability of these models at a global level, mainly because their success coincides with large trade surpluses, which in turn mean large deficits for others (ie an unsustainable condition).

## Example 2: Democratic institutions

For Nobel Laureate Milton Friedman (1962) the case for competitive capitalism is that it creates economic freedom while at the same time promoting political freedom because it separates economic power from political power. K Polanyi (1944) had also noted this separation, but he denounced it as the foundation of economic uncertainty (and not freedom) leading to humankind's addiction to economic activities. In this line, the crucial question, raised by Bowles and Gintis (1986), is why voters do not elect governments to implement extensive redistributive policies. After all, at least 50 per cent of the voters (assuming that all adults have the right to vote) would necessarily benefit from an extensive redistribution scheme.

The answer to this paradox lies in the existing consensus in democratic Northern countries around economic growth. In short, it is the prospects of redistribution through economic growth that alleviates the tension arising from economic inequality and political equality, which Bowles and Gintis (ibid) call the Keynesian accommodation. The corollary is that economic growth is necessary for preserving the separation between economic and political power. Growth is not just an outcome of a particular framework, but plays an active role in stabilizing this framework.

## Example 3: Consumption and needs

Straightforward neo-classical theory would have it that as people get richer, they would wish to consume more leisure and therefore to work less. By contrast, the experience in developed countries is one in which the 'hunger for more' is insatiable. The French sociologist Baudrillard (1970) even argued that overconsumption and waste are structural components of capitalism. One explanation proposed is that consumption is, in essence, competitive or that at least an ever increasing part of consumption is competitive by nature (see also Veblen, 1899).

The point is that the very goal of economic growth, the satiation of needs, cannot be attained as long as economic growth does not alleviate the sense of scarcity but in contrast exacerbates it. Hence one objective of the transition process must be to re-examine profoundly the link between consumption and needs.

## CONCLUSION

There are basically two issues: one is the organization of the North itself; the other is North–South domination. As for the first issue, there is an inner contradiction in speaking about Northern sustainability. This is because 'Northern', inasmuch as it stands for the political and economic organization of 'developed' countries, is built on unsustainability. This is in part what this chapter has tried to argue by considering colonization as an essential property of Northern societies. It notably challenged the commonly held view (at least among economists) that the establishment of rights over global commons would be sufficient to ensure sustainable development. Three major problems have been discussed: the question of legitimacy of these rights; the possibility of regulating the rights created; the insufficiency of this approach on matters concerning a trade-off between present and future.

The need for rights is a consequence of the colonialistic behaviour of modern societies. However, in our view, the establishment of rights will be insufficient to curtail the environmental crisis if it is not accompanied by a restructuring of institutions that have been built in and for the context of unrestrained growth. The issue is not between more or less economic growth. The issue is to be able to choose between different paths.

The second issue reverts back to the first one, because even the very form of North–South domination depends upon what is perceived as being in the interest of the North. One of the lessons of the breakdown of the Soviet Empire is precisely that the South was, and is, demarcated along the lines of Northern interests. As has been well documented by Ruffin (1989), that which falls outside of these interests also falls outside of the South, which tends to be divided into two zones. One could be called the buffer zone in which the North will remain very present for strategic regions – access to natural resources for instance. The other will eventually become the land of 'the new barbarians', in which the North will have less and less interest, and thus less influence. A number of countries and regions of the world already fall into this category: Sudan, Afghanistan, a large part of Peru and Nigeria, and inner cities, including those of Northern countries, like New York and Los Angeles.

It is not relevant in these conditions therefore to speak of Southern sustainability. The North has set the rules, which carry within them the germs of unsustainability and the South, or at least most of it, can only abide by them in its effort to survive. In the game of sustainability, the North has the ball.

# REFERENCES

Agarwal, A and S Narain, *Global Warming in an Unequal World: A Case of Environmental Colonialism*, Delhi: Centre for Science and Environment, 1991.

Amalric, F and T Banuri, 'Population, Environment and De-Responsibilisation' in T Banuri and F Amalric (eds), *Population, Environment, and De-Responsibilisation: Case Studies from the Rural Areas of Pakistan*, Islamabad: SDPI, 1992.

Banuri, T (ed), *Economic Liberalization: No Panacea*, Oxford: Clarendon Press, 1992.

Banuri, T and J Holmberg, *Governance for Sustainable Development*, London: IIED, 1992.

Baudrillard, J, *La Société de Consommation*, Paris: Denoel, 1970.

Bowles, S and H Gintis, *Democracy and Capitalism: Property, Community, and the Contradictions of Modern Social Thought*, New York: Basic Books, 1986.

Boyer, R, *Labor Institutions and Economic Growth: The 'Regulation' Approach*, paper presented at the international workshop on 'Labour Institutions and Economic Development in Asia', Geneva: IILS, 1992.

Coase, R H, 'The Problem of Social Cost', *Journal of Law and Economics*, vol 3, 1960, pp 1–44.

Daly, H E and J B Cobb Jun, *For the Common Good*, London: Berlin Press, 1990.

Fernow, B, *A History of Forestry*, Toronto: University of Toronto Press, 1902.

Friedman, M, *Capitalism and Freedom*, Chicago: University of Chicago Press, 1962.

Hardin, G, 'The Tragedy of the Commons', *Science*, vol 162, 1968, pp 124–38.

Hirsch, F, *Social Limits to Growth*, Cambridge, MA: Harvard University Press, 1977.

Keynes, J M, *Essays in Persuasion*, New York: Norton, (1931) 1963.

Lipietz, A, *La Préparation de la Conférence des Nations Unies sur l'Environnement et le Développement (Rio de Janeiro, 1992) comme Processus de Négociation: Rapport á l'UNESCO*, Paris: Unesco, 1992.

Marglin, S, *Alternative Approaches to the Greening of Economics: A Research Proposal*, Helsinki: WIDER (mimeo), 1991.

Max-Neef, M, *From the Outside Looking in: Experiences in 'Barefoot Economics'*, Uppsala: Dag Hammarskjoeld Foundation, 1982.

Meadows, D H, *The Limits to Growth*, New York: Universe Books, 1972.

Meadows, D H, *Beyond the Limits*, London: Earthscan Publications, 1992.

Pearce, D (ed), *Blueprint 2, Greening the World Economy*, London: Earthscan Publications, 1991.

Polanyi, K, *The Great Transformation*, Boston: Beacon Press, 1944.

Rostow, W W, *The Stages of Economic Growth*, Cambridge: Cambridge University Press, 1960.

Ruffin, J-C, *L'Empire et les Nouveaux Barbares*, Paris: Pluriel, 1989.

Shames, L, *The Hunger for More: Searching for Values in an Age of Greed*, New York: Times Books, 1986.

Veblen, T, *Theory of the Leisure Class: An Economic Study of Institutions*, New York: Macmillan Company, 1899; reprinted by New American Library, New York, 1953.

WCED (World Commission on Environment and Development), *Our Common Future*, Oxford: Oxford University Press, 1987.

Zaman, A and R M Zaman, *Psychology and Development: A Conceptual Itinerary*, Islamabad: NIP, 1991.

*Chapter Seven*

# People's Empowerment

## A Condition for a Sustainable, Equitable and Liveable World?

*Grazia Borrini Feyerabend*

'Empowerment' refers to a process by which people – as individuals, in groups and in organized communities – exercise an active and direct control over the factors influencing their life and their local environment. Is, in this sense, empowerment of local people a necessary condition for achieving a sustainable, equitable and liveable world? Exploring this question opens up an immense variety of issues, from populist theories in political sciences to comparative analysis of ecological impacts of different social systems, from models of communal formation to psychology of small groups, from economic analysis of historical phenomena (eg enclosure of the commons) to the current debate on development indicators. It would require the knowledge and experience of an anthropologist, an economic historian, a political scientist, a human ecologist, a demographer and a humorist to make a minimum of sense of the immense area opened up by that question. Even if I was all these people at once (and I am not even one of them), for every assertion I would have made I surely could find many excellent colleagues who disagreed. Therefore, this chapter will not provide a definite answer, but only offer some suggestive examples and general considerations on the matter.

### IT CAN BE DONE!

My first example comes from India: a self-help sanitation project that covered 12,000 hectares on the eastern periphery of the city of Calcutta.[1]

---

1. Further information on the Fishermen's Cooperative Society and the CAMPFIRE project can be found in C Pye-Smith and G Borrini Feyerabend, *The Wealth of Communities*, London: Earthscan, 1994.

To begin with there were poor people, sunshine and lots of sewage water (elements rarely missing in the South). There was an environment in need of sanitation, and there were people in need of employment and food. Combining the desperation, strength, patience and ingenuity of poverty, these people – without any help from 'development' agencies – managed to set up an energy intensive, efficient and renewable system in which they now use the power of nature to transform sewage into food for themselves and cash crops for the market. The system comprises different kinds of productive activities. After a first sorting of garbage, what is recyclable (glass, metal etc) is collected and sold. Most of the rest is organic refuse, which is composted and combined with soil to create beds where vegetables are grown. Irrigation for the vegetables is provided by waste water, while sewage is left first to 'mature' separately, then conveyed to fish ponds where it offers excellent nutrients for algae and fish. The effluents from the fish ponds are finally used to periodically fill some paddy fields, where rice and other crops are grown.

The system is run by poor farmers (some organized in cooperatives) and could certainly benefit from various improvements. In the words of a scholar who has studied it, however, it possesses a kind of 'rustic grace' (Ghosh, 1991). Most importantly, it is environmentally beneficial, economically viable, and sustained by the ingenuity and the will of the local people. In fact, it is a telling example of the culture of conserving and reusing resources which usually thrives among the poor. The system is 'liveable'. People like it, earn good money with it, and have dedicated time and resources to grow trees and flowers around the fish ponds to make the area more attractive. The system is 'equitable'. It has provided an opportunity for many poor families. The system is 'sustainable'. It is ecologically sound (it actually cleans up the environment) and has been in operation for decades (the first families of fishermen settled in the area in the 1930s).

This example tells us that it can be done: there are viable ways by which people, the economy and the environment can all win, and this even in extremely poor and difficult conditions.

## COMMUNITIES SHOULD HAVE A SAY

'Development's spoiled fruits: reforestation project for India's poor wastes millions' is the title of an article in the *Herald Tribune* which appeared in the month of May 1992. The story tells of the failure of an ambitious, US$30 million plan to reforest denuded hills and mountains in the Indian Himalayan range. The plan – financed by the World Bank and implemented by the Indian government – provided thousands of trees and seedlings to local villagers, expecting them to be eager to plant, protect and take care of them. In reality villagers could not care less about the new initiative and continued struggling for their needs the old way, finding firewood wherever they could and paying little attention to the reforestation efforts, which could do nothing but fail. A few villagers interviewed by the *Herald Tribune* said that they were never consulted about the programme. They had much more pressing needs than trees, they could not afford wasting time with them and – to tell the truth – they were not at all amused by the fact that so much money was spent on something of no concern for them.

The example illustrates a typical clash between lofty environmental (or development) plans and the everyday concerns of people struggling to survive. It is an old story. Problems and solutions are identified and concocted by experts and high level officials in well-heated or air-conditioned capital offices. Finances and technologies are obtained through national and international deals, with trade issues, political ends and personal interest playing powerful roles. The local people are not even consulted prior to the starting of the programme. They come in only when it is time to 'implement' something, when there is a need for their 'enthusiastic participation' in the activities designed to 'benefit' them. Fat chance! Typically, such programmes absorb lots of time and resources, and then fail miserably.

What does this example tell us? It tells us that local people should be at least consulted and at best actively involved in any programme meant to benefit them. The alternative is a loss of time and resources, and often a loss of credibility for the agencies involved.

## PEOPLE AND THE ENVIRONMENT CAN BENEFIT TOGETHER

A third example deals with a typical case of environmental conservation: the protection of wildlife species and their habitats.

The country of Zimbabwe possesses some of the finest populations of wildlife in Africa, a unique patrimony of biological diversity. The country has also a large and growing human population, much of which lives in unproductive rural areas, beset by economic and environmental problems. From time immemorial, people viewed wildlife as a threat to themselves and their crops, but also as a common resource which could be exploited for food, clothing and medicines. During colonial rule, however, rural people were prohibited from making any use of it. Wildlife was declared state property and the state took action to conserve it on a strictly 'protectionist' basis, following an ecological aesthetic and moral rationale. Such a rationale viewed human communities only as a threat to wildlife (poachers, hunters, encroachers of habitats), while the communities started viewing wildlife only as a threat to themselves (destruction of crops, injuries to cattle and people, limitation of land for agricultural production).

This state of real and/or feared mutual damage was unproductive and untenable. Slowly, different experiences and a new approach towards environmental conservation emerged. From this new perspective, wildlife is a communal resource that can and should be used by rural communities to generate income and improve the quality of local lives. These benefits encourage people to change their attitudes towards wildlife, and turn them into voluntary caretakers of natural ecosystems and habitats.

The many economic, legal, social, institutional and ethical complexities of the new approach have been worked out during the evolution of Zimbabwe's Communal Areas Management Programme for Indigenous Resources (CAMPFIRE), now implemented in many of Zimbabwe's communal lands (see Zimbabwe Trust et al, 1990; Zimbabwe Trust, 1992; Murphree, 1991; Child and Peterson, 1991). The programme – rooted in ideas and experiments of the 1960s and 1970s – took off after a legislative act of 1975 that assigned authority over local wildlife to selected district councils. Only the councils which could demonstrate their ability to manage and conserve natural resources for the benefit of their local communities were eligible. In the districts that obtained the special status, rural communities soon took initiatives to generate income.

Some initiatives involved non-consumptive uses of wildlife (such as tourism and photo safari). Others – often the most productive – involved the culling of wild animals (for safari hunting, for meat and other products, to get rid of problem animals etc). In the latter initiatives, a culling 'quota' was carefully calculated to be sustainable and well below the point of ecological stress. While culling practices have a sound ecological basis and excellent economic results, not everyone agrees on the philosophy of sustainable use rather than 'non-consumptive conservation'. In particular, opponents are found among people in industrialized societies (which profited in the past from the destruction of most of their own wildlife and are often unaware of the current plight for survival of people in developing countries).

The key characteristic of CAMPFIRE is that – unlike previous schemes in which the central government controlled all permits and revenues regarding wildlife – it involves local districts and communities as managers and decision makers. The system is not perfect and many of its supporters would like to see the local communities assuming greater control. At the moment private owners or district authorities still retain much power and institutions at ward or village level cannot make totally independent decisions over wildlife management. What counts, however, is that the principle that local people should directly benefit from local wildlife is now well established and widely accepted.

When people can genuinely profit from the sound management of environmental resources, they prove to be successful planners and managers. In fact, the programme demonstrates that – contrary to the opinion of prior colonial administrations – poor and formally uneducated rural communities are perfectly capable of articulating their problems, evaluating options and reaching a solid consensus over profitable solutions.

CAMPFIRE's income from safari and tourist operators, and from the culling of animals already provides management funds, revenues for the district council and cash for each household in the programme communities. Households often devote part of their income to communal projects (schools, clinics etc), but most of it is kept for family use. People damaged by wildlife (eg when their crops are destroyed by wild animals) are compensated. The working principles are that benefits should go to the communities on whose land they are generated (wildlife is usually migratory), and income should be distributed according to the efforts put into gaining it and to offset the losses incurred in the process.

Ecological, economic and social indicators demonstrate the success of CAMPFIRE. The ecological success is shown by an increase in the range of land dedicated to wildlife, by the conservation of habitats and by the full viability of culled wildlife species. In some countries where hunting is forbidden and the police are used to kill poachers, elephants and other endangered species are disappearing. On the contrary, in Zimbabwe, there are more elephants and other animal species than the land theoretically could support. Economic success is shown by the very good income of community members and district councils, while the country as a whole earns valuable currency from tourism. Social success – a most significant and rarely assessed result – is shown by the desire of CAMPFIRE communities to maintain and expand the programme operations, while other districts pressure the government to be assigned authority over wildlife. A telling example is one of the CAMP-FIRE communities to whom the governmental agencies recently proposed to set up a cattle raising scheme. The people objected strongly and insisted that the land should be devoted to wildlife management instead (Zimbabwe Trust et al, 1991).

The CAMPFIRE programme profited from outside assistance (in particular from the Centre for Applied Social Studies of the University of Zimbabwe, the World-wide Fund for Nature and the Zimbabwe Trust, a development oriented institution) and it can be maintained that without such assistance it would not exist today. It could develop, however, only through the full involvement of local communities, who manage to make their interests and the interests of their environment coincide.

Apart from a variety of specific lessons of concern for professionals in the field of environmental management, the experience of CAMPFIRE tells us that combining environmental protection and economic advantages ensures that local people participate voluntarily and actively, and care for the long term sustainability of results.

The experience also shows that external support (political, legal, financial, technical etc) may be essential to establish the preconditions and provide the initial impulse for community-based management of environmental resources.

## SOME ARGUMENTS BEYOND ANECDOTAL EVIDENCE

The examples make sense and show interesting details, but they are just anecdotal evidence. Yet, there are also general reasons why communities should exercise a good amount of control over the factors influencing their life and local environment, and play a key role in the decisions that affect them.

- People usually know their environment and society better than any outsider. Given the appropriate conditions they can put their local knowledge to work with excellent results (see also Chapter 5 on the neglect of indigenous knowledge in Sri Lanka).
- Local people are more directly interested and more strongly motivated than anyone else to act for their quality of life and the sustainable use of their local resources. If they decide what to do and how to do it, they are likely to succeed.
- Local people can be quick to respond and adapt to local circumstances, and they can easily monitor and enforce compliance with rules.
- When people control the local resources, they can fend off those external interests that may end up impoverishing both the local environment and economy.
- When people have security of tenure over the local resources, they feel more

responsible towards the environment and manage it with an eye to the future.

- Often local communities have a measure of stability and commitment that centralized governments cannot duplicate.
- Community-based projects tend to be economically viable; they usually recover costs, and use human and material resources in an efficient way.
- Many communities possess idle human resources and poorly utilized economic resources; by organizing and pulling those resources together, people can create new job opportunities and innovate and diversify the basis of local livelihood.
- By organizing and pulling resources together, people acquire a working experience of communal processes; they may be encouraged to participate more actively in all sorts of social activities.

## COMMUNAL PROPERTY REGIMES

The management of environmental resources (a forest, a fishery, a grazing area, a water source) is an activity in which people naturally participate, sharing interests and efforts. Historical records show that some communities failed and that their fortune as a society has followed the destiny of their ecological surroundings.[2] In most cases, however, communities evolved successful practices in which institutional arrangements and socio-cultural regulations played a part as important as methods, technologies and tools of resource use (Simmons, 1989; Goudie, 1981).

A multitude of customary and legal arrangements regulate the communal management of environmental resources (McCay and Acheson, 1987; Beikes, 1988; Bromley and Cernea, 1989). They span from informal rules of exploitation of migratory resources (for instance fish and game) to formal sharing of profits from the selling of local oil and gas; from tribal property to co-management with a state government; from internal subdivisions of seasonal grazing rights to agreements over the use of timber on a rotational basis over long periods (even several decades); from long-term village leases to concessional rights assigned to ad hoc user groups. The more formal communal property regimes are property arrangements that restrict access to well-defined groups of users, and that establish rules of management, incentives and sanctions that promote a sound exploitation of the common resources. A comparable multitude of local organizations and institutions can be in charge of such customary and/or formal arrangements (Ostrom, 1990; Uphoff, 1992). Ad hoc user-groups are quite common, but cooperatives, protection societies or village councils can also play that role. Their main tasks are to agree upon, regulate and oversee the rights, duties and behaviour of resource users.

It is only by neglecting the historical, social and institutional analysis that models such as the 'tragedy of the commons' have come to enjoy vast recognition and support (Hardin, 1968; Feeny et al, 1990). Such models locate the source of much resource degradation in 'common property', which is simply interpreted as a less

---

2. A typical example of management failure is the degradation of the once extremely fertile soils of Mesopotamia. It is believed that several thousands of years ago they were salinated beyond recovery due to the faulty irrigation practices of their resident population.

effective and efficient system than private property. The models, however, do not consider that:

- private property is no guarantee against abuse and waste of resources;
- the commons are usually highly regulated;
- interdependence and cooperation are essential features of well-functioning societies;
- both individual and collective interests are best balanced not by abstract property systems but by the concrete facts and conditions of resource use.

In risky and unpredictable situations, for instance, there are important advantages in maintaining access rights to a variety of micro-environments in common lands. In cases of crop failure, people can diversify production by making use of such micro-environments (Chambers, 1991). In this sense, communal use rights provide equitable access to resources that would otherwise be used only by a privileged few. (It is not uncommon, however, that those with greater power and wealth attempt to make a disproportional use of common resources. Such people may actually be the strongest advocates of unregulated 'open access' regimes.) In all, more than adherence to tradition or a romantic view of communal societies, preserving common property regimes is a matter of sound social and economic sense. This has also been shown by cost-benefit analyses (Stevenson, 1991), and is particularly true for resources that are diffuse, of unpredictable yield and low in unit value. In this sense, resource degradation is better defined as the 'tragedy of the open access' (the term is used by Bromley and Cernea, 1989) in places where communal management has broken down.

Unfortunately, modern historical developments have often acted against communal property arrangements, violently imposing change.[3] Colonial powers and national governments undercut local authorities (in particular, the ones who specified rules of access and use to communal properties) and acquired formal sovereignty over many local resources they could not possibly manage or control (Feeny et al, 1990; Bromley and Cernea, 1989).[4] Monetary relations replace local moral economies (reciprocity, solidarity, conviviality, 'the common good' etc) and contribute to create social crises (see, for African examples, Franke and Chasin, 1980; Watts, 1983). Development programmes put the accent on short-term profits

---

3. Changes in communal property regimes are not necessarily 'imposed'. Often they are initiated by the commoners themselves in response to changing conditions of resource management and use. Conversely there are instances in which private property shifts back to communal property or there is alternance of regimes in long cycles. The management of common resources, in fact, is one of the central areas of collaboration and conflict of all societies. There exist many possible outcomes, varying with time, while a society changes together with the external conditions of its existence. Unfortunately, it is not uncommon that governmental interventions 'close off all possible avenues for the (local people) to work things out and replaced them with next to nothing' (Anderson, 1987: 333).
4. Often governments find themselves in situations in which they cannot manage all the land they formally own. Yet they will not relinquish it either. At times they expect that – while continuing to own the land – local people will manage it voluntarily. These hybrid arrangements invariably fail (Shepherd et al, 1991).

instead of long-term sustainable yields, taking much of the best land out of the control of local people (eg Burbach and Flynn, 1980). On top of this, the growth of population has in places forced communities to intensify production, and modify social arrangements and land uses.[5]

Despite these problems, communal management of environmental resources – possibly in co-management arrangements involving public and private interests – still offers one of the best options available for ecologically and socially sound development (Jodha, 1990; Agarwal and Narain, 1990; Renard, 1991; Murphree, 1991).[6] Such an option requires the existence of a number of favourable conditions. The first and most important one is the political support necessary to secure the entitlement to the resources to be managed, such as land tenure rights, rights to grazing, fishing, collecting products etc (in the Zimbabwe example it meant legalizing local authority over wildlife). This has important legal and organizational aspects. Another form of political support is the unrestricted right to organize and develop local institutions. Crucial assistance may also be needed to integrate the local knowledge with external information, know-how and relevant research results (in the Zimbabwe example, for instance, information to calculate the appropriate culling quota for each animal species), to offer training opportunities, to provide market infrastructures, and access to loan and credit facilities.

In general it is about time to renounce the 'scientific' prejudices which say that experts by definition know things better than anyone else, and have the right to regulate and direct what other people do. The experts who wish to be useful and to contribute what they know, need to learn how to interact – sincerely and effectively – with the local people they would like to assist.

Participatory methods of appraisal, planning, monitoring and evaluation of 'development' programmes have recently been developed and applied in fields as different as forestry and public health, tourism, water and sanitation, adult education and agriculture. These methods seek ways by which 'experts' from governmental and non-governmental agencies can provide genuine technical assistance in a collaborative and non-imposing way. They offer the basis of a 'quiet' – but extremely promising – 'methodological revolution' in development activities. (An excellent assessment is provided by Chambers, 1992.)

Up to now, a genuine and effective practice of the participatory approach has been the exception rather than the rule. Non-governmental organizations have gathered important experience on the matter, but most countries' governmental agencies have lagged far behind. A critical and difficult task ahead is to reform agencies in the realm of agricultural extension, water and sanitation, health, education, trade and commerce etc, so that their personnel can effectively interact and collaborate with local people, learn from them and support them according to their needs (Korten, 1980; Nichter, 1984; Fritschi, 1986; Peluso and Poffenberger, 1989; Gronow and Shrestha, 1990; Renard, 1991; COOPIBO, 1991). In more than one

---

5. See the case studies reported in the special issue of *Ambio*, vol 21, no 1, 1992, on 'Population, Natural Resources and Development'.

6. There is also the vast literature reviewed in *The Common Property Resource Digest*, available from 332e COB, 1994, Bulard Ave, St Paul, MN 55108-6038, USA.

way, a genuine, widespread participatory approach would foster a more equitable and sustainable society.

## EMPOWERMENT FOR POOR AND AFFLUENT COMMUNITIES

These examples and conditions of local empowerment seem to apply principally to poor communities in developing countries. Thus, is 'empowerment' a recipe for poor communities only? Has it anything to do with affluent societies or the middle class in developing countries? I believe it may have much to do with them. One may even speculate that the large-scale environmental problems of industrial societies are related to having lost too large a measure of local and communal control over life and resources. Life in industrial societies is dominated by forces that have little to do with local neighbourhoods. They are either on a very large-scale – the state, the market, the news and advertising industry – or on the scale of the individual – private property, education and career. Very little is left of communal activities and of a community-based management of local environments. In a modern society the commons are barely inhabited. Many people use them just as a place to park their car. Control of resources is either fully privatized or fully delegated to professionals. Only rarely is an urban neighbourhood sufficiently organized to restrict the movement of vehicles through its area. Only rarely is a rural neighbourhood sufficiently organized to self-regulate access to the products of a local forest.

Local communal activities and communal spaces have been, through millennia, the breeding ground of culture. Without them something is lost. It may turn out that that something is quite important if we want to develop a sustainable, equitable and liveable world. Perhaps the 'better, ecologically sustainable, 1.5 kilowatt society' that Hans-Peter Dürr (see Chapter 2) talks about, and the 'appropriate institutions of resource management' that Franck Amalric and Tariq Banuri (see Chapter 6) talk about, have much to do with a revival of the local commons, of their capacity for local governance, conviviality and sense of limits in both so-called poor and so-called affluent societies.

Perhaps we should not speak any more of 'global problems'. No problem – even those that invest planetary conditions like the climate or the composition of the atmosphere – is or will be felt equally by every community on the planet. The climate warming and sea-level rise that could cause havoc in New York and Naples may pleasantly warm up the Siberian spring and autumn. The accumulation of toxic waste in the Sahel may leave purer water for European children to drink. The population growth that could push an Ethiopian village beyond the brink of local carrying capacity may revitalize a community in the Italian Alps. In fact, the most serious problems of today – from starving to civil violence, from deforestation to deadly infant diseases, from toxic pollution to mafia killings, from soil degradation to child prostitution, from flooding to political violence – all have characterizing and critical local dimensions. Their solutions require a variety of international agreements and national resolutions, but cannot do without the local knowledge, work and care of local people and communities. These should be acknowledged and facilitated in any possible way.

The menus for a liveable, equitable and sustainable world may ultimately have to be cooked in millions of local ovens.

## REFERENCES

Agarwal, A and S Narain, *Towards Green Villages*, New Delhi: Centre for Science and Environment, 1990.

Anderson, E N, 'A Malaysian Tragedy of the Commons' in McCay and Acheson, 1987, pp 327–43.

Beikes, F (ed) *Common Property Resources*, London: Belhaven Press, 1988.

Borrini, G (ed), *Lessons Learned in Community Based Environmental Management*, Rome: ICHM, 1991.

Bromley, D W and M M Cernea, *The Management of Common Property Natural Resources*, Discussion Paper no 57, Washington, DC: The World Bank, 1989.

Burbach, R and P Flynn, *Agribusiness in the Americas*, London: Monthly Review Press, 1980.

Chambers, R, *Micro-Environment Unobserved*, IIED, Gatekeeper Series, no 22, London, 1991.

Chambers, R, *Rural Appraisal: Rapid, Relaxed and Participatory*, Brighton (UK): Institute of Development Studies, University of Sussex, 1992.

Child, B and J H Peterson, *CAMPFIRE in Rural Development: the Beitenbridge Experience*, Department of National Parks and Wildlife Management and Centre for Applied Social Sciences, Harare, 1991.

COOPIBO, *Participatory Research and Extension: The Experience of the Agricultural Project Muganza*, COOBIBO, Kigali (Rwanda), 1991.

Feeny, D, F Berkes, B J McCay, and J M Acheson, 'The Tragedy of the Commons: Twenty-Two Years Later', *Human Ecology*, vol 18, no 1, 1990.

Franke, R W and B H Chasin, *Seeds of Famine*, New York: Universe Books, 1980.

Fritschi, B, *Cooperation Between Communities and Agencies*, IRC, The Hague, 1986.

Ghosh, D, 'Self-Help Sanitation; Towards a Third World Option', *Global 500 Newsletter*, UNEP, 1991.

Goudi, A, *The Human Impact on the Natural Environment*, Oxford: Basil Blackwell, 1981.

Gronow, J and N K Shrestha, 'From Policing to Participation: Reorientation of Forest Department Field Staff in Nepal', Nepalese Ministry of Agriculture and Winrock International, Katmandu, 1990.

Hardin, G, 'The Tragedy of the Commons', *Science*, 162, 1968, pp 1243–8.

Jodha, N S, *Rural Common Property Resources: Contributions and Crisis*, Katmandu: ICIMOD, 1990.

Korten, D C, 'Community Organization and Rural Development: A Learning Process Approach', *Public Administration Review*, September–October 1980, pp 480–511.

McCay, B J and J M Acheson (eds), *The Question of the Commons*, Tucson, AZ: University of Arizona Press, 1987.

Murphree, M W, 'Communities as Institutions for Resource Management', occasional paper of the Centre for Applied Social Sciences, University of Zimbabwe, Harare, 1991.

Nichter, M, 'Project Community Diagnosis: Participatory Research as a First Step Toward Community Involvement in Primary Health Care', *Social Science and Medicine*, vol 19, no 3, 1984, pp 237–52.

Ostrom, E, *Governing the Commons: the Evolution of Institutions for Collective Action*, New York: Cambridge University Press, 1990.

Peluso, N and M Poffenberger, 'Social Forestry in Java: Reorienting Management Systems', *Human Organization*, vol 48, no 4, 1989, pp 333–44.

Renard, Y, 'Institutional Challenges for Community Based Management in the Caribbean', *Nature and Resources*, vol 27, no 4, 1991, pp 4–9.

Shepherd, G, E Shanks and M Hobley, *National Experiences in Managing Tropical and Subtropical Dry Forests*, Proceedings of the Technical Workshop to Explore Options for Global Forestry Management (Bangkok, 1991), London: IIED, 1991.

Simmons, I G, *Changing the Face of the Earth: Culture, Environment, History*, Oxford: Basil Blackwell, 1989.

Stevenson, G G, *Common Property Economics: A General Theory and Land Use Application*, New York: Cambridge University Press, 1991.

Uphoff, N, *Local Institutions and Participation for Sustainable Development*, IIED Gatekeeper Series, no 31, 1992.

Watts, M, *Silent Violence*, Berkeley, CA: University of California Press, 1983.

Zimbabwe Trust, Department of National Parks and Wildlife Management and CAMPFIRE Association, *People, Wildlife and Natural Resources the CAMPFIRE. Approach to Rural Development in Zimbabwe*, Harare, 1990.

Zimbabwe Trust, *Wildlife: Relic of the Past or Resource of the Future?*, Zimbabwe Trust Pub, Harare 1992.

*Chapter Eight*

# Improving Health

## A Key Factor in Sustainable Development

*Andrew Haines*

Many studies show that there is a link between ill-health and poverty. According to the *Human Development Report 1992* (UNDP, 1992) 1.2 billion people live in absolute poverty, 2.3 billion lack access to sanitation and over a hundred million people were affected by famine in 1990. Fourteen million children die every year before they reach the age of five; many of them of preventable conditions, including gastro-enteritis, acute respiratory infections, measles and tetanus. Nevertheless, there have been some improvements. The average life expectancy in developing countries is now 63 years – 17 years more than in 1960. In 26 developing countries, it is above 70 years. Access to safe water has increased in the past 20 years by more than two-thirds and average daily calorie supply is now about 110 per cent of the overall requirement, compared with 90 per cent some 25 years ago. The male/female disparity in primary education has decreased by half in the past 20 to 30 years, and in literacy by one-third in the past 20 years, although on average females receive only half the higher education of males. In the case of industrial countries, average life expectancy is 75 years and there is an average of one doctor for every 460 people. Overall, nearly three-quarters of health bills are paid by public insurance.

But world population will reach 6 billion by 1998, meaning that the average annual addition to the world's population will be around 97 million people. Nearly all of this addition will be in Africa, Asia and Latin America. The (medium) UN projection is 10 billion by 2050, but numbers could be as high as 12.6 billion by 2050, peaking at over 20 billion in the next century. Over 80 per cent of the population growth in the 1990s will take place in cities (UNFPA, 1992). How to assess the overall impact on health of these factors, and how to influence these trends by improving health care measures, are the central questions in this chapter.

# HEALTH AND DEVELOPMENT: THE HUMAN DEVELOPMENT INDEX

In the past, development has frequently been equated with economic growth, but the goal of development is to improve the quality of human life. Health is a key contributing factor to quality of life and thus to liveability. The World Health Organization's (WHO) definition of health is: 'a state of complete physical, mental and social well-being and not merely the absence of disease or infirmity' (WHO, 1992, p 6). It is clear from this definition that while the prevention and treatment of disease and rehabilitation are clearly within the remit of health care professionals, the promotion of health also depends on wider societal factors. These include government policy in a range of sectors, such as education, housing, energy and transport, as well as the availability of resources to meet human needs.

Although there is no universally accepted measure of the quality of life, the United Nations Development Programme (UNDP) introduced a new Human Development Index (HDI) in their 1990 report (UNDP, 1990). This combines life expectancy, educational attainment and income indicators in a single index. Clearly, a single number cannot express the complexity of human development, but such indicators are important because they emphasize the importance of other factors besides conventional economic indicators such as gross national product (GNP) when assessing the performance of nations in addressing the needs and aspirations of their populations.

The HDI has three components: longevity, knowledge and income. These are combined in a three-phase procedure to obtain a single figure with a maximum value of one. Longevity is measured by life expectancy at birth. Knowledge is measured by two standard educational variables: adult literacy and mean years of schooling, giving a weight of two-thirds to the former and one-third to the latter. In the case of income, the HDI uses the Atkinson formulation; a formula for the utility of income. The index can be further modified to make it gender sensitive. Although women typically live longer than men, once they have lived beyond childhood when the differential treatment of girl children in some societies has an adverse impact on survival, they tend to work harder with longer hours than men, often undertaking work in the home or in the community, which is unpaid or inadequately remunerated. The HDI can also be adjusted for income distribution within a society. Clearly, the more variables that are introduced in such an index, the less likely it is that the data will be available across a range of countries, particularly among poorer nations.

Although in the case of life expectancy the gap between developed and developing countries has narrowed, in ten countries there have been falls in the HDI between 1970 and 1990. As the HDI ranks countries relative to each other over a time period, a decline may not invariably mean an absolute deterioration. Twenty-one of the 38 countries which have experienced declines or marginal increases of between 0 and 0.049 in HDI between 1970 and 1990 are from Sub-Saharan Africa, 7 from Latin America and 7 from Asia. Twenty-three of the countries started with an HDI of below 0.300 in 1970 and remained below that level in 1990. Structural adjustment programmes in a range of countries in the 1980s resulted in a declining expenditure on education and health, but more recently most governments' adjustment programmes have tried to compensate by maintaining cost-effective expenditures in health and education. In general, the least developed countries tended to improve their level of development at a lower rate than the rest of the developing world. In the 1980s, there was greater polarization between rich and poor than in the 1960s. In 1960, the top 20 per cent of the world population received 30 times more income than the bottom 20 per cent, but by 1989, the difference was 60-fold. Even if real purchasing power rather than nominal GNP were used, there would probably be a real difference in income of more than 50 to 1 between rich and poor nations (UNDP, 1992: 35).

There are many mechanisms by which poverty results in ill-health. They clearly include educational disadvantage and lack of health care, adequate nutrition, clean water and shelter. Cultural factors and the deleterious effects of war and conflict may also contribute. Differences in life expectancy and other indicators of health between developed and developing nations are largely due to diseases of poverty resulting from poor sanitation, inadequate food etc. Within developed countries, there is also a pronounced gradient in health between rich and poor. For instance in the UK, a working group under the leadership of Sir Douglas Black completed a review on inequalities and health in 1980. They noted that the gap in mortality rates between occupational groups had increased within the 20 years up to the early 1970s. In the case of infant mortality, a three-fold difference between the children of unskilled manual workers compared with children of professionals was particularly due to marked disparities in deaths from accidents and respiratory disease. Among adults, the social class difference is particularly large for those in their 20s and 30s (Black et al, 1982). A major study of over 17,000 UK civil servants showed that people in the lowest employment grade had three times the mortality than the highest grade from coronary heart disease (Marmot, Shipley and Rose, 1984). Conventional risk factors such as smoking, obesity, physical inactivity and blood pressure explained only part of the difference in mortality. Early environmental influences have been suggested by a number of studies, particularly by Barker and colleagues in Southampton. For instance, they have shown that among men born 70 years previously, those who had lower birth weights and weights at one year subsequently had higher death rates from coronary heart disease (Barker and Martyn, 1992). Since low birth weight is commoner among women from lower social classes, this could be a mechanism by which deprivation has a long-term impact on health.

The Black Report (1982) described four types of explanations for inequalities in health between rich and poor: artefactual, selection, cultural or behavioural, and materialist. An artefactual relationship might occur, for example, if social class were recorded differently on death certificates than at the census. If unhealthy people move down the social scale, this could explain in terms of selection the association between poor health and socio-economic status. Behavioural factors include cigarette smoking and materialist explanations for socio-economic variations in health involve differences in exposure to hazards, including occupational factors, toxins, inadequate diet, poor quality housing etc. The major factors are probably behavioural and materialist. The role of differential access to health care is still controversial, but probably explains only a relatively small part of the social class gradients in health, at least in developed countries, although clearly the differences in access to primary care and preventive measures in particular are likely to be responsible for some of the differences between developing and developed countries in health indicators. Unemployment has been associated with poor health in a number of studies. For instance, in the UK, Moser and colleagues demonstrated an excess mortality among unemployed people which did not seem to be due to health-related selection for unemployment (Moser et al, 1987).

There is a higher prevalence of mental illness in poorer areas. There is also a tendency for patients with schizophrenia to drift into the centres of cities and down the social scale (Goldberg and Morrison, 1963). Working class women are more susceptible to depression than women of higher social class. Life events such as marital breakdown and death of a close relative can trigger a depressive episode (Brown, 1979).

## HEALTH AND DEVELOPMENT: ECONOMIC FACTORS

The total external debt of developing countries has multiplied 13-fold in the last 20 years and was around US $1,350 billion in 1990. It levelled off following a period of rapid growth up to 1987. Between 1983–9, there was a net flow of US$242 billion from poor to rich as a result of debt-related transfer. The debt of Sub-Saharan Africa is currently around US$150 billion – 100 per cent of its GNP (UNDP, 1992: 45). Many other factors contribute to the economic disparities between rich and poor nations, including differences in interest rates, a tendency for multinational companies to channel most of their investments towards better-off countries, trade barriers for manufactured goods and agricultural produce, and the brain drain from poor countries to the rich. Africa as a whole is estimated to have lost up to 60,000 middle and high level managers between 1985 and 1990 (UNDP, 1992: 57). In Ghana for example, 60 per cent of doctors trained in the early 1980s are now abroad, resulting in severe shortages in the Ghanaian health service.

While there is an obvious tendency for countries with a higher GNP per capita to have longer life expectancies and lower rates of infant mortality than poorer countries, this does not prove that it is invariably necessary to increase GNP in order to achieve improvements in health. A study which investigated the relationship between income distribution and life expectancy in a number of developed countries suggested that the association was closest between life expectancy and the proportion of income going to the least well-off 70 per cent of the population (Wilkinson, 1992). The United Nations (International) Children's (Emergency) Fund (UNICEF) has argued that the per capita GNP of the poorest 40 per cent of the population is an appropriate indicator of development (Unicef, 1989). In the case of Japan, where people have the highest life expectancy in the world, no obvious explanation for the rapid improvement in Japanese life expectancy has been found in terms of changing diet, health services and other aspects of life. However, Japan now has possibly the most egalitarian income distribution of any country on record (Marmot and Davey Smith, 1989).

It is clear that countries with low per capita income can have a life expectancy comparable with much richer countries. For instance, the life expectancy at birth in the case of Cuba is 75.4 years, slightly above that of much richer countries such as Austria, Germany, Belgium and New Zealand. Its GDP per capita (using purchasing power parities to adjust for differences in the relative domestic purchasing powers of currencies) is only US$2500 (UNDP, 1992: 12). Other countries with an average real GDP per capita of less than US$5000 also have life expectancies of well over 70 years, including Costa Rica, Argentina, Jamaica, Dominica and several other Caribbean islands. China and Sri Lanka both have life expectancies of over 70, with average real GDP per capita of US$2656 and US$2253 respectively (UNDP, 1992: 126). Many of these countries compare favourably with the average in 'high human development countries' (those with a HDI of 0.8 to 1.0).

Attempts to determine the relationship between measures such as life expectancy and indicators of environmental sustainability are fraught with difficulty because of inadequate data and the lack of a clear definition of sustainability in statistical terms. In some countries with relatively low incomes but long life expectancies, the statistics indicate rapid deforestation and a high greenhouse index. (The greenhouse index is a measure of net emissions of three major greenhouse gases–carbon dioxide, methane and chlorofluorocarbons (CFC's). Each gas is weighted according to its warming properties in carbon dioxide equivalents and expressed in metric tons per capita.) For instance, Costa Rica had an annual rate of deforestation of 6.9 per cent between 1980 and 1990, and a greenhouse index of 4.1 metric tons per capita, carbon heating equivalents (compared with an average of 1.6 for countries of 'high human development'). By comparison, Sri Lanka has an annual rate of deforestation of around 3.5 per cent, but a greenhouse index of only 0.5, probably because it has lower commercial energy use (UNDP, 1992: 172).

Thus, it is unlikely that any country currently has a truly sustainable life-style combined with a high life expectancy, but there is good evidence that relatively low average per capita income is compatible with longevity.

There are a number of factors which cast a shadow over those beneficial trends of health which have occurred. These include the health effects of climate change and stratospheric ozone depletion, and the spread of AIDS. In addition, there has been concern that improved child survival through the use of simple techniques, such as oral rehydration and immunization programmes, may accelerate population growth and exacerbate the danger of populations being caught in a 'demographic trap' (King, 1990). According to this hypothesis, population growth in some areas could exceed locally available resources and result in further increases in mortality because of the inability to provide for basic human needs.

## CLIMATE CHANGE AND HEALTH

The greenhouse effect is responsible for the fact that the mean temperature of the earth's surface is warmer by about 33°C than it would be if natural greenhouse gases were not present. The concern now is about the enhanced greenhouse effect which is occurring as a result of anthropogenic emissions of greenhouse gas, particularly carbon dioxide, methane and nitrous oxide. Recently, it has been suggested that CFCs may not contribute as much as was previously believed to greenhouse warming. This is because depletion of ozone in the lower stratosphere in the middle and high latitudes leads to a reduction in radiative forcing, which is thought to be approximately the equivalent to the radiative forcing resulting from CFCs over the last ten years or so (*IPPC Report*, Houghton et al, 1992). In addition, the updated *IPCC Report* pointed out that the cooling effect of aerosols from sulphur emissions due to fossil fuel use may have counterbalanced a significant part of greenhouse warming in the northern hemisphere. Nevertheless, the report also noted that the high global mean surface temperatures of the late 1980s have continued into 1990 and 1991, which were the warmest years on record. The warming is particularly characterized by increases in nightime rather than daytime temperatures. Sulphur emissions, while reducing greenhouse warming, are also responsible for acid rain and other adverse environmental effects. The IPCC scientists concluded that the estimation of a rate of warming of 0.3°C per decade for the emissions scenario A of the earlier *IPCC Report* might be revised downward somewhat, but reductions in sulphur emissions would result in a rapid loss of their cooling effect.

There are a number of feedback mechanisms which may play a role both in determining the rate of increase of concentrations of greenhouse gases and the response of climate to increases in greenhouse gases. Feedback mechanisms which could affect concentrations of greenhouse gases in the atmosphere include the capacity of the ocean and of plants to take up carbon dioxide, and the impact of temperature rise on emissions of methane from rice paddies and natural wetlands. Because the oceans act as a buffer to climate change, distinction has to be made between the temperature realized at any particular point in time and the final rise in temperature to which the world has already been committed as a result of the greenhouse gas concentrations at a particular point in time. The realized temperature at a given point in time is around 60–80 per cent of the committed rise.

There are several mechanisms by which climate change could have an impact on health. Effects could be direct and indirect. Increases in mortality from cardio- and cerebrovascular disease during hot spells have been documented in a number of studies. A study of the relationship between temperature and mortality from coronary disease and stroke in a range of American cities found an inverse association between temperature and mortality between about –5°C and 25°C, but above and below this range, there were increases in mortality (Rogot and Padgett, 1976). An increase in mortality was also observed in the UK during heat waves in the summers of 1975 and 1976 (MacFarlane and Waller, 1976). The overall effects on mortality will depend on the magnitude of the reduction in winter deaths, particularly in temperate countries where mortality is higher in the winter months. Estimates for the US suggest an overall increase in deaths (Kalkstein et al, 1986). Recent evidence indicates that heat-related deaths are also a significant problem in some developing countries, for example, in Shanghai, China (Kalkstein, 1993). The elderly and perhaps the very young are particularly at risk for heat-related morbidity and mortality because their capacity for adaptation is less than young and middle-aged adults.

Potential adverse indirect effects on health include the spread of vector-borne diseases. The most notable include malaria, dengue, filariasis, yellow fever, arbovirus encephalitides – viral diseases affecting the central nervous system – and possibly leishmaniasis (WHO, 1990). It is likely that the spread will occur principally to areas which border on currently endemic regions. But temperate, industrialized countries such as the US could be at risk of a number of conditions, including dengue, yellow fever and Rift Valley fever. In the case of Australia, there may be a spread of Australian encephalitis and epidemic polyarthritis (causing inflammation of joints). It is also possible that cholera epidemics might be more likely in some parts of the world (Shope, 1991; Epstein, 1992). Other diseases which could be affected include schistosomiasis, which is also dependent on the spread of irrigation systems, bringing humans and infected snails into increased contact.

The rise in sea level will threaten the viability of a number of low-lying island states such as the Maldives, Kiribati and Tokelau. Five of the ten countries most threatened are densely populated and relatively poor, including Bangladesh, Indonesia, Egypt, Thailand and Pakistan. In the case of Bangladesh, 300,000 were killed in the 1970s as a result of floods. The livelihoods of 46 million people living in the Nile and Ganges deltas are at risk (Jacobson, 1990).

Climate change is likely to have an overall adverse effect on food production, particularly because of impacts on precipitation patterns in some regions which, when accompanied by rises in temperature, will lead to loss of soil moisture. Although the prediction of regional climatic patterns is fraught with difficulty, work using a number of global circulation models (GCMs) suggests that the number of people at risk of hunger could increase by between 5 and 50 per cent by 2060 (Rosenzweig and Parry, 1992). In *Vital Signs* from the Worldwatch Institute (Brown et al, 1992) it is reported that grain land shrank in 1991 by 0.3 per cent. Combined with the addition of 92 million people to the world population, this resulted in a decrease of 2 per cent in grain land per person. In addition, the expansion of irrigation is slowing and the use of fertilizer fell in 1991. Reduced availability of water in some regions could also result in an increase of diseases related to lack of water for washing ('water-washed') or clean water for drinking ('water-borne'), including gastroenteritis, dysentery and some worm infestations. Many other potential adverse effects of climate change exist, including effects on respiratory (Ayres, 1990) and skin diseases. The major effects on health are likely to be borne particularly by developing nations, at least initially (Haines, 1991; Haines and Fuchs, 1991), but no part of the world will remain unaffected, particularly by the indirect impacts. These will include increased movements of refugees, conflicts over, for instance, limited water resources (Myers, 1989) and economic damage.

## OZONE DEPLETION AND POLLUTION

The depletion of stratospheric ozone which has been increasing since its discovery in 1985 is attributed to CFCs and other substances such as the halons used in fire fighting and solvents such as carbon tetrachloride and methyl chloroform. The seasonal appearance of ozone holes in the Antarctic is now being accompanied by an appreciable depletion of stratospheric ozone in the northern hemisphere. Health concerns focus on the effects of the consequent increase in ultraviolet radiation on skin cancer, particularly in pale skinned individuals, and possibly on cataracts (Longstrech et al, 1991). Squamous cell and basal cell carcinomas are generally of local malignancy. Much more dangerous is malignant melanoma, which is probably related to intense brief exposures to sun, particularly in individuals who tan poorly or not at all. In addition, there is concern about the possibility of immunosuppression, which may occur irrespective of skin pigmentation and might theoretically lead to increased susceptibility to some communicable diseases. Although international action has resulted in the 1987 Montreal Protocol to the Vienna Convention on the Protection of the Ozone Layer and its subsequent amendments, there is still concern that ozone depleting chemicals should be phased out more quickly than is currently the case and that appreciable stratospheric ozone depletion will occur well into the twenty-first century (Jones and Wigley, 1989). There is also concern about the potential impact of stratospheric ozone depletion on the growth of phytoplankton in the Antarctic with subsequent implications for the food chain, and for animals which may also be susceptible to skin cancer and cataracts.

There are growing problems of disposal of hazardous wastes and toxic chemicals. For instance, in the US there are around 50,000 land sites where hazardous wastes may have been dumped in an unregulated way (WHO, 1992). Lead and cadmium concentrations in drinking water were in excess of guideline values in around 25 per cent of the 344 monitoring stations of the Global Environmental Monitoring System Network (WHO/UNEP, 1987). The discharge of mercury contaminated wastes has resulted in mercury pollution at a number of sites, including parts of China, Brazil and India. The most notorious episode occurred at Minamata in Japan, where hundreds of deaths occurred and thousands of people were disabled. The cleaning operation involved 1.5 million m$^2$ of seabed and cost nearly 48 thousand million yen.

Inadequate legal and institutional structures make developing countries particularly vulnerable to the dumping of chemical wastes (Michaels et al, 1985). Hazardous industries may transfer their operations to developing countries because of tax regulations. For example, many industries manufacturing asbestos moved from the US to Latin America. There is an estimated 338 million tonnes of hazardous waste produced every year, 80 per cent of which comes from the US (OECD, 1991). Available figures for 1988 suggest that 230,000 tonnes of hazardous wastes were exported from the US. Annually, 200–300,000 tonnes are shipped from EC countries to east European countries and about 120,000 tonnes from Europe to the Third World (Crump, 1991). Although transfrontier movements of hazardous wastes were regulated under EC law and endorsed by the OECD in 1988, this has resulted in an increase of illegal dumping, particularly in developing countries (UN, 1989).

## HIV

The first description of AIDS was in 1981 (Gottlieb et al, 1981). Since that time, there has been rapid spread in much of Africa with a variable rate of spread in other regions. There was a decreasing rate of growth of the epidemic in male homosexuals in developed countries in the late 1980s, although there is recent evidence that unsafe sexual behaviour and HIV transmissions have increased among homosexual men (Evans et al, 1993). There has been rapid spread among intravenous drug users in Europe, north America and parts of south-east Asia (Des Jarlais et al, 1989), and a steady rise in heterosexual populations in some developed countries, South America and parts of Asia (Cortes et al, 1989). Mathematical models of the spread of HIV-1 in Africa show a range of possible outcomes, depending on the specific patterns of sexual behaviour and contact in a particular population (Anderson et al, 1991). The development of mathematical models has surpassed the information available about patterns of sexual contact. A number of studies have shown a doubling time of the prevalence of HIV-1 infection ranging from less than 1 to 2.8 years in some groups in Africa (US Bureau of the Census, 1990; Piot et al, 1987). Simple models based on such doubling times suggested AIDS is potentially able to reverse population growth rates over a timescale ranging from a few to many decades. Already, the disease is a leading cause of mortality in a number of urban centres in Africa. If efforts to control the spread of HIV fail, by the year 2000 an additional one million people will be dying from AIDS annually (World Bank, 1993) in Sub-Saharan Africa.

## MEASURES TO PROMOTE HEALTH CARE AND DEVELOPMENT

Despite a bleak picture for many, there are a number of concrete steps that could be taken to improve health. They are not only compatible with sustainability, but essential for its achievement.

### A more equitable income distribution

Given that poverty lies behind much of the world's ill-health, redistribution of wealth is a necessity both between and within countries. Although there have been a number of debt cancellation schemes, these are not sufficient to have much impact on the current level of indebtedness. As long as indebtedness continues at levels equivalent to 40 per cent of the collective gross national product (GNP) of the Third World, progress for the majority of the world's population is likely to remain problematic. Clearly, in many parts of the world, the pendulum has moved away from political systems which tend to redistribute wealth along equitable lines. Nevertheless, as countries like Japan show, a relatively equitable income distribution is compatible with economic development, relatively low fossil fuel use and exceptional longevity. However, perpetuation of the current system which equates economic growth with development is likely to pose a serious threat to the quality of life for all. A high GNP per capita is not necessary for the attainment of longevity and low infant mortality rates, but the removal of outright poverty is essential.

### A reduction in pollution

Although local air pollution from fossil fuels may be ameliorated by pollution control measures, these do not deal with the contribution of fossil fuels to global warming. In view of the potential climate change to impact adversely on human health, increased energy efficiency, growth in renewable sources of energy and consequently reduction in carbon emissions, until they return at least to the 1950 level of less than 2 billion tons annually, is necessary. A transfer of energy-efficient technologies to Third World nations could be of mutual benefit to rich and poor nations alike, and particularly if they are accompanied by reductions in fossil fuel use, could have significant benefits for health. The potentially important role of primary environmental care is described by Grazia Borrini (1991 and Chapter 7 of this book). Illegal transfer of toxic wastes could be reduced by increasing the penalties and policing. Legal regulation of pollution by governments in the South could prevent transfer of polluting industries.

## The promotion of family planning

While global population growth is at an unprecedented level, overall fertility is now falling, albeit slowly, almost everywhere. A number of countries have shown that a rapid fall in population growth is feasible without coercion. The UN has advocated the universal right to reproductive health care, including family planning. Three hundred million couples still lack access to adequate family planning. An annual investment of only $US9 billion would be sufficient to provide contraception to those who wish to use it (Sadik, 1992). This small sum is equivalent to less than three days' world-wide military expenditure and should be made available as a matter of urgency. A reduction in family size can help to improve the health of mothers and children. Avoiding motherhood under 20 could reduce the deaths of children under 5 by 17 per cent and spacing births by 2 years or more could have a similar impact.

## The development of primary health care

In 1990, a number of goals were adopted by the World Summit for Children which, if achieved, would significantly reduce under-5 death rates among children (by one-third or to a level of 70/1,000 live births) and death rates among women (halving of maternal mortality). Many of them can best be achieved through primary care services. These include:

- the eradication of polio;
- the elimination of neonatal tetanus by 1995;
- a 90 per cent reduction in measles cases;
- virtual elimination of vitamin A and iodine deficiency;
- the implementation of growth monitoring and promotion in all countries;
- education of all families about the importance of exclusive breast feeding for the first four to six months of a child's life;
- basic education for all children, access to prenatal care for all women;
- the provision of a trained attendant during childbirth and referral where appropriate.

A 'best guess' for the cost of reaching the goals is around US$20 billion per annum for ten years from 1990 – this is approximately equivalent to one-eighth of 1 per cent of world income. One-third of this sum (equivalent to only ten days' debt repayments currently transferred from the developing to the developed world) might come from the industrialized world in a number of ways, including the linkage of debt relief to investments aimed at attaining the goals (UNICEF, 1991).

## *The organization of district health systems*
The World Bank has calculated that a basic package of effective public health measures and minimum essential clinical services in poor countries would cost US$4 to US$8 per capita respectively (World Bank, 1993). Many governments spend too much on sophisticated hospital services of low cost-effectiveness, and too little on essential public health measures and clinical services. Health systems can be organized around defined populations in the form of districts. District health systems include primary care and hospital(s), and aim for an integration of the two with appropriate mechanisms for planning and management to ensure efficient use of limited resources. In this way, uncoordinated vertical programmes dealing with specific problems such as tuberculosis, diabetes, nutrition, and mother and child health, should be able to be incorporated into a more comprehensive and flexible health care system without loss of effectiveness.

## *Reform of official development assistance*
Official development assistance (ODA) has had a disappointing record. Currently, the industrial countries give ODA equivalent to only around 0.35 per cent of their combined GNP (UNDP, 1992). Only a quarter of the aid goes to the ten countries which have about 75 per cent of the world's poorest people. More than two-thirds of ODA is given directly from one country to another and therefore is potentially able to be influenced by political considerations – which may have nothing to do with the needs of populations of those countries. Importantly, basic education, primary health care, safe drinking water, family planning and nutrition programmes are only given 6.5 per cent of bilateral ODA, and the percentage is probably not much better than this for aid given through multilateral agencies. In any event, the sums of money transferred as part of ODA are dwarfed by transfers of resources from South to North due to debt repayment, trade barriers and inequitable financial markets etc. Thus, if ODA is to play a significant role in promoting sustainable health care systems, it will have to be fundamentally reformed.

## *The improvement of public information and education*
While no cure or effective vaccine for HIV infection is currently in sight, much more could be done to limit the spread by public education about methods of transmission and encouraging the use of condoms. Promotion of increasing use of condoms might also help to reduce unwanted pregnancies, providing condom use does not displace more effective means of contraception. Education programmes about sexual health could be linked to expansion of literacy and basic education programmes.

The suggestion that basic primary health care measures should not be promoted to populations who threaten to outgrow their resources is not logically, morally or practically supportable. It is the rich countries of the North who, by their high per capita consumption of resources, are particularly threatening of global sustainability. In many cases, their populations' consumption patterns have long since outgrown the resource base within their own national boundaries. In any event, it would be impossible to prevent the diffusion of knowledge about the use of simple primary care measures. There are a number of examples of countries, eg Sri Lanka, and states, eg Kerala in India, which have, over comparatively short periods, made a successful transition from high infant mortality and high fertility into a state of low infant mortality and fertility. An increasing emphasis on the education and advancement of the position of women in society, the development of primary health care programmes, incorporating family planning and organized in health districts, have important roles to play in moving towards a sustainable, liveable and equitable world.

Human development, without prejudicing the capacity of the environment to support future generations on earth should be the key aim. While there is likely to be continuing debate about the most appropriate indicators of human development, it is clear that health plays a crucial role. Without a reasonable prospect of survival into old age in a society which cares for the sick, the disabled and the vulnerable, human development will be frustrated.

## REFERENCES

Anderson, R M, R M May, M C Boily, G P Garnett and J T Rowley, 'The Spread of HIV-1 in Africa: Sexual Contact Patterns and the Predicted Demographic Impact of AIDS', *Nature*, vol 352, 1991, pp 581–9.

Ayres, J G, 'Meteorology and Respiratory Disease', *Update*, 1990, pp 596–605.

Barker, D J P and C N Martyn, 'The Maternal and Fetal Origins of Cardiovascular Disease', *Journal of Epidemiology and Community Health*, vol 46, 1992, pp 8–11.

Black, D, J Morris, C Smith and P Townsend, 'The Black Report' in P Townsend and N Davidson (eds), *Inequalities in Health*, Harmondsworth: Penguin, 1982.

Borrini, G (ed), *Lessons Learned in Community Based Environmental Management*, Rome: ICHM, 1991.

Brown, G W, 'Life Events, Psychiatric Disorder and Physical Illness', *Journal of Psychosomatic Research*, vol 23, 1979, pp 461–73.

Brown, L R, C Flavin, H Kane, *Vital Signs. The Trends that are Shaping Our Future, 1992, 1993*, London: Earthscan, 1992.

Cortes, E, R Detels, D Aboulafia, L Xi, T Moudgil, M Alam et al, 'HIV-1, HIV-2 and HTLV-1 Infection in High Risk Groups in Brazil', *New England Journal of Medicine*, vol 320, 1989, pp 953–8.

Crump, A, *Dictionary of Environment and Development*, London: Earthscan, 1991.

Des Jarlais, D C, R Samuel et al, 'HIV-1 Infection Among Intravenous Drug Users in Manhattan, New York City, from 1977 through 1987', *Journal of the American Medical Association*, vol 261, 1989, pp 1008–12.

Epstein, P R, 'Cholera and the Environment', *Lancet*, vol 339, 1992, pp 1167–8.

Evans, B G, M A Catchpole, J Heptonstall et al, 'Sexually Transmitted Diseases and HIV-1 Infection among Homosexual Men in England and Wales', *British Medical Journal*, vol 306, 1993, pp 426–8.

Goldberg, E M and S L Morrison, 'Schizophrenia and Social Class', *British Journal of*

*Psychiatry*, vol 109, 1963, pp 785–802.

Gottlieb, M S, R Schross, H M Schanker, J D Weisman et al, 'Pneumocystis Carinii. Pneumonia and Mucosal Candidiasis in Previously Healthy Homosexual Men. Evidence of a New Acquired Cellular Immunodeficiency', *New England Journal of Medicine*, vol 305, 1981, pp 1425–31.

Haines, A, 'Global Warming and Health', *British Medical Journal*, vol 302, 1991, pp 669–70.

Haines, A and C Fuchs, 'Potential Impacts on Health of Atmospheric Change', *Journal of Public Health Medicine*, vol 13, 1991, pp 69–80.

Houghton, J T, B A Callander and S K Varney (eds), *Climate Change 1992*, The supplementary report of the IPCC Scientific Assessment World Meteorological Organisation/UNEP Intergovernmental Panel on Climate Change, Cambridge: Cambridge University Press, 1992.

Jacobson, J, 'Holding Back the Sea' in L.R. Brown et al, *State of the World*, New York: W W Norton, 1990.

Jones, R. R and T Wigley (eds), *Ozone Depletion – Health and Environmental Consequences*, West Sussex: John Wiley and Sons, 1989.

Kalkstein, L S, R E Davis, J A Skindlov and K M Valimont, 'The Impact of Human-Induced Climate Warming upon Human Mortality – A New York Case Study', Washington, DC: Proceedings of the International Conference on Health and Environmental Effects of Ozone Modification and Climate Change, June 1986.

Kalkstein, L S, 'Global Warming and Human Health: International Implications' in L.S. Kalkstein and J Smith (eds), *International Implications of Global Warming*, Cambridge: Cambridge University Press, 1993.

King, M, 'Health is a Sustainable State', *Lancet*, vol 336, 1990, pp 664–7.

Longstrech, J, F de Gruijl and Y Takizawa, 'Human Health' in UNEP, *Environmental Effects of Ozone Depletion*, 1991 update, Nairobi: UNEP, 1991, pp 14-24.

MacFarlane, A and R E Waller, 'Short-term Increases in Mortality During Heatwaves', *Nature*, vol 264, 1976, pp 434–6.

Marmot, M G, M J Shipley and G Rose, 'Inequalities in Death – Specific Explanations of a General Pattern?', *Lancet*, vol 1, 1984, pp 1003–6.

Marmot, M G and G Davey Smith, 'Why are the Japanese Living Longer?', *British Medical Journal*, vol 299, 1989, pp 1547–51.

Michaels, D et al, 'Economic Development and Occupational Health in Latin America: New Directions for Public Health in Less Developed Countries', *American Journal of Public Health*, vol 75, 1985, pp 536–42.

Moser, K A, P O Goldblatt, A J Fox and D R Jones, 'Unemployment and Mortality. Comparison of the 1971 and 81 Longitudinal Study Census Samples', *British Medical Journal*, vol 294, 1990, pp 86–90.

Myers, N, 'Environment and Security', *Foreign Policy*, vol 74, 1989, pp 23–41.

OECD (Organization for Economic Cooperation and Development), *The State of the Environment 1991*, Paris: OECD, 1991.

Piot, P, S A Plummer, M-A Rey, E N Ngugi et al, 'Retrospective Seroepidemiology of AIDS Virus Infection in Nairobi Populations', *Journal of Infectious Disease*, vol 155, 1987, pp 1108–12.

Rogot, E and S J Padgett, 'Associations of Coronary and Stroke Mortality with Temperature and Snowfall in Selected Areas of the US, 1952–1966', *American Journal of Epidemiology*, vol 103, 1976, pp 565–75.

Rosenzweig, C and M Parry, with G Fischer and K Frohberg, *Climate Change and World Food Supply. A Preliminary Report*, Oxford: Environmental Change Unit, 1992.

Shope, R, 'Global Climate Change and Infectious Diseases', *Environmental Health Perspectives*, vol 96, 1991, pp 171–4.

UN Doc A/33/362, 'Illegal Traffic in Toxic and Dangerous Products and Wastes', *Report of the Secretary General*, New York: United Nations, 1989.

UNDP (United Nations Development Programme), *Human Development Report 1990*, Oxford: Oxford University Press, 1990.

UNDP, *Human Development Report 1992*, Oxford: Oxford University Press, 1992.

UNFPA (UN Fund for Population Activities), *State of the World Population 1992*, New York: UNFPA, 1992.

UNICEF, *State of the World's Children 1989*, Oxford: Oxford University Press, 1989.

UNICEF, *State of the World's Children 1991*, Oxford: Oxford University Press, 1991.

US Bureau of Census, *HIV/AIDS Surveillance Database, 9th Update*, Washington, DC: United States Bureau of the Census, 1990.

WHO/UNEP, *Global Environment Monitoring System. Global Pollution and Health. Results of Health-Related Environmental Monitoring*, Geneva: WHO/UNEP, 1987.

WHO (World Health Organization), *Potential Health Effects of Climatic Change. Report of WHO Task Group*, Geneva: WHO, 1990.

WHO, *Our Planet, Our Health. Report of the WHO Commission on Health and the Environment*, Geneva: WHO, 1992.

Wilkinson, R G, 'Income Distribution and Life Expectancy', *British Medical Journal*, vol 304, 1992, pp 165–8.

World Bank, *World Development Report 1993. Investing in Health, World Development Indicators*, New York: Oxford University Press, 1993.

*Chapter Nine*

# The Relevance of Military Expenditures to Sustainable and Equitable Development

*Samuel E Okoye[1]*

It is useful to be reminded that the question of an equitable and sustainable development is, in the final analysis, an enquiry about human development and that human development is a people oriented exercise. Indeed it is a process of enlarging people's choices. No matter the level of development, the three major issues are for people to live a long and healthy life, to acquire knowledge and to have access to resources needed for a decent standard of living. These choices are essential in that if they are not available, many other opportunities become inaccessible. But it must be noted that human development does not end with these essential choices. Further choices range from political, economic and social freedoms to individual opportunities for enjoying personal respect and guaranteed human rights.

It is against this background that one must consider any effort geared towards equitable and sustainable development on a global scale. But the reality is that the global family is a divided community. About three-quarters of this community live in the so-called developing countries. They are often referred to as 'the South'. Largely bypassed by the benefits of prosperity and progress, they exist on the peripheries of the advanced or developed countries, also referred to as 'the North'.[2] While most countries of the North are affluent, most countries of the South are poor. While the countries of the North have strong economies and are in

1. The author thanks the principal of Homerton College, Cambridge, UK for a Senior Research Associateship, and Robert Hinde, Phil Smith and Jaap de Wilde for useful comments on an earlier draft of this chapter.

control of their destinies, the countries of the South in contrast have weak economies and as a group are very vulnerable to external factors, and they are generally not in control of their destinies. The South Commission (1990) has described the situation in the following graphic words:

> *Were all humanity a single nation state, the present North–South divide would make it an unviable, semi-feudal entity split by internal conflicts. Its small part is advanced, prosperous, powerful; its much bigger part is underdeveloped, poor, powerless. A nation so divided within itself would be recognised as unstable. Likewise a world so divided should be recognised as inherently unstable.*

Thus any effort towards equitable and sustainable development on a global scale must address the issue of global poverty. Any plan for equitable development must specifically address the incidence of human deprivation on a global scale. Such a plan must take into account that:[3]

- more than a billion people live in absolute poverty in the world today;
- the average life expectancy in the South is still 12 years shorter than that in the North;
- there still are about 100 million children of primary school age in the South not attending school;
- nearly 9 hundred million adults in the South are illiterate;
- 1.5 billion people are still deprived of primary health care;
- 1.75 billion people still have no access to a safe source of drinking water;
- 14 million children still die annually before reaching their fifth birthday;
- 150 million children under 5 years of age suffer from malnutrition;
- nearly 3 million children die each year from preventable diseases;
- nearly 3 billion people (ie more than 50 per cent of the world's population) still live without adequate sanitation;
- the South's maternal mortality rate is 12 times that of the North.

## THE DEBT CRISIS AND MILITARY EXPENDITURES

As mounting evidence from around the world suggests, the South's economy is plagued by the debt crisis, and its consequences have taken a heavy toll on human development. Indeed the South owed foreign creditors US$1.3 trillion at the start

---

2. Strictly speaking, the world cannot be divided into just a 'North' and a 'South'. The North in reality corresponds to the G7 countries (Canada, France, Germany, the UK, Italy, Japan and the US) as well as other countries of Western Europe. The former Soviet Union and its satellite countries which formed the Second World are in dire straits and conditions in these countries are not much better than in the 'South'. In the second world, therefore, some countries would approximate more to the 'North', and others more to the 'South', which would thus enable the discussion to proceed as if we had a bipolar world. This is, incidentally, the approach chosen in Chapter 3 by Biesiot and Mulder.
3. The following figures are taken from UNDP (1990), Box 2.2: 27.

of 1989 – a figure that represents half their combined GNP and is two-thirds more than their annual export earnings. The annual interest obligations on the debt are approaching US$100 billion while, with debt amortization, the debt service bill is US$200 billion. This has meant that the mounting debt burden of the South has reversed the North–South resource flows, from a positive flow of US$35.2 billion in 1981 to a negative flow of US$32.5 billion in 1988.[4]

Before the early 1970s, the external debt of the South was relatively small and purely an official phenomenon; the majority of creditors being foreign governments and international financial institutions, such as the International Monetary Fund (IMF), the World Bank and regional development banks. Most loans obtained during this period were on concessional (or low interest) terms. Indeed these debts were incurred in the climate of the then conventional development strategy in which Third World nations had to operate sizeable current account deficits for the imports of capital and intermediate goods which were required to provide the machinery and equipment needed for industrialization. Export earnings paid for most, but not all, of these imports. The financing of most of these deficits was therefore facilitated by large resource transfers in the capital account in the form of bilateral aid between governments, as well as by direct private investments by multinational corporations.

However, during the late 1970s and early 1980s, the commercial banks began playing a large role in international lending by recycling the so-called surplus Organization of Petroleum Exporting Countries (OPEC) petrodollars. The commercial banks eventually went as far as providing general purpose loans to developing countries for balance of payments support, as well as for some productive ventures, such as the expansion of export sectors, and loans for dubious purposes which often facilitated misuse if not fraud and corruption. Indeed, in the approximately ten-year period between 1979 and 1989, the external debt of the South escalated from US$68.4 billion to US$1283 billion – a total increase of 1846 per cent. At the same time, debt service payments increased by 1400 per cent, and had risen to almost US$200 billion by the end of the 1980s. However, it must be remarked that a great deal of this debt is concentrated in 4 Latin American countries (Brazil, Mexico, Argentina and Venezuela), with 17 countries, including one in Africa (Nigeria), being designated by the World Bank as 'highly indebted' countries because their debts are deemed most vulnerable to default on account of the large share that is owed to the commercial creditors at variable rates of interest.

Faced with this critical debt situation, some economics pundits (eg Todaro, 1991) suggest that Third World countries in reality had only two policy options out of this economic quagmire. To wit, they could either control imports and at the same time impose restrictive fiscal and monetary policies, thus impeding growth and development objectives, or they could finance their widening current account deficits through more external borrowing. Most developing countries, afraid of the social costs of adopting the first option as a means of solving the balance of payments crisis, were forced in the early 1980s to rely on the second option. Hence

---

4. Unless otherwise indicated, these and all subsequent data are taken from World Bank (1990 and 1992) and Todaro (1991 and 1992).

they went on to borrow even more. Debts and the concomitant debt service obligations accumulated quickly. By the middle of the 1980s the situation had become so bad that some countries like Brazil, Mexico, Argentina, the Philippines and Chile faced such severe difficulties that they could not even pay the interests on their debt out of their export earnings.

In this situation, many developing countries were no longer in any position to borrow more funds from the world's capital markets. Indeed, not only did private lending dry up, but during the 1980s the South was paying US$11.3 billion more to the commercial banks than it was receiving loans. When paybacks to the international lenders (IMF and World Bank) are included, the net resource flow (ie new lending minus debt service) for all indebted developing countries went, in only two years, from a positive US$35.2 billion in 1981 to a negative US$30.7 billion in 1983. Five years later, in 1988, the negative flow remained at US$32.5 billion. The highly indebted countries had no recourse but to seek IMF assistance and were obliged to accept the so-called IMF conditionalities or stabilization programme – also referred to as the Structural Adjustment Programme (SAP). This was nothing other than the abandoned policy option for economic recovery indicated above. In such circumstances, most countries in the South are effectively caught in the so-called debt trap, with the net effect of their productive potential being overdrained by their debt requirements. Their pleas for 'debt forgiveness', apart from token responses from the North, have so far fallen on deaf ears, and the hope of achieving a standard of living remotely near the level prevalent in the North remains a pipe dream.

It is with the above background in mind that one must consider that about 5 per cent of the world's GNP goes directly into military spending. Significantly, both the North and the South alike spend about 5 per cent of their GNPs on their military machines, thus making the world's military industry a significant economic sector. It is doubtful whether even the North can afford to spend so much on the military (US$466.7 billion in 1980, for example), when so much remains to be done for the underprivileged in the inner cities of the North and while so many do not have good access to basic health care, even in the US (an economic superpower), not to talk of unemployment levels which are running at all-time highs, with about 17 million people being jobless in the EC countries alone. It is all the more difficult to understand when it is remembered that many countries in the North (Japan excluded) are currently struggling with huge budget deficits as well. The economy of the North, which serves as the engine of the global economy, is itself showing signs of instability with global recession occurring relatively more frequently in recent times. Indeed, the US, a leading economic power in the North, has been cutting back on its social and educational programmes for 12 years now because of the overburdening budget deficits.

It is therefore nothing short of folly for the South to attempt to spend the same proportion of its GNP on the military as the North does. Although at US$129.1 billion in 1980, the military expenditure of the South is in absolute terms only 21.7 per cent of the world's military expenditure. Yet this amount must be viewed against the fact that the South's debt to export ratio is very large and rising (from 99.4 per cent in 1970 to 139 per cent in 1989), while the debt to GDP ratio is also rising (from

13.3 per cent in 1970 to 34.5 per cent in 1989). For Africa, the figures are much worse, with the debt to GDP ratio standing at 53.2 per cent in 1989. Indeed, according to the World Bank, military debt is more than a third of the total debt for many countries in the South.

Overall the South spent more in per capita terms on the military (in 1979 eg US$34 per capita) than on their education (in 1979: US$27 per capita) or health (in 1979: US$11 per capita). These figures are not surprising when one remembers the huge debt service burdens that the South must contend with. By contrast, the North, in the same year, spent the greatest share on education, US$428 per capita, compared to US$345 per capita on the military and US$320 per capita on the health sector. This demonstrates that although the South has achieved parity with the North in military spending (relative to their GNPs), nevertheless the South lags behind by a factor of about ten in the combined per capita expenditures on education and health. Curiously, among the developing countries with the highest shares of military expenditures are some of the poorest and least developed countries – Angola, Burundi, Sudan, Uganda, Yemen and Zaire. Despite the more than 800 million in absolute poverty in South Asia and Sub-Saharan Africa, we find that South Asia spends US$10 billion a year on the military and Sub-Saharan Africa US$5 billion. If past trends continue, the level of military expenditure in the South will increase between US$15 billion to 20 billion every year in the 1990s.

Resources channelled into military spending mean less resources for investment, and less investment is likely to mean less growth in the civil components of income and output. In these circumstances, the global security environment and consequent expense of resources to maintain it, play a not insignificant part in the quest for a global family that develops not only equitably but ultimately sustainably.

## DISARMAMENT AND DEVELOPMENT

One of the intriguing features of the state of underdevelopment of the South is that military spending is in relative terms (ie as a proportion of the GNP) the same as in the North. Equally alarming is the fact that in the last three decades or so, there has been a rapid rise of military spending in the South. Surprisingly, military spending in the South continued to rise even in the 1980s despite faltering economic growth which saw major cutbacks in education and health expenditures. The total annual military spending of the South increased by a factor of seven – from US$24 billion in 1960 to 160 billion in 1986 – compared with only a doubling for the North. Furthermore, of the incremental growth of US$500 billion in annual global military expenditures between 1960 and 1986, nearly 30 per cent was additional spending by the South. As a result, the share of the South in global military expenditures rose from 7 per cent in 1960 to 21.7 per cent in 1980. Whereas the North reduced its share of the GNP allocation to the military from 6.3 per cent in 1960 to 5.4 per cent in 1986, the South increased its share from 4.2 per cent in 1960 to 5.5 per cent in 1986. Most surprising of all is the fact that during this period the least developed countries of the South nearly doubled the percentage of their GNP spent on their military from 2.1 per cent to 3.8 per cent.

It is worth recalling in this context that the average per capita income of the South is only 6 per cent of that of the North. Indeed at the 1985 levels of GNP per capita, the annual military costs in the South represented nearly 160 million person years of income in the South, which is three times the equivalent military burden of the North. One may conclude therefore that the poverty of the South has been no barrier to the affluence of her military.

The sharp increases in military expenditures have not only led to diminishing budget resources, but have also squeezed social services and economic growth. Military expenditures have also consumed considerable amounts of foreign exchange. The arms imports by the South sky-rocketed from US$1.1 billion in 1960 to 35 billion in 1987, thus accounting for three-quarters of the global arms trade.

The above trends have had serious consequences for human development. Apart from its political implications, the recent military expansion in the South has evoked debate over the economic impact of military expenditures on developing countries, where resources are scarce and the opportunity costs of military spending may be considered light. Indeed, empirical work supports the view that military spending has had a negative effect on economic growth. For example, Lim (1983) has examined the relationship between defence spending and economic growth for 54 developing countries, and concluded that there is a negative correlation between military spending and economic growth rate in the developing countries. Similar results have also been obtained by Faine, Annez and Taylor (1984) in a study of 69 developing countries. More striking, however, is Maizels and Nissanke's (1986) definitive empirical study of 83 developing countries, which clearly demonstrates that the impact of military spending on economic growth is unambiguously negative. Although an earlier study by Benoit (1973) had found that military spending and economic growth had a positive correlation, this result may be regarded as spurious in view of the fact that high military spending in the South was positively correlated with the high foreign aid obtained during the period examined. But, with the decline in foreign aid in the 1970s and 1980s, the relationship between military expenditure and economic growth has been reversed.

The expectation that the rediversion of resources, allocated through disarmament to development could universally be positive and beneficial is difficult to fault since the deployment of increased resources to development could only be to the good of all. Indeed the end of the Cold War between the superpowers is leading to a careful reassessment of past military spending, as well as an open dialogue about future options. But immense problems remain to be solved, as everything depends on the nature of the resources now devoted to produce armaments and how they are used. The resources released may, in some cases, be particularly unsuitable for meeting development needs. Furthermore the transfer of highly advanced technology from military industry (even when adapted for peaceful purposes) to the South would exacerbate existing problems of the technological subordination of the South to the North. Besides it is yet to be demonstrated that the transfer of this kind of technology would in any case meet basic needs.

The responsibility of some major world powers and a few other arms exporters in the South for the rising military expenditures of the South must also be recog-

---

nized. In this regard the defence assistance budgets of major countries of the North have often increased even when net economic assistance has declined (Todaro, 1991). Defence industries in the North have often aggressively sought willing clients in the South by offering soft credits and on occasion even illegal gratuities. Many countries of the South have in the past served as convenient battle grounds for the Cold War rivalries between the superpowers. To put this in bold relief, the military budget of just one superpower currently exceeds the combined military spending of the South by more than 50 per cent. This shows that in absolute terms a lot of resources are trapped in the military spending of the North. Such a huge reservoir of resources, however, can be mobilized into a 'peace dividend' to the benefit of the South, if the appropriate security measures on a global scale to cover both the North and the South can be put in place. This is not an easy proposition, but the recently proposed deep cuts in the strategic nuclear arsenals of the US and countries that make up the former Soviet Union provide a basis for looking towards the future with hope.

## TOWARDS A SUSTAINABLE WORLD

At 5 per cent of the world's GNP, military expenditure is an important parameter in any discussion of global socio-economic development. Disarmament as a global process must thus be viewed not only as an important goal from the point of view of world peace and security, but also as an important mechanism that should facilitate the release of resources presently inaccessible to basic human needs, and therefore useful in promoting equitable global development. Since equity is the basis on which can be built, the importance of decreased military spending in any consideration of global sustainability cannot be overemphasized. It therefore behoves the international community to ensure that all effort is mounted towards curbing the existing and future armed conflicts in the various regions of the world, since any reduction in the world's military expenditures can only be sustained over an extended period of time when the parts that make up the whole are at peace with each other. The major world powers (ie the permanent members of the Security Council – China, France, the UK, the US and the Russian Federation) have an important obligation to fulfil in this regard. They should seize the initiative in promoting peaceful developments in the world by defusing regional tensions, particularly in Southern Africa, the Middle East and Africa. They should also facilitate world peace and security through establishing a standing UN Peacemaking/Peacekeeping Force.

---

## REFERENCES

Benoit, E, *Defence and Economic Growth in Developing Countries*, Boston: DC Heath, 1973.
Faine, R, P Annez and R Taylor, 'Defence Spending, Economic Structure and Growth: Evidence Among Countries over Time', *Economic Development and Cultural Change*, vol 32, no 3, 1984, pp 487–98.

International Monetary Fund (IMF), *World Development Report*, Oxford: Oxford University Press, 1989.

Kruger, A O, 'Debt, Capital Flows and LDC Growth', *American Economic Review*, vol 77, no 2, 1978.

Lim, D, 'Another Look at Growth and Defence in Less Developed Countries', *Economic Development and Cultural Change*, vol 35, no 22, 1978.

Lever, C and C Huhne, *Debt and Danger: The World Financial Crisis*, New York: Atlantic Monthly Press, 1978.

Maizels, A and M Nissanke, 'The Determinants of Military Expenditures in Developing Countries', *World Development*, no 9, 1986.

Pool, J C and S Stamos, *The ABC of International Finance*, Lexington, Massachusetts: DC Heath, 1987.

South Commission, *The Challenge to the South : The Report of the South Commission*, Oxford: Oxford University Press, 1990.

Todaro, M P, *Economic Development in the Third World*, New York: Longman, 1991.

Todaro, M P, *Economics of a Developing World*, New York: Longman, 1992.

UN Development Programme (UNDP), *Human Development Report*, Oxford: Oxford University Press, 1990.

World Bank, *World Debt Tables, 1987–1988, vol I*, Washington, DC: The World Bank, 1988.

*Chapter Ten*

# The Power Politics of Sustainability, Equity and Liveability

## *Jaap de Wilde[1]*

How can every human being on earth live a decent life within a world order that is symbiotic with the rest of nature? This will be the essence of politics for the coming decades.

Realpolitik, or power politics, in the second half of the twentieth century was dominated by the question of how to avoid a global nuclear war. Related questions were how to end the Cold War in Europe and how to stop the arms race among the superpowers. The guiding motive for almost all actors concerned was the 'national interest'. There were of course other questions, like how to raise living standards in the Third World, how to improve the socio-economic and political position of women, how to improve human rights records, how to restrain nuclear proliferation, how to guarantee full employment, how to guarantee monetary stability or how to use 'commodity power'. Most of these questions still stand. New questions will arise. But, as in preceding decades, some will dominate others because they involve collective existential dimensions.

The most important issues cn the agenda are covered by the question that opened this chapter. Politics will be dominated by problems of (in)equity ('How can every human being on earth...'), (un)liveability ('...live a decent life...') and (un)sustainability ('...within a world order that is symbiotic with the rest of nature?').

These are the themes that will fill the vacuum left behind by the bankruptcy of the ideological division of the Cold War. There is a new dialectic in the making: the combined ideals of sustainability, equity and liveability versus the ideals of liveability and survival for the time being on a selfish scale – or, phrased differently, a comprehensive reaction versus a superficial one. Whether the traditional motive behind realpolitik, the national interest, will be on the one side or the other, will differ from government to government.

1. The author would like to thank the Pugwash 'Crossroads' study group and the Copenhagen Research Group of the Centre for Peace and Conflict Research for comments on earlier drafts of this chapter and Professor Robert Hinde for editing the English.

The argument of this chapter is that a change in traditional power politics is required to prevent societal dominance of political extremism in dealing with the main issues of the coming decades.

## KEY CONCEPTS AND A GLOBAL CHALLENGES AGENDA

Sustainability is a keyword for the long-term macroperspective of politics. The main question is: how can we create and maintain conditions of life that will last beyond the temporal perspective of the present generations? Sustainability is most directly concerned with humankind's relationship with its natural environment. The ideal is a symbiosis, a relationship of mutual advantage. Thanks to the Brundt-land Report, sustainability has secondarily become an adjective of development (WCED, 1987). This is to stress a shift from growth policies to policies of unfolding, that is the provision of space to develop one's own potential – development in a qualitative sense. (See also Hans-Peter Dürr's description of sustainability in Chapter 2.) In this meaning sustainable development is as urgent for the 'West' as it is for the 'East' and the 'South'; and as urgent for the élites and the middle classes as for the poor. It is a universal value. The concrete course may differ from place to place and from group to group, depending on the winds, the streams, the pirates ahead, the state of the ship and the skills of the crew. But the horizon towards which to steer is clear enough.

Liveability refers to the quality of life, both now and in the future. It is the key-word for the short term microperspective. How can each person live a decent life within the limits of his or her own perspective? The ideal is, first of all, a guarantee of basic needs: clean air and clean water, food providing necessary energy and essential nutrients, shelter and living space, a hospitable environment and contacts with others (see Chapter 1). Secondly, liveability requires the satisfaction of additional needs, ie emotional, intellectual, and spiritual needs, including culture, social norms, beliefs, values and principles. If sustainability refers to the course of the ship, liveability refers to the life on deck. Cultural diversity can and should be optimal, but within the limits posed by universal values. (To define these universal values is a dangerous affair, because they are, like all normative structures, discriminative and restrictive. Moreover, well-defined universal values can easily be misused for rhetorical purposes, to conceal policies of repression. Therefore a continuous debate about the validity of universal values is required. Only when dominant values are under constant pressure from deviating convictions can their degeneration be prevented. Obviously this makes freedom of speech and the press one of the universal values.) Preferably, the discrepancies between perceived additional needs and the constraints given by sustainability and equity will disappear from all cultures and belief systems.

Equity refers to the social scope of sustainability and liveability. Both at the macro- and the micro-level of social life, both in the long- and the short-term perspective, both at the basic needs and the cultural level of social life, people share the same rights and obligations as far as universal values are concerned. In practice, equity is strongly linked to human rights issues, social security issues, distributional problems, problems of ingroup/outgroup attitudes and economic dynamics. These key concepts merge in the leading question: how can every single person on earth live a decent life within a world order that is symbiotic with the rest of nature? Such a general question generally provokes unrealistic, Utopian answers; blue prints without scenarios. It is wrong, however, to conceive the answer in terms of some articulated paradise that has to be created. Paradise is beyond any present horizon, as it probably will be beyond any future one. But the question is important as such. It is a yardstick for the public struggle about the hierarchy of issues on the policy agenda. It replaces (or gives new meaning to) the value of the national interest as a decisive criterion for realpolitik.

Given this yardstick, it becomes possible to define the more concrete issues that will dominate politics. At a macro-level, six categories of global challenges can be identified.

- **Demographic problems**   These include population growth and consumption beyond the earth's carrying capacity; uncontrollable migrations; unmanageable urbanization; epidemics (including AIDS); rising criminality and social disorder; declining literacy rates.
- **Food problems**   These include poverty, famines, overconsumption and related diseases; loss of fertile soils and water resources; scarcities and uneven distribution.
- **Energy problems**   These include depletion of natural resources; local, regional and global forms of pollution; management disasters (in particular related to nuclear energy and oil transportation); scarcities and uneven distribution.
- **Disruption of ecosystems**   This includes deforestation; desertification and other forms of erosion; loss of biodiversity; acid rains; depletion of the ozone layer; the greenhouse effect.
- **Militarization of societies**   This includes growing human rights violations; increased spending on military and police forces by governments; increased spending on armaments and combat training by oppositional groups/organizations; growing investments in security measures by business firms and individuals; growth of armed criminality and crime syndicates; growing repression of pluralism and freedom of speech; a growing social legitimization of violence.
- **Economic problems**   These include social instability inherent in the growth imperative (leading to cyclical and hegemonical breakdowns); the social poverty of the monetary price and reward system; growing unemployment (in GNP terms), eg through increasing automatization of industries and services; continued legitimization of greed inherent in economic theory; monetary and trade instability; protectionism of unsustainable production modes.

Obviously, these points are interrelated in terms of cause and effect, overlapping, perhaps exaggerating, definitely not exhaustive. Many of them are defined as crucial by authoritative politico-scientific task forces, including the World Commission on Environment and Development (WCED), UN Environment Programme (UNEP), World Bank, Club of Rome, Stockholm International Peace Research Institute (SIPRI), Worldwatch Institute and Amnesty International. Others are developed throughout this book. As such the list is presentable enough for the point made here. It should be recognized that these issues in one form or another will dominate politics in the coming decades. They will do so, thanks to the disasters they imply, or they can do so, if common concern develops early enough.

Some of the disasters are already taking place, and the people involved cannot afford the luxury to read books like this to theorize about the best way out – for them it is sink or swim. In many countries, however, at least the élites and at best the bulk of all the inhabitants are in a position to make up their minds.

## COMPREHENSIVE VERSUS SUPERFICIAL REACTIONS

Scenarios for a sustainable, liveable and equitable world only make sense when they are embedded in realpolitik. No one will oppose these interests in general, but when they boil down to concrete stakes, conflict starts. There are prices to be paid, investments to be made – and these are not automatically distributed equally. To compensate costs equitably is not easy, as the present world order with all its structural economic imbalances does not offer a fair point of reference. But pay-offs will be necessary to prevent social disturbances beyond the point of social elasticity in any given society. One needs to identify, as has been argued by Homer-Dixon (1991), the thresholds beyond which societies cannot respond to the pressures put on them.

The recent experience with the end of the Cold War underlines this. The obvious improvements at the global level took their toll at local levels, especially in the East. Communist rule left a political vacuum and the West was not prepared, able or willing to fill it. Populations not educated in democratic practices, unfamiliar with basic economic skills and faced with massive unemployment, scarcities and, above all, existential uncertainties about their immediate future, returned to the sacred values of the historic periods when they were 'independent' or at least 'glorious'. Moreover, in times of crisis the family – 'your own blood' – comes first. The size of the family is determined by nationalistic myth. And, because it is a myth, people tend to fight rather than to argue about it.

These developments can be stereotyped as 'natural' reactions. They refer to the behavioural and cognitive patterns that result from unprepared, improvised answers to crises with existential dimensions. As a policy, they are superficial, but tempting because they appeal to the public instinct. Reactions similar to those in Central Europe, Eastern Europe and Western Asia are to be expected world-wide when the scenarios inherent in the global challenges agenda are spelled out. Moreover, they feed upon one another. Now already, in parts of Africa, India, and the megalopolises of North and Latin America, examples can be found of the chaos and anarchy inherent in such circumstances.

The dynamics of the superficial reactions to existential crises point towards self-help at the regional, national, neighbourhood, family and individual levels – depending on the specific mixtures of social identities and perceived interests. Superficial reactions are directed by short-term interests and imply a return to primitive, survival of the fittest tactics. The rich build fences around their houses, the middle classes arm themselves and form or hire militias, and the not too poor organize themselves in plundering gangs, sometimes headed by so-called 'war-lords'. (The very poor probably do nothing in political terms – they simply continue to suffer.) Extremism, whether left wing, right wing or religious, will flourish.

Superficial reactions tend to be regressive and are culturally embedded. But they do not refer to the finest and most creative aspects of culture. They follow a romantic fall-back principle: let's return to the safe world of before; let's restore the good old days. Additionally, scapegoats and enemy images will return. Angus MacKay (quoted in Homer-Dixon, 1991: 81–2) noted in a study about climate change and civil violence in the kingdom of Castile (in the fifteenth century) that the anger over food scarcity led to pogroms against Jews: their unchristian life-style was held responsible for the problems. Superficial reactions reduce complex issues to such monocausal dimensions that exclude or play down in-group responsibility and that tend towards extremist solutions, because of the predictable failure to deal with complex causes.

Somalia, former Yugoslavia and some 40 other conflict-ridden regions and cities show the way.[2] The result is political chaos, a negative spiral of destruction and the deterioration of societies. Less extreme, but nevertheless the same, tendencies are evident throughout Western Europe: fences, burglar alarms, security services in shopping centres and business firms, robbing gangs, crime syndicates, jungle capitalism, xenophobia, extremist political parties or individual politicians – it is all there, slowly gaining public legitimacy and waiting for a profitable social climate to escalate. To some extent these tendencies are reactions to statistically proved increased insecurity, but to a larger extent they reflect disproportionate perceptions of insecurity and carry the risk of turning themselves into self-fulfilling prophecies.

Whether the superficial reactions can be avoided depends on the ability to turn the tides, and on the resilience of civilization. In the absence of mature alternatives many people will sympathize with the logic of superficial reactions – even though their success may be short term, people may argue that they at least offer an option.

Political science ought to contribute to the attempts to temper these dynamics. This must not merely involve sketching out the problems that lie ahead or the violence societies have to prepare for and the fortresses they can build. People need no research and hardly any education to develop 'policies' like ethnic

---

2. In 1991/2 more than 1000 victims of several forms of political violence were registered in each of the following countries: Burundi, Ethiopia, Liberia, Mali, Mozambique, Sudan, Somalia, Uganda, South Africa, Afghanistan, Bangladesh, India (Kashmir), India (Punjab), Pakistan (Sindh), Azerbaijan, Armenia, Bosnia-Herzegovina, Croatia, Moldova (Dnestria), Uzbekistan/Kirgistan, Russia, Serbia, Turkmenistan, Turkey, Colombia, El Salvador, Guatemala, Haiti, Peru, Iran, Iraq (Gulf War), Iraq (Kurds), Iraq (Shiites), Kuwait (Gulf War), China (in particular Xinjiang Uygur), Indonesia (Atjeh), Myanmar (Karen, Mon) and Sri Lanka, See Jongman (1992: 34–7). Less well documented is the amount of yearly inner-city violence. The *International Herald Tribune* (17 August 1993) mentions eg 1995 killings in New York City in 1992.

cleansing, nuclear blackmail, terrorism, repression in the name of law and order, occupation of regions with scarce resources, extreme nationalism or religious fundamentalism. Neither is it enough to point out the reciprocal, often middle term, negative effects of such survival strategies. It is illusory as well to think that state power can control all this with its monopoly on the legitimate use of violence. At best police and military forces can temper the fever. But this has only a temporary effect as it cannot deal with the causes. It may even aggravate them. Military expenditures are already part of the problem (see Chapter 9), while, as Pirages (1991: 132) correctly remarks, 'modern military equipment from tanks to aircraft is not designed with energy conservation in mind'. (See also Westing, 1990, on the environmental effects of warfare in industrialized regions.) Moreover, military action, even if it is intended as peace-keeping or peace-enforcing, in the longer run may corrupt politics. Repressive state behaviour is a superficial type of reaction.

There is a need to develop comprehensive policies to deal with the crises ahead. These involve careful planning, the ability to negotiate and to cooperate, and the ability to combine local, regional and global interests in well-balanced scenarios. In this respect political science may have something to offer. There are enough clues and well-developed insights in the existing literature to build on. Some of these clues are elaborated upon here.

## MEANS OF POWER ARE CULTURE AND SITUATION BOUND

The term power politics refers to the view that politics is a struggle for power (implying that political power is defined as the relative advantage of one or more actors over others in a given period of time). Whatever actors want to achieve once they have the power, they first have to get it. In this struggle virtually all means are allowed, as long as they seem to serve the final objectives. This lesson can be learnt from a vast amount of literature, ranging from the work of Thucydides, Machiavelli and Marx to Morgenthau and Kissinger.[3] Though this power thesis is certainly not true for all politics (the policies of people like Gandhi, Martin Luther King and others are fundamentally different), it can be argued that those who recklessly strive for power have an advantage over those who restrict themselves on moral grounds. On the average, realpolitik will dominate.

Some may renounce this, but that will not be of much help in the practical struggle for sustainability, equity and liveability. To achieve these values the Bismarcks and Machiavellian princes must be on our side. As a minimum they must realize the practical political advantage of supporting these ideals. Sometimes this may result in monstrous alliances, but in general the strategy aims at altering the contents of the struggle for power. This is not only feasible, it is already happening.

---

3. Power politics is generally associated with the Realist school of IR-theory. To the extent that the paradigm debate is at stake here, the present argument fits in the tradition of E H Carr (1939) more than that of Hans J Morgenthau (1948) or Kenneth N Waltz (1979).

Politics may be a struggle for power, but it is wrong and mischievous to think that people throughout history have always struggled for similar things and with similar means. Even if we accept the restricted definition of power as 'the ability to make actors do what they otherwise would not have done', it should be remembered that this inherent enforcement did not involve identical instruments throughout history. Simply compare the power of Julius Caesar with that of Franklin D Roosevelt: Caesar would never have made the history books if he had been confined to a wheelchair. In the Roman age, horse-riding and physical strength were important qualities for rulers. In the twentieth century they are still of value for the Olympic games, but virtually meaningless for political power. Managerial skills and media performance have become crucial.

In the academic debate similar developments can be traced. Neo-Realists, like Robert Gilpin, argue that political power is based on military, economic and technological capabilities simultaneously. As a result the market is as important in their work as the state (Gilpin, 1987). The next step would be to give the environment a similar status in political theory. The ability of a state to base its military, economic and technological capabilities on environmentally sustainable structures has become vital to its power – even though this is hardly recognized in practice. Additionally, it could be discovered that long-lasting, stable international organizations in the realm of sustainability, equity and liveability will serve the national interest. Again this is not illusory. Similar developments took place in the military, the economic and the technological realms; they were accompanied and facilitated by the development of international law. The Public Unions of the nineteenth century, like the International Postal Union, were an answer to technical inconveniences of the state system. The League of Nations, the United Nations, the North Atlantic Treaty Organization (NATO), the Warsaw Treaty Organization, the Association of South-East Asian Nations (ASEAN), the Organization of African Unity (OAU) and the Organization of American States (OAS) were answers to the politico-military inconveniences of the state-system. The Bretton Woods system, OPEC and the OECD were answers to the economic inconveniences of the state system. Present networks of intergovernmental organizations (IGOs), non-governmental organizations (NGOs) and grassroot movements in the realm of environment and development form a similar attempt to deal with the inconveniences of the state system in these sectors. Just like organizations such as NATO, OECD or the UN system, they will gain momentum and political impact (ie power) the more the inconveniences of the state system grow apparent.

It may take some inconvenient lessons, but governments have the ability to learn and adapt. From 1918–38, the alleged idealist Sir Norman Angell (winner of the Nobel Peace Prize in 1933) urged the democracies of the world to form a NATO-like alliance to stop the emergence of totalitarian regimes in Germany, Japan, Italy and Spain (De Wilde, 1991: 75–83). It took a second world war to make them see the wisdom of such an alliance and to build firm international cooperation – which implied a comprehensive demilitarization of their diplomatic relations. Similarly, the Great Depression of 1929 made governments understand the necessity of international economic cooperation, which materialized in the Bretton Woods system. NATO, IMF, World Bank, GATT – they have become concrete powerful political realities. They are in the power game and their policies or lack of policies matter. They make a bigger difference than many of the sovereign national states.

These developments were related to military and economic security. Similar developments may take place in the realm of sustainability, equity and liveability.

Means of power are culture and situation bound; they change. The nature of power may have an absolute value at a high level of abstraction (in philosophy), but as soon as one descends to lower levels it becomes variable. In practice, power coincides with the possession or the presence of the concrete means necessary to dominate within a specific culture or to handle a specific situation. Phrased differently, power is a derivative of specific human skills, of resources that are instrumental to these skills and of their cultural appreciation by a given population. Even an apologist of traditional power politics, like Hans J Morgenthau, starts from this premise.

> *The kind of interest determining political action in a particular period of history depends upon the political and cultural context. ... The same observations apply to the concept of power. Its content and the manner of its use are determined by the political and cultural environment.*
>
> Morgenthau, 1973: 9

## CHERNOBYL AND *SILENT SPRING* TYPE LESSONS

The more the ideals of sustainability, equity and liveability are valued positively in society (ie the more they dominate culture), the more they will be at stake in the struggle for power. The ability to serve these ideals will then become a new criterion in politics.

This is a development similar to the historical development from medieval feudal power structures to modern economic power structures – where the sword has largely been replaced by currency. It is similar to the development from dictatorship and authoritarian rule (where they have political power who can effectively exploit their subjects) to modern welfare communities and pluralistic rule (where they have political power who can serve their subjects best).

There are two main ways along which sustainability, equity and liveability can grow dominant in the struggle for power. One track is formed by the 'Chernobyl type lessons' or shock therapy (for those who survive the shock). Public debate about nuclear energy was strongly affected by the disaster that took place in Chernobyl (1986) and the safety of nuclear power stations, especially those in Eastern Europe, has become a concern for the whole of Europe. The authority (political power) of watchdogs like the International Atomic Energy Agency (IAEA) profits from this.

The second track is formed by the '*Silent Spring* type lessons' or the provision of information: public debate is slowly being transformed by the reports drawn up by the Club of Rome, Brandt Commission, Brundtland Commission, Worldwatch Institute, UNEP etcetera. (The book *Silent Spring* by Rachel Carson (Fawcett, 1962), was among the first publications that to draw attention to the environmental crises ahead.)

In between are mixed forms. First of all there are the Greenpeace type initiatives, where public attention is drawn to specific issues by sensational and often dramatic acts. Secondly, one can think of intergovernmental initiatives, like UNCED in Rio de Janeiro (June 1992), where public attention was drawn to the interplay of political forces for and against sustainability. Events like these, if they are not too frequent, stimulate people to make up their minds and rethink previous political attitudes.

Provision of information is an important aspect of the new power politics. It enhances and exploits the power of sound reasoning and scientific knowledge (Rosenau, 1990, Ch 13: 'Powerful People: The Expansion of Analytic Skills': 333–87). This makes freedom of speech and press an essential element of the new power politics. It is, for instance, hardly imaginable that the pollution and environmental disasters in the former Soviet empire could have taken on such enormous proportions if people had not remained silent about them.

## POWER BY FORCE VERSUS POWER BY PARTICIPATION

It is important to notice that the political climatic change is already on the right track. There are *Silent Spring*, Greenpeace and UNCED type lessons. Less fortunately, there are also Chernobyls. But even so, the process might be too slow or too uneven. It is quite idealistic indeed to expect that a transition to a sustainable, liveable and equitable world can be based on global consensus and understanding. Such a transition involves conflict and a certain measure of enforcement will be necessary.

Here, however, lies a dangerous trap. Perhaps history will judge the many present reports, theories and studies in the same way that it has judged the 'Utopians' of the nineteenth century. These Utopians strove for a socialist world, and allowed for more and more enforcement strategies in their theories, culminating in a plea for global revolution (which didn't work either). But if ideals of sustainability, liveability and equity are not going to dominate culture, policies to pursue them will have to be accompanied by enforcement or one has to accept failure. Moreover, even if cultural dominance is achieved some enforcement remains unavoidable, as is the case with all collective measures. Obviously, there lurks a fall-back to superficial reactions.

Apart from the ideological trap of radicalization through political failure, and apart from ethical arguments, enforcement costs should be kept low for two pragmatic reasons. First, enforcement raises the social-economic price of sustainability. The higher this price, the less remains of the other ideals: liveability and equity. There is a real danger that rhetorics of sustainability will be misused to support narrow-minded self-help types of policy (a superficial reaction in disguise). This shows why it is essential to deal with sustainability, equity and liveability comprehensively.

Secondly, enforcement has its social limits. It does not work under all circumstances. A striking example of failing enforcement is the prohibition of the production, trade and use of drugs. It doesn't work. Supply and demand and the profits are too high. Probably, a certain measure of tolerance (as some aspects of the Dutch policy on soft drugs show) might be more effective than suppression: covert activities are more difficult to control than overt ones; underground activities involve more criminals and draw more people into crime. Indeed, gangster dominance in the US in the 1930s coincided with the prohibition of alcohol; and among the first failures of Gorbachev's perestroika was the enforcement of a prohibition of alcohol in the Soviet Union. Similarly, it might be impossible to force people into effective birth control or to force them to pay huge energy prices (which would limit their mobility). They must see the need for the new standards.

To minimize the risks of radicalization, the main resources and instruments for sustainable power politics have to be of a constructional nature (as opposed to enforcement which is of a confrontational nature).

There is a vast literature on the nature of power. But despite the different labels used some aspects are common to most of them. Power is based on different pillars. Force is one of them. Policies based on it are coercive, destructive, exclusionist, aggressive, brutal, discriminative, in short confrontational. Ruling is based on political violence towards active actors and submissive obedience by passive actors.

At the other end of the spectre stands participation. This pillar of power is characterized by constructional interdependence (De Wilde, 1991, Ch 1). Two can do more than one. The policies based on it are not without conflict but on balance they are cooperative, integrative and functionalistic. Ruling is based on political participation by active actors and willing compliance by passive actors.

The more a government pursues policies which the public understands to be in its interests, the less a government has to invest in sanctions and threats, control and inspections, policing and military enforcement.

## A REAPPRAISAL OF GEOPOLITICS

'Environmental trends are beginning to shape both economic *and* political trends' (MacNeill, Winsemius and Yakushiji, 1991: 52). This has also been the case before.

Adolf Hitler was influenced by the theories of Friedrich Ratzel (1844–1904), Rudolf Kjellén (1864–1922) and especially Karl Haushofer (1869–1946). Kjellén coined the term geopolitics and saw the state as an living organism; Ratzel's anthropogeographie led to the idea of superior civilizations; Haushofer developed the terms lebensraum and 'dynamic frontiers'. Together with the application of social Darwinism to nation states this formed the legitimization of Nazism. Geopolitics meant that states were seen as animals caught in a relentless struggle for survival (Dougherty and Pfaltzgraff, 1990: 65). It is important to realize that 'geopolitics is a creature of militarism and a tool of war' (Whittlesey, 1971: 388). War, according to Haushofer, was the natural state of affairs in international relations. As a consequence, he deemed national economic autarchy as essential (Van der Pijl, 1992: 105–12). A revival of this logic and war spirit can be expected.

These types of theories loom in all state-centric and nationalist attempts to deal with unsustainability, inequity and impoverished living conditions. In particular public anxieties in Western Europe about migrations call into remembrance Hitler's view on what he called the 'Vernegerung' of France (*Mein Kampf,* Ch 14). A revival of traditional geopolitics can easily legitimize such superficial, culturally embedded points of view.

The attractiveness of traditional geopolitics lies in the severe environmental, geographic and demographic characteristics of the problems we face. Pollution, migration, urbanization, global warming, scarce resources, energy supply, ozone depletion etc have clear geopolitical dimensions: they affect the geographical base of a society, and thereby its functioning and prospects for further development. Combined with the attractiveness of nationalist simplification, skinhead logic ('Ausländer raus') and Serbo-Croatian logic ('ethnic cleansing') will become endemic. Also, at the interstate level traditional geopolitical motives are present. The defence of Western oil interests in the Middle East is partly an expression of geopolitical concerns. Writers on environmental security have emphasized the risk of major conflicts over clean water, environmental refugees, costs of pollution etc (see WCED, 1987; Brown, 1989; Brock, 1991; Homer-Dixon, 1991; Thomas, 1992; Homer-Dixon et al, 1993).

The chance that global challenges will automatically create a 'brotherhood of men' or be taken as a signal for the 'people of the world to unite' is rather Utopian. In a historical perspective, imperialism and isolationism (conquer and control what you need and forget about the rest) have appeared to be frequent answers to forms of global interdependence (De Wilde, 1991: 217–19). Though a process of social learning is on its way, there is no reason to assume that, in face of the collective problems ahead, collectively profitable solutions will be preferred or even sought.

On the other hand, there is no use denying the political significance of spatial factors. Geopolitical arguments should not be left to the new Hitlers. Instead, the spatial factors should be highlighted in their proper context. (Harold and Margaret Sprout, 1968 and 1971, were among the first to develop more sophisticated insights into humankind's political place within the ecology.) The crucial alteration to traditional geopolitics is due to the impossibility of applying its logic successfully to the international state system because of the present levels of global interdependence.

During the twentieth century a world society is emerging as a consequence of two processes: first, 'the conquest of distance', the physical unification of different societies into one whole – this is the structural dimension of global interdependence; and secondly, the psychological awareness of this unification – the cognitive dimension of global interdependence (De Wilde, 1991: Ch 2). The structural dimension can be related to geopolitics. Its first successes date back as far as the Persian and Mongolian empires, about 2000 BC (Buzan and Little, *An Introduction to the International System: Theory Meets History,* forthcoming). It became a dominant aspect of European affairs, from the eleventh century onwards with the Crusades and the colonization of the Baltics. It globalized in the sixteenth century, when 'the European peoples began to expand their trade, their ideas and their methods of organization over the rest of the world' (Muir, 1971: 2). It accelerated in the nineteenth century and continued in the twentieth century, though less a strictly Euro-centric affair. The results have been tremendous. Here is an illustration: in 1790 a traveller from Boston needed five days to get to Philadelphia; in 1938 he or she could reach London, Paris or Rio de Janeiro in that time (Staley, 1939: 11); in 1993 he or she can visit any place on earth, or may even stay at home to telephone, fax or e-mail world-wide, and watch the world news in between. These physical changes have political consequences, but these are not perceived automatically.

One of the main political problems during the twentieth century has been getting accustomed to the new structural conditions. Nazism and traditional geopolitics fit in to this learning process. The awareness of global interdependence in general leads to three possible types of reaction. The most realistic one is to understand it, to accept it and to deal with it. The foundation of the League of Nations after the disaster of the First World War, and the foundation of the United Nations with its specialized agencies after the disaster of the Second World War, belong to this scheme.

This realist reaction has to compete, however, with two ultimately inadequate yet easy alternatives. The first is isolationism. In general this is a Utopian attempt to withdraw from global interdependence by seeking autarchy and absolute sovereignty. Only if one is forced or willing to accept very primitive living standards (think of Albania and tribes from the Amazon river basin) is this option viable in economic terms. But even then, in political terms, isolationism remains an illusion. It is illustrative that in February 1989 the Kayapó from the basin of the Amazon river, in order to save their land, demonstrated at a meeting of the World Bank to protest against international financing of the plans of 'their' Brazilian government to build dams in the Amazon river with the aim of improving the Brazilian economic infrastructure in order to pay its huge debts to bankers in America, whose bankruptcy could in turn escalate into a global monetary crisis. It is illustrative, too, that the Albanians have been at the brink of war since 1991 despite their isolationist behaviour. For their peace and quiet they are more dependent on (in)action by the rest of the world than ever before.

A similar danger of the isolationist track is illustrated by the interbellum experience with North American policy. Eventually, Canada and the US were forced into the war; political isolationism failed.

The other extreme is imperialism. Like isolationism, imperialism is an attempt to escape from the complexity of world politics, this time not by neglecting other actors, but by denying their right to exist. Complexity is killed. This is what Germany and Japan tried during the Second World War. There was only partial understanding of structural interdependence. Mostly the dependence was seen – in Japan's case for instance the complete dependence on foreign resources. The reciprocity was not recognized, nor the complexity. Rosecrance (1981: 700) caught the illusion of imperialism clearly, when he wrote: 'So many sources of dependency exist, even for the most independent countries, that the agenda of necessary conquests becomes implausibly long.' This is the losing track of traditional geopolitics and 'Blut und Boden' theories.

A reappraisal of geopolitical thinking therefore leads to the conclusion that it must start from an awareness and acceptance of structural global interdependence. Nationalist extremism is at odds with geopolitical logic, whereas the management of global interdependence is in tune with it. Realizing the global dimension of national problems is a crucial element of the new power politics. This means that, for example, the solution for uncontrolled massive migrations between and within countries (at present by far a greater problem in Africa and parts of India than in Europe) cannot be found in isolationist measures like lower immigration quotas, complicated criteria for achieving a refugee status or the actual fencing of borders to reduce illegal crossing as between Texas and Mexico. Such measures try to deny or ignore the causes of the migrations, they may temper the immediate fever but will solve nothing and in the longer run often fuel violent conflicts.

## THE POWER OF INTERNATIONAL ORGANIZATION

A concrete obstacle to overcome is the problem that policy making is concentrated in the hands of national governments. The mandates of governments are not based on global interests. They are based on élite interests, electoral interests or a combination of both. Global interests are an additional dimension, a luxury, unless acute crises have concrete domestic impacts. One way of getting around this problem is to stress the self-interest of treating the outside world as part of 'us'. This means stretching the national interest. But this plea for globalization of domestic politics has to compete with nationalistic reactions, ie the tendency to fall back on parochialism in the face of problems too complex to handle by well-intentioned governments. Large countries will probably suffer more from this than smaller ones, because the latter are traditionally forced to accept a mixture of domestic and foreign affairs.

Despite a century of global interdependence, foreign policy and domestic policy are still separate worlds in the people's minds. It is illustrative that President Clinton seemed to revolutionize traditional politics when he tried to convince the American people that development aid to the Russian Federation served the national interest (*International Herald Tribune*, 2 April 1993).[4] But the logic is simple: neo-Stalinism or chaos in Russia means a threat to Clinton's domestic reform policies (to be financed through cuts on military spending). If this is true for Russia, it is true for other regions, countries or continents. It implies a plea for Marshall Plans all around the world (preferably on the 'people to people' basis Clinton promised). But examples like these are scarce, and also in the Clinton-case rhetoric is partly mischievous: the American grain exporters get most of the US$1.6 billion Clinton promised to Yeltsin (*International Herald Tribune*, April 5, 1993).

---

4. A similar logic, but less overt, was applied by the Kennedy administration, when it decided, after the Cuban missile crisis, to provide the Soviets with the high tech knowledge of the PAL system. (This is an electronic system to seal off nuclear weapon launching systems, thus preventing them from being launched through a technical failure or without the political approval of those who hold the 'keys'.) This 'development' aid clearly served the 'national interest' as it prevented a nuclear launch by accident.

In general it is because of their national mandates that governments seldom play the first violin in relation to global challenges and why an appeal to global interests often tends to be mere rhetoric. The problems in making national governments champions of the 'green movement' are twofold. First of all, the issues are too complex to handle at domestic levels, which implies that effective action involves loss of sovereignty, while success depends on the loyal behaviour of other governments. The more international cooperation is needed, the more the 'power to say no' (MacNeill et al, 1991: 61) increases. Moreover, without an immediate crisis, the costs of pre-emptive crisis management are the only aspect that counts. (Unfortunately, pre-emptive investment in sustainability, equity and liveability lacks the historical tradition of pre-emptive military spending. A lot may be learned from the lobby techniques in these circles.)

In the second place, the cognitive maps of politicians and governmental bureaucrats are, at least in the West, dominated by state-centric variants of power politics. Homer-Dixon (1991: 84–5) summarized the problem nicely.

> *Realism focuses on states as rational maximizers of power in an anarchic system; state behaviour is mainly a function of the structure of power relations in the system.... Realism thus encourages scholars to deemphasize transboundary environmental problems, because such problems ... do not have any easily conceptualized impact on the structure of economic and military power relations between states. Realism induces scholars to squeeze environmental issues into a structure of concepts including "state", "sovereignty", "territory", "national interest" and "balance of power". The fit is bad, which may lead theorists to ignore, distort, and misunderstand important aspects of global environmental problems.*

As a result, politics of sustainability, equity and liveability are dominated by non-governmental movements and international organizations. This is obvious, for instance, in the realm of environmental politics (for documentation see Thomas, 1992) and also in the realm of human rights. The new power politics do depend partly on governments but mostly on international organization. Where possible, national or local governments can be, and should be, the vehicles for concrete policies, but one need not wait for their initiatives and can work behind their backs if necessary (though in most cases this will imply a measure of tolerance and willing compliance by local officials and police). Precisely because IGOs, NGOs and social movements are issue-specific functionalistic actors they are less suspicious than governments who, because of their mandates, first and foremost have to serve the short-term 'national interest', and who, because of their historical roots, are often involved in mutual competition and zero-sum games. Especially in the North–South context, NGOs and IGOs are important bridges. Finally, it should be realized that the political role of international organization has been growing anyhow, both in quantitative and qualitative terms, throughout the twentieth century.

The increasing importance of international organization does not necessarily imply a decline of state power. Up to now, international organization has had a double effect on the state: it has improved the functioning of the state system but it has also undermined the functioning of the state system. The improvement comes about because it offers an answer to increased systemic interdependence in economic, military, ecological and social affairs. The undermining comes about because it makes the juridical foundation of the state system – national sovereignty – arbitrary and even more artificial than it was from the very beginning in 1648. It is especially the rule that governments are not allowed to intervene in one another's domestic affairs that is in crisis.

But governments have shown great flexibility in adjusting to changing circumstances. Perhaps they will find a balance in the future as well (compare the century-long survival of the European aristocracy after its almost monopolistic political dominance disappeared). There is no reason to assume that the state system will disappear. Moreover, international organizations are not perfect either: many of them are hampered by malfunctioning, oversized bureaucracies and complicated procedures. But nevertheless, for the time being, the development of international organization offers the best trump for the pursuit of sustainability, equity and liveability.

## THE GLOBE ON A SURVEY MAP SCALE

International organizations may also prove crucial in solving the dilemma of how to deal with the micro/macro dimension of world politics (Rosenau, 1990; De Wilde, 1993). In contemporary politics sometimes almost the whole world population (5.5 billion people) is at stake – for instance in case of imminent escalations of wars, ecological and epidemical disasters, economic crises or the effects of large-scale migrations. But, simultaneously, contemporary politics is about individuals: the chances for education and self-development, food security, social security, health care, freedom of speech, equal rights, in short the quality of life (or liveability). Politics in the twentieth century is characterized by these two extremes: the global and the individual scale. It is unclear how these scales relate. Metaphorically speaking, political theory has no satellites in orbit that can zoom in on any required square metre, thus smoothly relating the scale of a survey map to that of the globe and vice versa. In the absence of such a perspective many policy proposals will fall short on one or the other end of the scale. Scenarios for global solutions, with appeals for world government or a world federation as the extreme, tend to play down the value of the particular communitarian circumstances. Scenarios for a local approach tend to overestimate the spillover effects to regional and global levels, and to underestimate the structural effects of the larger social, political and economic context.

How, for instance, can an individual deal with the problems that are caused by the dynamics of collective behaviour? The individual responsibility for this is small, though still an aspect. Marching soldiers can cause bridges to collapse, but none of the soldiers can be held individually responsible; it is the sum which counts (and as long as the nature of bridges is unknown, even the collective cannot be blamed). The new power politics in this context is about how to get enough people out of step. But how many is enough is not known.

To get people out of step implies partly a change in the command structure and partly a change in the individual soldier, who for his or her own reasons marches in step. The optimal strategic mixture of these top-down and bottom-up approaches is unknown. The present process is one of trial and error in which the nation state system and the networks of non-governmental organizations seem to serve as competing theatres for political action. This spectre was for instance manifest at UNCED in Rio de Janeiro (1992). Here it was visible how the micro- and macro-worlds try to interact, compete and flirt with one another. Rio was organized by an IGO, the United Nations, for the actors of the nation state system – a top-down approach. More than a hundred heads of governments participated, 'the largest gathering of national political leaders in history', according to Lester Brown (1993: 3). Even great powers (especially the US), who considered Agenda 21 exaggerated, felt themselves compelled to participate to prevent loss of face in the eyes of the NGO and grassroots worlds, who advocated the bottom-up approach of 'think globally, act locally' during their own parallel meetings. An important aspect in this interaction is that Rio was a media event (mostly run by non-governmental actors). Among the 35,000 people in Rio de Janeiro, there were about 9000 journalists (Brown, 1993: 3). The summit had a global audience (of groups and individuals) and modern politics is very sensitive to that. In the background business interests (mostly defended by non-governmental actors as well) were evidently present. In its results UNCED may have been a disappointment – it took a year just to create the UN Commission on Sustainable Development, charged with the implementation of Agenda 21; the promised technology transfer to the Third World has not yet started; and the good intentions to release more funds has been drowned in the swamps of national deficits (*de Volkskrant*, 5 June 1993). But the 'circus and chaos' in Rio (as a spokesperson of the American administration called it) represents much of the contemporary world order.

## COMPENSATION PROGRAMMES

The UNCED type lessons show that it is important to know who has to pay a price for policies that serve collective interests. In this respect, also, the micro- and macro-dimensions of world politics have to be linked. At a practical level this could lead to debates about the possibilities to create safety nets for the losers.

Compensation for the direct losers of collective political improvements would take the wind out of the sails of oppositional groups who may subscribe to the goals of sustainability and equity in general, but who fear for their own liveability in practice. It also divides the political debate into more accurate stakes: first, the contents of policy proposals; secondly, the nature of compensation. At present, the first debate is confused by arguments that belong to the second. As a result sustainability and equity are frequently dealt with as so-called add-on policies (MacNeill et al, 1991).

Safety nets are also needed to preserve the social equilibrium – both nationally and internationally. The losers may include Brazilian or Indonesian farmers who cut down the rainforest, American or Arabian industrialists who drill for oil or transport it, Russian nuclear scientists, Japanese whalers, Dutch fishermen and farmers, or whoever's work is based on unsustainable production. If they are put out of work by a measure for the common good, they need to fall back on a social security system, if not on moral grounds, then on pragmatic ones. Compensation programmes, providing social security, are an aspect of the new power politics.

## CONCLUSION

Compensation programmes and schemes for social learning are but two small examples of the new power politics at a practical level. Others, mentioned in this book, are plans for an eco-trust and a personal eco-budget, empowerment of local people, recognition of indigenous knowledge, adoption of 'organic' or 'low-input' farming methods, reduction in consumption of animal products, priority to subsistence farming, restoration of community rights over the local commons, deinstitutionalization of the economic growth myth, the release of resources by disarmament, plans for district health systems, reform of official development assistance and the provision of information and education.

Together they may fit a pragmatic but normative political programme that offers a realistic alternative for political extremism in response to crises; a comprehensive alternative for superficial reactions. Political science can contribute to the coherence of such a programme. By understanding that power is a culture and situation bound property, by understanding the importance of constructional interdependence, by recognizing the globalization of geopolitics, by counting on the growing role of IGOs and NGOs, by recognizing the discrepancy between global and individual dimensions, it may become possible to deal comprehensively with the population, food, energy and economic problems that will dominate politics for the coming decades, and to help stop the disruption of ecosystems and the militarization of societies.

---

## REFERENCES

Brock, Lothar, 'Peace through Parks. The Environment on the Peace Research Agenda', *Journal of Peace Research*, vol 28, no 4, 1991, pp 407–22.

Brown, Lester R, 'A New Era Unfolds', in L R Brown, et al, (eds), *State of the World, 1993*, London: Earthscan Publications, 1993, pp 3–21.

Brown, Neville, 'Climate, Ecology and International Security', *Survival*, vol 31, no 6, 1989, pp 519–32.

Carr, E H, *The Twenty Years' Crisis, 1919-1939. An Introduction to the Study of International Relations*, London: Macmillan, (1939) 1940[2].

Dougherty, James E and Robert L Pfaltzgraff, Jun, *Contending Theories of International Relations. A Comprehensive Survey*, New York: HarperCollins, 1990[3].

Gilpin, Robert, *The Political Economy of International Relations*, Princeton: Princeton University Press, 1987.

Homer-Dixon, T, 'On the Threshold: Environmental Changes and Acute Conflict', *International Security*, vol 16, no 2, 1991, pp 76–116.

Homer-Dixon, T, J H Boutwell and G Rathjens, 'Environmental Change and Violent Conflict', *Scientific American*, February 1993, pp 16-23.

Jongman, Berto, 'Oorlog en politiek geweld' in Bert Bomert and Herman de Lange (eds), *Jaarboek Vrede en Veiligheid 1992*, Nijmegen: SVV Cahier 56, pp 27–39.

MacNeill, Jim, Pieter Winsemius and Taizo Yakushiji, *Beyond Interdependence. The Meshing of the World's Economy and the Earth's Ecology* (A trilateral commission book), New York/Oxford: Oxford University Press, 1991.

Morgenthau, Hans J, *Politics Among Nations. The Struggle for Power and Peace*, New York: Alfred Knopf, (1948) 1973[5].

Muir, Ramsay, *The Interdependent World and its Problems*, Washington/London: Kennikat Press, (1933) 1971.

Pijl, Kees van der, *Wereldorde en machtspolitiek. Visies op de internationale betrekkingen van Dante tot Fukuyama*, Amsterdam: Het Spinhuis, 1992.

Pirages, Dennis Clark, 'The Greening of Peace Research', *Journal of Peace Research*, vol 28, no 2, 1991, pp 129–33.

Rosecrance, Richard, 'International Theory Revisited', *International Organization*, vol 35, no 4, 1981, pp 691–713.

Rosenau, J N, *Turbulence in World Politics. A Theory of Change and Continuity*, New York/London etc: Harvester Wheatsheaf, 1990.

Sprout, Harold and Margaret Sprout, *An Ecological Paradigm for the Study of International Politics*, Princeton, Center for International Studies, 1968.

Sprout, Harold and Margaret Sprout, *Toward a Politics of the Planet Earth*, New York: Van Nostrand, 1971.

Staley, Eugene, *World Economy in Transition: Technology vs Politics, Laissez Faire vs Planning, Power vs Welfare*, New York: Council on Foreign Relations, 1939.

Thomas, Caroline, *The Environment in International Relations*, London: The Royal Institute of International Affairs, 1992.

Waltz, K N, *Theory of International Relations*, Reading, MA: Addison-Wesley, 1979.

WCED (World Commission on Environment and Development), *Our Common Future*, Oxford: Oxford University Press, 1987.

Westing, Arthur H (ed), *Environmental Hazards of War. Releasing Dangerous Forces in an Industrialized World*, London: Sage (PRIO, UNEP), 1990.

Whittlesey, Derwent, 'Haushofer: The Geopoliticians' in Edward Mead Earle (ed), *Makers of Modern Strategy. Military Thought from Machiavelli to Hitler*, Princeton: Princeton University Press, 1971 (1943), pp 388–411.

Wilde, J H de, *Saved from Oblivion: Interdependence Theory in the First Half of the 20th Century. A Study on the Causality between War and Complex Interdependence*, Aldershot: Dartmouth, 1991.

Wilde, J H de, 'Peace Research After the Cold War. An Essay on the Micro/Macro-Dimension of Security Issues' in Judit Balázs and Håkan Wiberg (eds), *Peace Research for the 1990s*, Budapest: Hungarian Academy of Sciences, 1993 (forthcoming), pp 41–50.

*Chapter Eleven*

# Can Societies Be Changed Quickly Enough?

*Robert A Hinde*

---

It seems likely that, if things go on as at present, many of the raw materials on which societies depend will be consumed in at most a few generations and our planet will become irreversibly polluted with the by-products of exploitation. Furthermore, the gap between rich and poor will widen. There are likely to be cultural clashes as nations jockey for position and there may be great suffering as the resources on which we all depend are eroded. There is some uncertainty as to which are the critical issues and the time-scales involved, but it is clear that the time available for change is limited. The question is, can change occur soon enough? It is easy to advocate a scenario of universal restraint and cooperation for the common good, but what precisely must be achieved and can it be achieved in time? We evolved slowly, a long time ago and in a quite different world, and natural selection operated to fit us to that world. The propensities acquired then, interacting with the cultures of the societies they produced, have given rise to the behaviour which produced the present situation. That situation requires radical and rapid changes in many of our attitudes, especially in the industrial societies. How can such changes be brought about?

It would be possible to draw up a list of key issues – environmental preservation and a sustainable world, a more equitable distribution of resources, the elimination of the rule of force, a stable world population, a sustainable per capita consumption – and analyse their interrelatedness, as has been done throughout this volume. All such issues depend ultimately on human behaviour as shaped by the beliefs, values and institutions of societies. But these values and institutions are not simple givens: rather they are continually being created, maintained and changed through the action of the individuals in each society. Just as advertisements both mirror and stimulate human desires, and both advertisements and human desires change with time, so the values and norms of a culture both affect and are affected by the behaviour of individuals, and both can be changed. Some basic aspects of human behaviour relevant to these issues are considered here, in order to illuminate their social and psychological dimension.

## ASSERTIVENESS AND COOPERATION

A prime candidate for concern is the balance between selfish assertiveness and cooperation. Depletion of the earth's resources depends ultimately on individual greed: sustainability requires cooperation with others for the common good and for that of future generations. Potentialities for both are part of our nature, but their relative strengths depend on experience in the culture in which we grew up.

In our evolution, natural selection acted on individuals to maximize their reproductive success. Among males, competing with each other for women, this meant especially selection for assertiveness and aggressiveness. In non-industrial societies, still, many of the more important goals that individuals seek are conducive to reproductive success. Thus studies have shown that male reproductive success was correlated with rank or wealth among the Turkmen of Persia, the Yanamamo Indians, the Melanesians of Ifaluk, the Kipsigis of Kenya, and even the Portuguese élite of the fifteenth and sixteenth centuries – though rank or wealth might depend on the possession of money, wives, cows or whatever was valued in the particular local culture (Betzig et al, 1988). Of course that does not mean that every individual's reproductive success was maximized: more wealth for X normally meant less for Y and some individuals were exploited. Nor does it mean that individuals consciously sought wealth in order to reproduce: the more immediate goals they pursued were culturally defined but correlated with reproductive success. Presumably any simple society in which the individual's primary goals were not conducive to reproductive success could soon become extinct.

But assertiveness and competition can easily overreach themselves. The resources necessary for survival and reproduction become goals in themselves, and what is perceived as necessary escalates, leading to waste of resources. In addition, since those perceived by others as succeeding in competition are liable to succeed further, they resort to ostentatious display, with the implication that those who can afford expensive cars or expensive jewellery must be successful. This leads to further waste and environmental degradation.

Turning to cooperation and affiliative behaviour, natural selection has fostered them primarily in two contexts. The first is when the behaviour is directed towards related individuals and thereby augments the survival of genes identical to the actor's own. Hence the sacrifices parents make unthinkingly for their children. The second is when it is likely to be reciprocated and thus contribute in due course to the actor's own success (Trivers, 1971). However, it isn't always obvious who is related or who is likely to reciprocate and in human societies individuals are most prone to cooperate with individuals perceived or deemed to be related, or to be likely to cooperate. Where cooperation involves exploitation of one group or category of individuals by another, the ingroup members tend to be marked as such by similarities in behaviour, language or adornments (Eibl Eibesfeldt, 1979; Johnson, 1989). There are wide societal differences in the nature of subgroups and the subgroup markers may be biological (eg skin colour), the product of early socialization (eg accent) or consciously acquired (eg dress, hairstyle).

Natural selection has enhanced cooperativeness within close relationships, especially in women. The lifetime reproductive success of a woman depends on the number of children she can rear, and in most societies that depends on cooperative relationships with a man or with other women, as well as on appropriate assertiveness. Thus while men tend to be more assertive and aggressive than women, women tend to be more affiliative and cooperative than men. The differences in basic propensities are, however, probably small: those we see have been much magnified by experience, itself shaped by cultural values. Indeed, as is obvious enough, women can be aggressive and males cooperative, both sexes showing an amalgam of masculinity and femininity with one or the other predominating. Furthermore, because individual characteristics are shaped by diverse forces – genetic, experiential and cultural – all present to differing extents in different individuals, it is inevitable that individuals should vary. There will always be some individuals who are, relative to the societal norm, extremely assertive or non-assertive, cooperative or selfish and so on (Hinde, 1987).

Not only do individuals differ, but so also do societies. Western capitalist societies emphasize assertiveness/acquisitiveness while some Eastern societies tend to place more weight on cooperation, at least within the family or group. Furthermore, in complex societies individuals may seek after goals which are neutral with respect to reproductive success or even deleterious to it (Vining, 1986). Such facts show that the relative strengths of assertiveness and cooperation, and the goals towards which they are directed, can be changed. In fact a great deal is known about the circumstances that make children and adults more or less assertive, more or less aggressive, more or less cooperative, more feminine and less masculine (eg Hinde and Groebel, 1991; Maccoby and Martin, 1983). We can try to shift the balance at least a little bit, ensuring that children are brought up in circumstances more conducive to cooperation and that adults live in a world less conducive to aggression. Tilting the balance towards cooperation would not necessarily involve minimizing assertiveness or initiative; we do not want and need not have a world of cabbages. But it is clear that we must seek to ensure that societies reward achievements consequent upon cooperation rather than reserving the bulk of rewards for the assertiveness of entrepreneurs. This would be facilitated if feminine values were no longer subordinated to masculine ones. There are two routes to this goal. One is increasing the role of women in local and national affairs, the other an increased emphasis on feminine values among males.

As well as changing the balance between assertiveness and cooperation, the goals towards which they are directed need to change. While for the foreseeable future limited competitiveness will remain a useful spur, the issue is competitiveness for what? We must judge 'success' less in terms of material goods or wealth accumulated or power over others, more in terms of contribution to the common good. Progress must be judged not in terms of increasing technical complexity but in terms of sustainability. These are massive tasks, involving changes at the family level, changes in values away from those of the unlimitedly competitive society and also massive political changes to ensure a more even distribution of wealth. But progress is not impossible. In the 1939–45 war values changed in the UK (and no doubt in other countries closely affected by the war). People were proud to limit themselves to 5 inches of bath water; waste was condemned and entrepreneurial activities frowned upon. Societies can and must change the way they distribute rewards and sanctions. This is not to say that moral exhortation will be sufficient, but it has its place.

## GROUP LOYALTIES

A related issue concerns the groups towards which individuals direct their loyalties. Individuals readily see themselves as members of small groups and people are more ready to cooperate with, and even to sacrifice themselves for, others if those others are perceived to be related to themselves. The importance of decentralization, with increased responsibility placed on local groups and organizations, is being increasingly recognised. For instance, Third World poverty cannot be alleviated by the imposition of Western agricultural methods, but requires sensitive liaison with the local scene (Bizot, 1992; Borrini, 1991 and Chapter 7 of this volume). What we now know about the dynamics of groups provides some indications of the routes that must be followed to augment the integration of groups. Some of this work has concerned the factors leading to the perception of another individual as an ingroup member. Perceived similarity may be adequate (Tajfel, 1978), but perceived interdependence is probably more fundamental (Rabbie, 1992). The integrity of local groups is also preserved in part by traditions, customs and rituals, and a certain amount is known about the ways in which propaganda and rituals can be used to channel feelings (eg Lane, 1981; Middleton, 1991). The more mutually enjoyable the shared customs, the more favourably the ingroup is perceived and the more do members of the ingroup identify with it. The more they identify with it, the more they strive to enhance their own self-image by enhancing its real or perceived characteristics (Doise et al, 1978; Tajfel and Turner, 1986).

But to achieve sustainability we need understanding and integration between individuals, between individuals and local groups, and so on up to the global community. People must come to terms with the fact that, while the consequences of an individual's consumption or pollution of the environment may be negligible, such acts repeated by millions of individuals can have a devastating effect. Reciprocally, regulations imposed by societies for the common good may have devastating effects on some individuals. (See Chapter 10 of this volume.) On a global scale, what happens in one part of the world may affect remote areas of other continents and reciprocally international restrictions may be good for some countries but not for others. It is necessary to strive for a recognition both of global interdependence and of societal diversity, and to maintain communication at all levels of the global system. This raises a problem: while ensuring an equitable distribution of the world's resources, we do not want a grey Coca-Cola world. Indeed the major sources of conflict in the world stem from attempts to increase cultural uniformity.

But the differences between societies within the global community need not lead to conflict: although loyalty to the ingroup is often associated with, and augmented by, hostility to one or more outgroups, the two can vary independently of each other. This is most likely to be possible if the outgroup is not seen to be frustrating the goals of the ingroup in an illegitimate way and if cooperation between the groups is seen to be mutually beneficial (Brewer, 1979; Van Knippenberg, 1984; Rabbie, 1989, 1992). The nature of the integration between communities and societies poses further problems. Local skills and local values must be preserved, and respect for other people's values and cultures is essential. Responses to global problems must be made at a local level, but coordinated at a global one.

## THE TIME-SCALE

In the course of evolution, humans became adapted to plan only a limited way ahead – enough for their own survival through the next winter, enough for the needs of their children or grandchildren, but rarely beyond that. If we are to achieve sustainability, the industrial societies must extend their time-scale, and plan for the indefinite future. In addition, planning must be based on the interests of future generations. In some contexts, such long-term planning is already in hand – environmental issues have provided a potent spur. But, so far as I am aware, there are no further guidelines. Perhaps we can build on the readiness of parents to sacrifice themselves for their children and extend that to the succeeding generations.

There is hope that the time-scale of the vision of the industrialized and industrializing nations can be extended. Some societies have lived on equal terms with nature; the classic example is the Iroquois Indian teaching that we should always act so that the seventh generation to come will also have a good life. In the West, many people have started to look further ahead since Rachel Carson's *Silent Spring* and our feeling of responsibility has extended at least in space: early in nineteenth-century Britain paupers could obtain assistance only from their own parish, but now aid is sent from the same parish to starving refugees in Central Africa. Such efforts can be facilitated by the media – starving refugees can be seen on television screens, inculcating a motivation to help. But future generations cannot be seen. The recognition that their well-being is of crucial importance to us requires a fundamental change in values.

## CHANGING INSTITUTIONS

Much of the planning in industrialized countries depends on misleading and outdated socio-economic indicators. Depletion of non-renewable resources must be seen as a cost and we must recognize that such indicators as per capita income bear at most a tenuous relation to the quality of life (Dasgupta and Weale, 1992).

Indeed, we need to change many of the institutions in industrialized societies if we are to achieve sustainability. Many of these grew up as a consequence of the assertiveness and acquisitiveness of individuals, and depend on short-term gains with a total disregard for longer-term losses to the community of which they form part. Some of the most obvious obstacles to the creation of a sustainable world are constituted by the vested interests of many large corporations and national governments. Some of the values that oppose progress in that direction have their roots in such institutions or their members. For instance the naïve belief in unlimited economic growth without further specification can be called institutionalized greed. Moreover, the career ambitions of many scientists may be in part responsible for the common but mistaken faith in the unfailing ultimate availability of technical fixes for all our woes, thus legitimizing unlimited economic growth. However, economic growth is acceptable only if it does not involve consumption of limited resources or intolerable environmental consequences. As usually assessed, without allowance for the costs of resource depletion or environmental pollution, economic growth is not compatible with an improved and sustainable quality of life. (The greed that is the consequence of institutional functioning is not necessarily due to greed of the individual incumbents of roles within the institution, though it often is.)

Changing institutions is an immense task, but not impossible. The socio-cultural structure of values, beliefs and institutions is not an entity enduring for all time, but is maintained through dialectical relations with the individuals and groups within the society. To take one example, modern war is an institution with numerous constituent roles – leaders, soldiers, politicians, transport workers, munitions workers and so on. Individual aggressiveness plays little part in the behaviour of soldiers: they fight because they are incumbents of a particular role in the institution of war with that duty assigned to it. But every institution is being continuously created, maintained and eroded by the actions of the incumbents of its roles and even by outsiders, while those actions are continuously affected by the institution. So if we are to minimize the effectiveness and respectability of the institution of war, we must understand the forces that maintain it. These can be sought in the group processes that maintain nationalism: in the flags and medals that glorify war; in propaganda that manipulates loyalties and sanitizes war; and in the defence mechanisms of the participants that help them to remember comradeship, and suppress memories of terror and suffering. Even more, the institution of war is maintained by its subinstitutions – the military, industry and weapons science establishments. Each of these subinstitutions has its own inertia, to which the career ambitions and assertiveness of the incumbents contribute in large measure (Hinde, 1991). It is difficult to put the issue in a few words that are not susceptible to facile interpretations of the type 'armies are unnecessary' or 'all soldiers and defence industrialists are bad'. There are many levels of complexity between the individual and the society, and the motivations of individuals are not constituted solely by their rights and duties as incumbents of particular roles. Nevertheless it is clear that, if we are to reduce the incidence of wars, it is not enough to patch up crises as they occur. Rather we must undermine the institution of war by understanding its bases and reducing their potency. And such changes have been effected: Sweden, at one time one of the most warlike nations of Europe, has become an example for others to follow.

In the same way we must seek to understand the institutions that contribute to the present world view and undermine their power to do so. But there is no necessary implication that we should dismantle existing systems and start again. We must work through existing institutions so far as we can, directing them towards appropriate new goals. Much could be achieved, with economic incentives and financial coercion affecting consumption choices and, where appropriate, compensation. In addition voluntary change in the face of the reality of the situation may also be both necessary and possible – as has effectively been the case with aerosol sprays.

## DEMOCRATIC CHANGE

Attempts to induce change are certain to meet fierce resistance, because of the vested interests involved. Any change achieved is likely to be accompanied by a backlash. Success is most likely if we concentrate on key issues, such as sustainability and the more equitable distribution of resources, though achieving these will require fundamental changes in attitude. If attitudes are to be changed while local cultures are preserved, a wide diversity of techniques will be needed to fit the diversity of local scenes. An equitable distribution of resources, for instance, will mean different things in different cultures. Local problems must be understood, local initiatives encouraged, local expertise valued, all within an integrated global perspective.

Authoritarian regimes not only inhibit civil rights, but also include no methods for error correction. In a few countries they have been successful, but Dasgupta and Weale (1992) have shown that in poorer countries, civil liberties are correlated with improvement in infant survival rates and life expectancy (although not, surprisingly, with improvement in literacy). It would thus seem to be essential that attempts to change attitudes should be neither autocratic nor totalitarian, but based on democratic principles. Experience shows that although cultural change can be facilitated by the use of ritual and other means (eg Hobsbawm and Ranger, 1983), ritual can only succeed if it responds in some degree to the emotional requirements of those who are to perform it (Lane, 1981). Thus the need is to harness popular sentiment to significant changes in policy, to talk with and listen to the people. Work at the grassroots of public opinion is going to be as important as converting the policy makers. If the changes in attitude indicated above are to be achieved, those who wish to bring them about must vigorously espouse new meanings for 'success', 'progress', 'us' and 'the future'.

Education is clearly the key, but since the need for change is acute, crash courses must be run. These must be geared appropriately to public and to policy makers at all levels from the United Nations to local groups. It may be more economical and efficient if they are directed first to the more influential groups.

The work to be done is urgent and demanding, and requires all the resources and expertise we can muster. But if the knowledge and techniques of social scientists can be tailored with humility to the needs of the different cultures of the world, we can achieve our goals and avert catastrophe.

## REFERENCES

Betzig, L L, M Borgerhoff Mulder and P M Turke (eds), *Human Reproductive Behaviour*, Cambridge: Cambridge University Press, 1988.

Bizot, J, 'In Review with Vandana Shiva', *UNESCO Courier*, vol 8, 1992, pp 8–11.

Borrini, G, *Lessons Learned in Community-Based Environmental Management*, Rome: International Course for Primary Health Care Managers, Istituto Superiore di Sanitá, 1991.

Brewer, J M, 'Ingroup Bias in the Minimal Intergroup Situation: A Cognitive-Motivational Analysis', *Psychological Bulletin*, vol 186, 1979, pp 307–24.

Dasgupta, P and M Weale, 'On Measuring the Quality of Life', *World Development*, vol 20, 1992, pp 119–31.

Doise, W, J-C Deschamps and G Meyer, 'The Accentuation of Intercategory Similarities' in Tajfel (1978), pp 159–68.

Eibl Eibesfeldt, I, *The Biology of Peace and War*, London: Thames & Hudson, 1978.

Hinde, R A, *Individuals, Relationships and Culture*, Cambridge: Cambridge University Press, 1987.

Hinde, R A, *The Institution of War*, London: Macmillan, 1991.

Hinde, R A and J Groebel (eds), *Cooperation and Prosocial Behaviour*, Cambridge: Cambridge University Press, 1992.

Hobsbawm, E and T Ranger (eds), *The Invention of Tradition*, Cambridge: Cambridge University Press, 1983.

Johnson, G R, 'The Role of Kin Recognition Mechanisms in Patriotic Socialisation: Further Reflections', *Politics and the Life Sciences*, vol 8, 1989, pp 62–9.

Lane, C, *The Rites of Rulers*, Cambridge: Cambridge University Press, 1981.

Maccoby, E E and J A Martin, '*Socialisation in the Context of the Family: Parent-Child Interaction*' in E M Hetherington (ed), *Mussen Handbook of Child Psychology*, vol 4, 1983, pp 1–101.

Middleton, H, 'Some Psychological Bases of the Institution of War' in Hinde (1991), pp 30–46.

Rabbie, J M, 'Group Processes as Stimulants of Aggression' in J Groebel and R A Hinde (eds), *Aggression and War*, Cambridge: Cambridge University Press, 1989, pp 141–55.

Rabbie, J M, 'Determinants of Instrumental Intra-Group Cooperation' in Hinde and Groebel (1992), pp 238–62.

Tajfel, H (ed), *Differentiation Between Social Groups*, London: Academic Press, 1978.

Tajfel, H and J C Turner, 'The Social Identity Theory of Intergroup Behaviour' in S Worchel and W G Austin (eds), *Psychology of Intergroup Relations*, Chicago: Nelson-Hall, 1986, pp 7–24.

Trivers, R L, 'The Evolution of Reciprocal Altruism', *Quarterly Review of Biology*, vol 46, 1971, pp 35–57.

Van Knippenberg, A F M, 'Intergroup Differences in Group Perceptions' in H Tajfel (ed), *The Social Dimension*, Cambridge: Cambridge University Press, vol 1, 1984, pp 560–78.

Vining, D R, 'Social vs Reproductive Success', *Behavioural and Brain Sciences*, vol 9, 1986, pp 167–216.

*Chapter Twelve*

# Summary and Recommendations

*Philip B Smith and Samuel E Okoye*

---

Just as there are many possible variations of the wrong fork of the crossroads, there are also many along the right fork. We are not so pretentious that we think that we alone have the right answers. The chapters of this volume are meant to be signposts, not detailed itineraries, on the road to sustainability, equity and liveability. The authors hope that they will be of some value in bringing humankind on to the right fork. Considering the diversity of cultural and geographical backgrounds from which the authors have come to this enterprise, it is not surprising that there are points of disagreement between them. Most remarkable, however, is how broad the areas are on which there is agreement. This is a positive sign for the future.

## AGRICULTURAL POLICIES

Even though no one can say what the earth's carrying capacity for humanity is, it is obvious that reducing it further is not desirable. Yet it is clearly being reduced to the extent that humanity degrades land and lowers its productivity, impoverishes the diversity of life, exposes its surface to increased ultraviolet radiation and alters biochemical cycles by emitting excess greenhouse gases to the atmosphere. Meanwhile the human population is headed towards doubling its size, unless social, political and economic reform measures are taken which will lead to slowing its growth. In the second half of the twentieth century agricultural techniques and economic regimes foreign to both land and people have been imposed upon many poor countries by the combined power of international agencies and a native élite acculturated to Western concepts. The consequences have wreaked havoc on both social structures and food sufficiency. On the other hand, in one case at least (Peru), serious study has made it possible to resurrect an ancient production technique capable of providing high yields even under harsh, unfavourable conditions. Much more work along these lines must be undertaken, proceeding from an attitude of respect for indigenous knowledge of proven value.

## Recommendations

- Globally, food production must be substantially increased to match the expected medium-term expansion of the human population by roughly a billion a decade.
- In most developing regions an urgent task is to improve food storage and transportation facilities.
- Much more research and extensive field trials in alternative farming and herding systems must be undertaken.
- Recognition of the value of indigenous knowledge that has proven to lead to sustainable agriculture in the past, even when it is not entirely understood, vis-à-vis imported Western agricultural concepts, is an important element of the revision of attitudes necessary to put agriculture in the tropics on a sustainable and socially equitable basis.
- 'Green revolution' yield techniques must be applied to crops other than the 'big three' – wheat, rice and maize. Tropical crops on which a large portion of the world's poor depend have, until recently, been neglected by plant breeders. Biotechnology could considerably speed up the process of developing higher yield varieties.
- Economic and agricultural policies can make or break the adequacy and sustainability of a nations food supply. Greater social investment in agriculture, especially in parts of Latin America and Africa can remedy lagging food production for domestic consumption.
- Reforestation and restoring local control over resources may be the keys to making areas of land degradation (eg deforestation and soil erosion) more sustainable. In many arid and semi-arid regions, reversing land degradation processes, improving and extending irrigation systems and improving livestock productivity will all be necessary elements in putting these regions on a sustainable basis.

## ENERGY POLICIES

In line with the goals of this book, the achievement of an equitable world order in the course of the twenty-first century is assumed in the discussion of energy policies. It is clear that continuation of the present energy policies of the industrialized countries is a dead-end road. Even leaving aside the tremendously increased demand from developing countries which is inevitable if an equitable world is reached, the existing known and speculative reserves of fossil fuels will be exhausted in less than a century by the industrialized countries alone if present growth trends continue. It must also be realized that the transition to renewables will cost a share of what now remains, so that any further delay in initiating the transition could lead to a cul de sac in which the possibility of ever carrying out the transition will have been sacrificed in order to satisfy the immediate demand for energy. Because this 'point of no return' will be passed before actual scarcity begins to drive prices up, the market mechanism is inadequate to provide an indicator of impending danger.

Nuclear energy, itself a non-renewable source, will not play a major role in effecting the transition, although under certain circumstances it could play a minor role. This conclusion is reached purely on the basis of energy availability considerations and is not related to either the burning technical questions of the safety of nuclear plants and the disposal of nuclear waste, nor the political problem of nuclear weapon proliferation.

These conclusions can be drawn independently of assumptions concerning the greenhouse effect. Even if the transition is taken to hand immediately it will not succeed unless there is a simultaneous substantial annual decrease in energy use per service and/or a significant annual decrease in the level of affluence (ie the average availability of services per capita) of the richer countries. These two desiderata work in the same direction and the division of effort between them can be influenced by policy decisions.

The issue of simpler life-styles is also relevant to the question of how much energy per capita can actually be used without causing irreparable damage to the ecosystem as a whole and to eco-diversity in particular. The permissible energy use per capita recommended here, 1.5 kW (continuous), must not be taken as a precise number; there are far too many approximations and imponderables, to make the calculation of a precise number feasible. It can only serve as a rough guideline for policy. Such a drastic reduction below present levels in Europe and North America would demand a reorganization of infrastructure, but it is entirely erroneous to think that this would mean a return to the Stone Age. It cannot be denied, however, that many everyday luxuries such as air travel at the present level would be impossible. The transition therefore becomes partly a cultural problem of how it might be possible to reshape institutions in the affluent countries so that the insatiable 'hunger for more', so characteristic of these societies today, could be sublimated towards spiritually more satisfying goals. Differential taxation policies will be essential in shifting priorities. It must be made clear that this would not mean an increased tax load – the funds would flow back to the taxpayer through subsidies of and rewards for ecologically sound developments. The way in which this is done is critical for acceptance by the public. It is unnecessary to wait until all countries do this. A single country or region could 'go it alone'; the temporary disadvantage in competitiveness would soon be turned into an advantage because the development of low energy intensive techniques would be stimulated, making the country or region a leader in ecologically sound technology.

We envisage, in our energy scenarios, that in an equitable world everyone on earth will have access to modern sources of energy, including modern forms of biomass energy conversion. In the meantime fuelwood, crop residues and dung will remain basic sources of, in principle, renewable energy for large segments of humankind. The levels of use in the world are extremely diverse, as are the social circumstances responsible for the biofuel entitlements of different segments of populations, so that policies intended to ensure a continuing supply of this important source of energy must not be based on aggregate calculations. Policies, to succeed, must be based on the local context, but integrated at national and international levels.

## Recommendations

- All sails must be set to effect the transition to renewable energy sources as rapidly as possible.
- The efficiency with which energy is used in the industrialized countries to provide services must be continuously increased and/or the level of services must be continuously decreased.
- Intense research efforts must be directed towards the increase of the efficiency of energy use and the results must be made available to developing countries.
- The adoption of simpler, more satisfying life-styles of the affluent must be stimulated by, on the one hand, differential taxation policies and, on the other, by educational measures. An effective measure in the category of education can be the stimulation of the idea of a 'personal energy budget' or 'eco-budget' making energy conservation into a game instead of a sacrifice. To make this game playable research is needed to determine the real energy costs of all of the components (activities and goods) of people's daily lives.
- The proceeds from differential taxation policies, which should raise the cost to the consumer of fossil fuels by a factor of at least three, should be placed in an 'eco-fund' or 'eco-trust' which would flow back to the taxpayer in such a way as to reward ecologically sound developments. This is necessary to make it acceptable to a public accustomed to wasting energy.
- In order to arrest irreversible destruction of biodiversity, and incidentally to slow down global warming and the exhaustion of fossil fuel stocks, the total per capita energy consumption must finally be reduced to around 1.5 kW (continuous) per capita – a factor of four below the present level in Europe and a factor of more than six below the present level in the US and Canada.
- In order to maintain a renewable supply of biofuel, until modern sources of energy are universally available, policies to stabilize its use and renewal must be built upon the local context, but integrated at national and international levels.

## THE ECONOMIC AND POLITICAL DIMENSIONS

Economic theories (whether of planned economy or free market type) advocated and implemented today are based on outmoded (nineteenth century) concepts. These theories perceive the environment as a reservoir which serves as an infinite source of materials and energy for human activities, and as an infinite sink for all their end products. They ignore the fact that all real productive power is derived directly or indirectly from nature and perceive capital as a primary factor in production. This stimulates a view of life in which only things that can be expressed in monetary terms count. All of the values that make life worth living are thereby devaluated to zero. This view of life has very negative consequences for the goals of sustainability, equity and liveability.

Modern economic theory, conceived as a study of production and consumption of (scarce) goods, has in the course of its development become in practice a formalization of greed. In addition, as ridiculous as it is mathematically, economic theory justifies the idea that endless economic growth is a normal and even necessary characteristic of society. There is therefore a great need for a transformation of, particularly Northern, economic institutions to facilitate a shift away from pro-growth concepts that stimulate people's 'hunger for more'. The point is that the very goal of economic growth does not alleviate the sense of scarcity, but in con-trast exacerbates it. Hence an important requisite of the transition process from unsustainability to sustainability is the examination of the link between consump-tion and needs.

Because the North has set the rules which carry within them the seeds of unsus-tainability, it is at present irrelevant to speak of economic or other measures that must be taken in the South to achieve sustainability. Indeed the South, if it is to survive, must abide by these rules, so that initiatives for change must originate in the North. The 'global enclosures' movement (illustrated by UNCED) now taking place will not – in contradiction to the tenets of conventional economic theory – create sustainability, because there is little assurance that the existing institutions are capable of, or even have the goal of, preserving the 'commons'. Another kind of enclosures movement, the 'colonization' of the future, is implied in the rapid depletion of the remaining natural resources. No political remedy for this 'colonial-ism' is possible because future generations cannot be politically empowered; self-restraint of the present generation is the only answer.

Self-restraint is also an essential element in creating a sustainable, equitable and liveable world order within the lives of the present generation. It is sad to see that the tendencies towards 'free-trade' and the market economy, dominant in the world today (eg GATT and NAFTA), are pushing in the opposite direction: ie towards a world governed by acquisitiveness, hardness and aggressiveness.

The existing international values are not of a high ethical standard. Partly because the international system is perceived to be basically anarchic, immoral val-ues of might, greed and profit travel almost unhindered under the cover of 'national interest' or ideological rhetoric. Indeed, much of the reality of prevailing geopolitics and the global economy is that a zero-sum game is being played between the industrialized and developing countries: what one side wins the other must lose. As long as this is the way the game is played, there is little hope of real change.

There is, therefore, a need to incorporate the goals of sustainability, equity and liveability into realpolitik. This requires optimal knowledge of the complexities involved, careful planning, diplomatic skills and the ability to combine local, global and regional interests in well-planned scenarios. The more sustainability, equity and liveability are valued positively in national societies, the more that they will be at stake in politics, both at the national and the international levels. The ability of political actors to serve these interests is already part of the struggle for power. The globalization of geopolitical factors has gone so far that there are no state-centric or nationalist tracks towards sustainability, equity and liveability. But international coordination, imperative as it is, only makes sense when focused on local circum-stances.

The most serious problems of today – from starving to civil violence, from defor-estation to deadly infant diseases, from toxic pollution to terrorist killings, from soil degradation to child prostitution, from flooding to political violence – all have characterizing and critical local dimensions. Their solutions require a variety of international agreements and national resolutions, but cannot do without the knowledge, work and care of local people and communities. Sustainable management of local resources requires efforts and care, which will be provided if people connect the protection of the environment with direct and sure benefits, in particular to satisfy their pressing needs. Such a link between environmental protection and benefits for the populace is assured when people have access and tenure to environmental resources. No problem is truly 'global', because the consequences of every global development will be felt differently in each of the millions of communities on earth. But given the chance, people will react in a way that is advantageous for themselves and for their immediate environment. That is why 'empowerment' of local people is an essential element in achieving sustainability.

But while international coordination and empowerment of local people are the key to a better future it is, in the last analysis, the national governments who, due to their special tasks as tax collectors, law makers, monopolizers of legitimate police and military forces, and providers of social security, occupy a strategic position between the local and the global level, and are therefore in a position either to become powerful catalysts of or formidable obstacles to change.

The global family is a divided community of rich (Northern) and overwhelmingly poor (Southern) societies. The economy of the South is still plagued by the debt crisis with the attendant curse of poor human development. In both North and South alike, military expenditure, high both in absolute terms and as a fraction of total state expenditures, constitutes an important parameter in any discussion of global socio-economic development. Roughly the same percentage of GDP goes to military expenditures in the South as in the North. If the present high level of military expenditure is hardly affordable in the North, it is sheer folly for the South to have achieved this kind of parity. Indeed recent studies suggest that military expenditures have had a negative effect on past economic development, particularly in the South. In spite of this, military expenditures in the South are on the rise and this is affecting the possibility of the South ever bridging the development gap between it and the North. The North is not entirely blameless in this affair because it is the major producer and vendor of most of the world's weaponry today, and at the same time is equally responsible for the present socio-economic arrangements that produce so much inequity between the North and the South.

## Recommendations

- The existential dependence of humankind on its special and highly diversified environment requires 'new rules of the game', in which recognition of the superior values characterizing the joint system of humanity and its environment are built in. The sustainability of the earth's ecosystem should be regarded as such a superior value.
- It is necessary to revise the principles of economics to allow economy to develop as a human activity without violating the essential conditions of sustainability of the earth's ecosphere. It must be widely recognized that it is nature in the first

place, and not capital, that furnishes all real productive power. To this end, a partial incorporation of nature into the monetary value system may be helpful. Although such a financial assessment of external nature will prove to be insufficient, it could none the less be an important instrument in moving the global economy towards sustainability. Economic 'growth' of a more balanced and equitable kind is as essential as social justice, if absolute poverty is to be eliminated and equity is to be achieved.

■ The greatest need at the political level is for insights into ways in which the institutions in the rich countries can be reformed so that a 'steady state' economy does not lead to collapse and the integrity of the commons can be maintained.

■ In order for developing countries to escape rapidly from the indignity of their poverty, a new ethical code is needed that allows for some redistribution of wealth and that must embody principles opposite from those towards which the world is now moving (GATT and NAFTA). Hardness, competitiveness and aggressiveness must give way to gentleness, sharing and compassion. The ultimate aim should be a sustainable development strategy that discounts the need for endless growth and ensures that the needs of the present generation are met without compromising the ability of future generations to meet their own needs.

■ 'Empowerment' of local populations is important for effective environmental protection and the realization of well thought-out national plans and international agreements. Policies should be adopted to reverse the tendency towards centralization of environmental control, particularly when this leads to interference by international organizations in the management, by local communities, of forests and wildlife.

■ To give political clout to the agenda defined by the leading question, 'how can every human being live a decent life within a world order that is symbiotic with the rest of nature?', the following steps and policies should be implemented.

— In the realm of public opinion, political parties, the media and scientific offices and governmental departments must provide optimal public information on the risks and opportunities of present developments and their alternatives. In addition, public awareness of the role played by international organizations must be enhanced in order that their (dis)functioning be at stake in domestic politics.

— The coordinating role of international organizations is crucial because of the globalization of geopolitical factors, but only makes sense when focused on local circumstances.

— In order for governments to become catalysts for change they should welcome and stimulate the process of international organization for its ability to overcome the inconveniences of the state system in the realm of environmental and demographic issues. They can also facilitate the translation of international initiatives and developments by setting up compensation programmes for domestic 'losers'. Domestic burden sharing, ie the creation of safety nets, will enhance public and business support for reorganizing unsustainable production modes and recasting life-styles.

■ To achieve a sustainable, equitable and liveable world, it makes sense for both the South and the North to redirect, through disarmament, a considerable portion of the resources now channelled into the military sector towards human development. Such disarmament is in its own right, of course, an important goal from the point of view of peace and security.

# HEALTH POLICIES

A most important factor in human development is health. A key aim should be health care which stimulates human development without prejudicing the capacity of the environment to support life on earth. Though there is a clear link between ill-health and poverty, there has also been a pronounced increase in life expectancy in developing countries over the last 30 years. International data show that a low average per capita income (US$5000 per annum or less) can be compatible with a long life expectancy (about 70 years), but the elimination of outright poverty is essential. A relatively equitable distribution of income within a country and the provision of education and basic health care contribute to prolonged life expectancy. If development is meant to improve the quality of human life, conventional economic data, such as GNP, are poor indicators. The Human Development Index (HDI) is more promising. It combines life expectancy, educational attainment and income, and can be used to compare countries.

Future threats to health include the impacts of global warming, stratospheric ozone depletion, population growth and the spread of HIV. The transfer of wealth from poor to rich countries via debt repayments, the transfer (dumping) of (toxic) waste and other forms of pollution are major barriers to sustainable health conditions.

## Recommendations

■ **A more equitable income distribution**   Given that poverty lies behind much of the world's ill-health, redistribution of wealth is a necessity both between and within countries.

■ **The promotion of family planning**   While global population growth is at an unprecedented level, overall fertility is now falling, albeit slowly, almost everywhere. A number of countries have shown that a rapid fall in population growth is feasible without coercion. The United Nations have advocated the universal right to reproductive health care, including family planning. Three hundred million couples still lack access to adequate family planning.

■ **The development of primary health care**   In 1990, a number of goals were adopted by the World Summit for Children which, if achieved, would significantly reduce under-5 death rates among children (by one-third or to a level of 70/1000 live births) and death rates among women (halving of maternal mortality). Many of them can best be achieved through primary care services. These include the eradication of polio, the elimination of neonatal tetanus by 1995, a 90 per cent reduction in measles cases, virtual elimination of vitamin A and iodine deficiency, education of all families about the importance of exclusive breast feeding for the first four to six months of a child's life, basic education for all children, access to prenatal care for all women, the provision of a trained attendant during childbirth and referral where appropriate.

- **The organisation of district health systems**   Health systems can be organized around defined populations in the form of districts. District health systems include primary care and hospital(s) and aim for an integration of the two with appropriate mechanisms for planning and management to ensure efficient use of limited resources. In this way, uncoordinated vertical programmes dealing with specific problems such as tuberculosis, diabetes, nutrition, and mother and child health, should be able to be incorporated into a more comprehensive and flexible health care system without loss of effectiveness.

- **The improvement of public information and education**   While no cure or effective vaccine for HIV infection is currently in sight, much more could be done to limit its spread by public education about methods of transmission and encouraging the use of condoms. Promotion of increasing use of condoms might also help to reduce unwanted pregnancies, providing condom use does not displace more effective means of contraception. Education programmes about sexual health could be linked to expansion of literacy and basic education programmes.

## POPULATION

There is no doubt that the prospects for the future would be brighter if there were fewer people on earth. At present almost half of the primary production of photosynthesis is appropriated by humanity. Yet the number of people living on earth is only one facet of the many problems which confront humanity. It cannot be considered separately from the interlocking relationships between the economic, political and cultural policies under which people live, the majority in poverty. Population growth is a symptom of a maladjusted world order. It is illusory, therefore, to prescribe solutions that focus solely on birth rate/death rate ratios. It is the societal context that counts.

The social context is exceedingly complex. For example the promotion of birth control, especially by foreign agencies, is patronizing, even when well intentioned. Furthermore, when population control programmes involve any form of coercion, and especially if they are tainted with mandatory sterilization, they constitute an inadmissible interference with human rights. The concern expressed by many in the North over the environmental threats of 'runaway population growth' in the South does not ring quite true. The most important threat to the environment is the exhaustion of natural resources and the production of pollution in the affluent societies, rooted in the ideology of consumerism.

Education programmes that help close the gap between men and women, primary health care programmes that give children a better chance for a healthy, productive life and family planning programmes set up to give families more control over the number of their children should be carried out in a context of the creation of a more just society, not the context of controlling population.

## THE BOTTOM LINE

When all is said and done it is human beings themselves who are, by their behaviour, sawing off the limbs that they are standing on. Given the current rates of resource depletion and pollution, is it possible to change society sufficiently quickly to avoid catastrophe? Achieving or not achieving sustainability, equity and liveability depends ultimately on human behaviour as shaped by the values and institutions of society. In order to reach solutions to the multitude of problems delineated above, the prospectives with which people view the world must be extended and behaviour patterns must change. Prospectives must be extended in time, taking account of not only the world as we want it to be in ten years' time, or in our own lifetimes, but as we want it to be generations ahead. Prospectives must likewise be extended in space, because what happens elsewhere matters. It will also be necessary to change both individual and institutional behaviour. It will be necessary to alter the balances between assertiveness and cooperation, and between male and female values. This is possible provided we can integrate a global perspective with respect for local diversity in knowledge and traditions, and achieve changes in the goals and values of both policy makers and populations. This does not mean aiming for uniformity – global interdependence can and should embrace local diversity. To achieve this there must be changes both at the grass roots level of public opinion, and in the minds and modes of action of policy makers and business leaders.

# Index

Acheson, J M 130
acid deposition 15
acid rain 142, 161
acquisitiveness 15, 189
aerosols 142, 182
affluence 3; of the military 156
Afghanistan 123, 163n
Africa: addition to world's population
  (1998) 137; biofuel shortages 79; Central
  32, 181; chaos and anarchy 162; debt to
  GDP ratio 155; degraded land 23;
  HIV/AIDS 144, 145; per capita food
  production 26; social crises 131; social
  investment in agriculture 28, 186;
  Southern 27, 157; Southern, regional
  tensions 157; Sub-Saharan 27, 32, 138,
  140, 145, 155; uncontrolled massive
  migrations 171; untapped potential 24;
  *see also under various country names*
Agarwal, A 118, 132
Agarwal, B 78, 81, 82, 89
aggressiveness 15, 189, 191
agriculture 11, 22–5, 33–4, 87, 105, 109;
  felling of forested land for 83; greater
  social investment in 186; less energy-
  intensive 13; limitation of land for
  production 127; neglect of traditional
  knowledge in 110; new development
  projects based on large reservoirs 101;
  policies 31, 32, 185–6; rain-fed 98;
  residues 83; shifting 32; social
  investment in 28, 186; sustainable 13,
  186; *see also* farming
agro-forestry 32, 90
Ahuja, D 78
AIDS (acquired-immune-deficiency
  syndrome) 141, 144–5, 147, 161, 192, 193
Albania 170
Alcántara, E M de la Peña 83, 84
Allende, Salvador 8

Altieri, M 32, 90
Amalric, Franck 14, 39, 117, 133
Amazon Basin 32, 170
*Ambio* 132n
AMDP (Accelerated Mahaweli
  Development Project) 105–6
Amnesty International 161
Anderson, C 79
Anderson, E N 131n
Anderson, R M 145
Andes 32
Angell, Sir Norman 165
Angola 155
animal products 31, 175
animal species 129; culling quota for each
  132; endangered 128; lost for ever 34;
  protection of 127; *see also* extinction
Annez, P 156
Antarctica 34, 143, 144
'anthropogeographie' 168
anti-agrarian policies 90
Antrobus, Peggy 16
aquifers 24, 32; overdrawn 25
Arbenz Guzman, Jacobo 8
Argentina 141, 153, 154
Arizpe, L 58
armaments 161; global trade 156
Armenia 163n
ASEAN (Association of South-East Asian
  Nations) 165
Asia 6, 138; addition to world's population
  (1998) 137; dragons 28; rapidly
  developing economies 73; South 27, 32,
  82, 155; South-East Asia 8, 32, 145;
  Western 32, 162; *see also under various
  country names*
Asian Development Bank 106
Atkinson formulation 138
Australia 143
Austria 141

IRRI (International Rice Research Institute) 22, 26
irrigation 24, 101, 126; ancient systems 95, 97–9, 107, 109; channel ecosystems 98; damage 23, 25; efficient systems 13–14; engineers 102; expansion slowing 143; faulty practices 130n; hydraulic engineering models for modern projects 109; improving and extending systems 32; inundation, on river banks 98; less wasteful practices 13; macro- and micro-ecosystems 105, 109; river diversion 100; spread of systems 143; traditional ecosystems 106–7
Islam, M N 81
isolationism 169, 170, 171
Italian Alps 133
Italy 165

Jackson, T 73
Jacobsen, J 28, 143
Jaffna 97
Jamaica 141
Janasaviya or Poverty Alleviation Programme 105
Japan 7, 28, 122, 140–1, 145, 165, 170; Minimata 144; whalers 175
Jayawardena, L R 102
Jews 163
job opportunities 130
Jodha, N S 84n, 132
Johansson, T B 58, 63
Johnson, G R 178
Jones, R R 144
Jongman, B 163n
Joseph, S 88
Julius Caesar 165

Kalaweva 97, 107
Kalkstein, L S 142
Kandy 97
Karekezi, S 90
Kates, R W 23, 27, 31, 32
Kayapó 170
Keepin, B 73
Kennedy J F 171n
Kennedy, J S 99
Kenya 82, 90; Kipsigis of 178
Keynes, J M 5, 120, 121, 122
King, M 141
King, Martin Luther 164

Kiribati 143
Kissinger, Henry 164
Kjellén, Rudolf 168
Knippenberg, A F M van 181
knowledge 138, 151; diffusion, about the use of simple primary care measures 148; indigenous 95–112, 185, 186; local diversity in 194; scientific 167; traditional, neglect in agriculture 110
Knox, R 98
Kondratieff's cycles 120
Koomey, J 63
Korten, D C 132
Kotte 97
Krause, F 63
Kuwait 163n

Laar, A van de 83, 88
labour markets 7; equilibrium 121; fluidity 122
land: agricultural 109; clearing 34; forested, felling of 83; grain 143; intensified pressures on 28; limitation for agricultural production 127; marginal 28, 30; pasture 23; potentially arable 22; suitable for farming 22–3; tenure 31, 87, 89; use requirements 64
land degradation 27, 28, 31, 116, 186; global extent 24; public 89; reduction of potential productivity from 29; reduction of potential productivity resulting from 29; reversing 32, 186; through salinization and waterlogging 24
landless people 84, 86, 89
Lane, C 180, 182
Latin America 23, 138, 145, 186; addition to world's population (1998) 137; chaos and anarchy 162; food production 26; social investment in agriculture 28, 186; *see also under various country names*
Latin Americanization 6
Lazarus, M 58
Leach, E R 97, 107
Leach, G 78, 81, 83, 86, 88, 89
League of Nations 165, 170
*lebensraum* 168
Lee, R 27, 28, 29, 31
legitimacy 118, 120, 123; explicit treatment and analysis of 119
legitimization 117; of violence 161; of greed

redistribution 122
reforestation 32, 63, 126; large scale 74
refugees: criteria for achieving status 171;
economic 3; major conflicts over 169;
starving 181
Reilly, J 58
religion 11, 99; fundamentalism 164
Renard, Y 132
renewable energy 13, 60, 63, 187–8;
construction of high sustainable yield
74; estimates of total realizable potential
64; extra energy for materials mostly
from 69n; feasible requirements for 74;
growth in sources 146; ingrowth of 67;
maximum supply from 74; phase-out of
sources 59; realizable potential from 68;
requirements for 72; traditional 64;
transition from fossil fuels to 61
Repetto, R C 22, 83
repression: in the name of law and order
164; of pluralism and freedom of speech
161
reservoirs 98–101, 105, 107–109
resources 9; biomass 81, 89; channelled into
the military sector 192;
commercialization of 84; communal
management of 132; consumption of 21;
distribution of 72, 182; energy 52, 53, 57,
58–9; environmental 5, 72, 132;
expropriation of 27; finite 21, 26; foreign,
complete dependence on 170; forest 79,
81, 87; fossil fuel, depletion of 72;
fuelwood 87; human-made 5; less for
investment 155; limited, efficient use of
193; local control over 32, 186; local,
sustainable management of 190; material
21; needed for a decent standard of
living, access to 151; non-renewable 52,
53, 57, 58–9; overconsumption of 34;
property 31, 84, 86, 87; redistribution of
34; release of 157, 175; renewable 34, 57;
scarce 164, 169; technologies 21;
traditional distribution mechanisms 87;
transfers of 153; use of 31; valuable 23;
waste of 178; water 161, 143; wood 81,
83; *see also* natural resources
reward systems 161
rice 26, 126, 142; crop declined 29
rights 9, 160, 161, 193; civil 182; community
175; concessional 130; customary,
forbidden to exercise 117; enforcement

of 118; equal 173; explicit treatment and
analysis of 119; global 116; grazing 130,
132; land tenure 87, 132; political 8;
property 84, 117, 118; sharing of 119;
traditional 84, 86; usage 117; *see also*
commons
Rio de Janeiro *see* UNCED
rivers: silting of 24; damming 98; diversion
of 98, 100, 105; perennial 98
Roberts, S 73
Rogot, E 142
Roosevelt, Franklin D 105, 165
Rose, D J 58
Rose, G 139
Rosecrance, R 170
Rosenau, J N 167, 173
Rosenzweig, C 143
Rostow, Walt 120
Ruberu, R 101
Ruffin, J-C 123
Ruhunurata 97, 98
Russell-Einstein Manifesto 15
Russia/Russian Federation 157, 163n, 171;
nuclear scientists 175

Sadik, 146
Sahara 22
Sahel 133
Sanchez, P 32
sanitation 90, 137, 139, 152; self-help
projects 125–6
SAPs (structural adjustment programmes)
138–9, 154
scarcities 161, 162; exacerbated by economic
growth 123; food 163; wind-rich areas
63; wood 83, 88
Schaatz, J 28, 31
scientific and technological know-how 47
sea-level rise 133, 143
'second law of thermodynamics' 40, 41
Second World 6, 152n; energy requirements
62
Second World War 120, 122, 170, 179
seeds 26, 32; high-yield 22, 25; improved 31
self-sufficiency 7, 8
Sen, A 28
Senanayake, D S 105
Serbia 163n, 169
SERI (Solar Energy Research Institute) 63
services: automization of 161; primary care
192; social 156

*Index compiled by Frank Pert*